DANGER CLOSE

DANGER CLOSE

MY EPIC JOURNEY AS A COMBAT
HELICOPTER PILOT IN IRAQ AND AFGHANISTAN

AMBER SMITH

ATRIA BOOKS

New York   London   Toronto   Sydney   New Delhi

ATRIA BOOKS

An Imprint of Simon & Schuster, Inc.
1230 Avenue of the Americas
New York, NY 10020

Copyright © 2016 by Amber Smith

First Atria Books hardcover edition September 2016

ATRIA BOOKS and colophon are trademarks of Simon & Schuster, Inc.

For information about special discounts for bulk purchases,
please contact Simon & Schuster Special Sales at 1-866-506-1949 or
business@simonandschuster.com.

The Simon & Schuster Speakers Bureau can bring authors to your live event.
For more information or to book an event, contact the Simon & Schuster Speakers Bureau at 1-866-248-3049 or visit our website at www.simonspeakers.com.

Interior design by Amy Trombat

Manufactured in the United States of America

10 9 8 7 6 5 4 3 2 1

Library of Congress Cataloging-in-Publication Control Number: 2016021638

ISBN 978-1-5011-1638-4
ISBN 978-1-5011-1640-7 (ebook)

For my parents, Lane and Betsy,
for always encouraging me to take the road less traveled
and to never, ever give up.

DANGER CLOSE: Ordnance delivery inside the 0.1 percent P^i [probability of incapacitation] distance will be considered "danger close." The supported commander must accept responsibility for the risk to friendly forces when targets are inside the 0.1 percent P^i distance.

—*Close Air Support*, Joint Publication 3-09.3

Contents

Author's Note

Kiowa Warriors played a critical role in the wars in Iraq and Afghanistan, yet few outside the modern military community know the impact they made on the battlefield every day. This book not only documents my journey through the Army and two wars, but the legacy of a helicopter that was essential to mission success on both fronts. Dialogue has been re-created through interviews and other forms of correspondence and is not intended to be word for word. Some names have been changed to protect the identity of certain individuals, as well as ground unit and aviator unit calls signs and route names. All events depicted in this book are told as accurately as possible and any unintentional deviations can be attributed to the chaos of combat.

—AMBER SMITH, Annihilator 24

DANGER CLOSE

Prologue

Survival. That's all that passes through your mind when you make it home from each flight mission. Every time your helicopter crosses over the fortifications of Hesco barriers that separate the sanctuary of the forward operating base (FOB) from the madness of Afghanistan, you realize that, somehow, you have lived to see another day.

Your whole body is sore from hours in a cramped cockpit. Your hand unclenches the cyclic flight control. Exhaustion washes over you as the adrenaline drains from your veins, the adrenaline that had flooded in with every crank of the helicopter engine before you took off into the Afghanistan sky.

Every mission is different, but the questions are always the same: *Is today my last day? Is today the last time I will lace up my boots? As we walk out to the flight line, is it the last time I will hear my fellow pilots say, "Have a safe flight"? The last time I will email my family and type, "Talk to you soon"?*

The uncertainty is the worst part. You never know if today is going to be your day—the day you won't come home.

Being immersed in war teaches you to accept death, to face the fear of the unknown that haunts you every day. It is an insidious form of torture. But it is also an addiction, something you crave. Once you break through the fear of dying, you eventually feel the thrill of dancing with death. When things are slow during a reconnaissance mission, you begin itching for some action. Any action. You think fatalistic thoughts: *You're never going home anyway, so if today is your day, so be it.* That's what you tell yourself to survive the unrelenting stress of the unknown dangers in your world every day.

Then you see the flag-draped caskets being carried on to a C-17 airplane, and you wonder, *Will I be on the next one?*

But you don't think of that in the air—maybe in the slow moments, the moments between flights that begin with the heaviness of the skids settling onto the pavement. You roll the throttle down to idle, the chatter of the blades slows, the high-pitched whine of flight bends an octave down. You're home, safe, and you can breathe again. You will live to see tomorrow.

But then tomorrow comes. Another flight, another mission. And you ask yourself again, *Is today my last day?*

1

THIS IS WHAT WAR FEELS LIKE

January 26, 2006

Near FOB Normandy, outside Baqubah, Iraq

The helicopter blades stuttered over the palm groves twenty miles east of our home base of LSA Anaconda, also known as Balad Air Base. An LSA—logistics support area— is similar to a FOB, but much larger. As one of the largest military bases in Iraq, Anaconda was one of the main air hubs for supplies, troops, and equipment into and out of the country, which made it a very busy airfield—and a natural target for enemy rockets and mortars.

In the doorless cockpit of our Kiowa, the frigid night air swept in, making our faces feel frozen and brittle. On the outskirts of Baqubah, the lights of civilization gave way to a velvet-black desolation, a flat, vast desert peppered with primitive mud huts clustered in small villages.

Through my night vision goggles—NVGs—I could see the grainy, green outlines of trees, dirt roads, and open fields. At night, we always flew fully blacked out during missions, cutting any lights on the aircraft that might make us visible targets. In the darkness, the constellation Orion shone brighter than I had ever seen it before.

I was flying right seat in our OH-58D Kiowa Warrior, trailing above the leader of our usual team of two helicopters. Small and nimble, Kiowas operate like an airborne extension of the infantry. We fly low and fast, within eyesight of friendly ground forces—and the enemy.

FOB Normandy—a tiny base on the eastern side of our area of operations toward the Iranian border—had been pummeled with rockets and mortar rounds in recent days. We were flying a reconnaissance and security mission to investigate the source of the attacks, looking for any suspicious activity—rockets set on timers, people placing them, any signs of movement—but the lush, impenetrable canopies of the palm groves gave the insurgents protective cover.

Then the lead pilot found something, a possible bunker, maybe a cache of weapons. He wanted to take a closer look. My left seater, CW3 Chris Rowley—the pilot in command (PC) and the air mission commander (AMC) for our flight—told lead to pick up an outer security pattern, to fly above us to overwatch our position while we dipped down for a closer look. Through our NVGs, we could see the something was nothing but trash. The other Kiowa resumed the lead flight position. But just as we were falling back in as trail, a blinding flash of light erupted under our aircraft.

The aircraft lurched forward with a sudden, violent kick.

"Taking fire! Taking fire!" yelled Chris.

I immediately dropped a waypoint, a digital marker that records in the navigation system the grid coordinates where we were hit. Chris broke right, away from the road, and began jinking, darting erratically to become an unpredictable target.

"You good?" Chris asked. "It's one hell of a rush, isn't it?"

I wasn't scared. I was *pissed*. Someone had just tried to kill me. We suspected small-arms fire—AK-47 rounds—but the concussion indicated it could have been something larger.

"Hey, Ambrosia," radioed Blane Hepfner, the pilot in the lead aircraft. "Hopefully there's not a UXO rolling around somewhere in the back of your aircraft right now." He was referring to an unexploded ordnance.

Thanks, jackass, I thought. He might have been messing with us, but he had a point. A concussion-type blast hit our aircraft, so it was possible that an RPG—rocket-propelled grenade—warhead had entered but not detonated. It was unlikely, but we had no way of knowing until we landed.

If we landed.

Even though neither Chris nor I was hit with a bullet, the aircraft may have sustained damage that could affect our flight between now and the time we were able to get the aircraft on the ground.

Chris and I looked at each other.

Shit!

The flight controls felt fine. There was no restricted movement or feedback indicating that the rotor head, engine, or transmission had received any battle damage, but you can never be too sure. We decided to fly to the nearest U.S. base to set our bird down and do a damage assessment.

Getting shot at is almost in the job description for a Kiowa Warrior pilot. When you are at war, it's not a matter of if you get shot at, it's *when*, and whether you'll walk away from it. Unfortunately, not everyone does.

I'd never been shot at before. Now I was in combat, and the reality of war hit home.

Someone is trying to kill me.

"Warhorse Base, Annihilator One-One, inbound for immediate landing to the FARP."

The FARP—forward arming and refueling point—was where helicopters landed to refuel and to rearm weapons systems, usually within the confines of a FOB or combat outpost.

We made a short final descent into FOB Warhorse, a tiny U.S. base in Baqubah, which was about halfway between where we had taken fire and our home base at Balad. Baqubah was only about ten minutes and a couple of miles from where we'd gotten shot at, but it felt like a lifetime.

Once we were safely on the ground inside the wire of a U.S. base, I lifted up my NVG and turned on the blue light inside the cockpit to give our eyes a break. I tightened my grip on the flight controls as Chris got out of the helicopter to do a walk-around to see if we'd been hit. The temperature and pressure levels on the instrument panel were still all in the green zone, indicating that a bullet hadn't severed a critical oil or hydraulic line.

Chris was only gone for a minute before he came back and plugged his helmet cord back into the aircraft radio.

"Yeah, we got hit a couple of times with small-arms fire," he said. "We have some damage in the aft electrical compartment, and I found an entry bullet hole on your side by the fuel cell." Luckily, there was no indication of an RPG—or anything larger than small-arms fire.

There was only one problem—we still had to make it back to Balad. Should we fly home or should we shut down there on the refuel pad? If we did the latter, our crew chiefs and maintenance personnel would have to come out to Warhorse and either fix the Kiowa there or put it on a low-boy flatbed semi truck and convoy it back to Balad. But driving in Iraq is a very dangerous thing to do. IEDs—improvised explosive devices—are everywhere. IEDs were often the weapon of choice against U.S. ground troops and usually litter their travel routes.

"I think we can fly it back," Chris said. "What do you think?"

I trusted Chris. An instructor pilot, my pilot in command of this flight, he was my stick buddy and had been to Iraq three years earlier, during the invasion in 2003. He always asked me—since I was still a newbie pilot—what I thought about different combat scenarios or emergency or procedural situations and what decision I would make. This was why he was so good. He was constantly trying to get me to think for myself and not just blindly agree with my PC. We were a crew, and crews made decisions together.

"I agree," I said. "I think we can fly it back."

And so we did.

As our aircraft skids touched down at Anaconda and eased the helicopter's weight onto the parking pad at Balad, I let out a huge sigh of relief. We had made it. Someone was looking out for us that day.

Our maintenance personnel assessed the aircraft and confirmed that we'd taken two direct hits. One 7.62mm AK-47 round had gone through the aft electrical compartment, where we kept our flight bags. The round had exploded on entry into the aircraft, sending shrapnel flying. I found a bullet hole that went through my flight bag, and I found shrapnel in our extra ammo magazines and flight gloves.

Another 7.62mm bullet had entered on the right side of the aircraft. It had pierced the fuel cell and continued its trajectory toward the cockpit until the armament control unit—the 12x12 computer box that controls the weapons system on the aircraft—finally stopped it about twelve inches behind my back. That was close.

After our damage assessments, Chris and I packed up our flight gear and called it a night. But I couldn't sleep much. I was still riding high from knowing that we had cheated death. I'd never felt that kind of rush before.

But the deployment was still young, and the enemy was out there, waiting for us. And I'd be back, looking for them.

2

BORN TO FLY

March 2003
Fort Jackson, South Carolina

You could say that flying is in my blood. My family's military and aviation legacy dates back three generations. My great-grandfather was an infantryman in World War I in Verdun, France. My grandfather flew an array of fixed-wing aircraft and was a test pilot on helicopter prototypes in the Army Air Corps (the predecessor to the Air Force) during World War II. My father was a paratrooper in the Army 82nd Airborne Division from 1960 to 1963. My mother was a gorgeous civilian pilot instructor who taught people to fly many types of aircraft in addition to being a Pan Am stewardess and purser. Female pilots were rare back in the 1960s, but my mom was fearless and wanted to fly. My father flew commercial jets for Pan Am, but he could pilot just about anything with fixed wings. He was also an instructor pilot and taught my two sisters and me to fly.

I grew up in the cockpit of my dad's planes, a Cessna 150 and an L-19 Bird Dog. It was a family tradition to "fly to breakfast" on the weekends. I loved taking off from the little grass airstrip on our family farm in White Salmon, a small town on the edge of the Columbia River in southern Washington State. We'd fly to nearby Trout Lake, Dallesport, or Hood River. The Cessna could seat only two people, so whichever kid got to fly with our dad always felt special. My sisters and I got our first flight lessons on those trips to breakfast, when Dad would let us talk on the radio, tiny voices announcing over the airspace frequency, "Cessna Three-Five-Zero Delta Echo, taking off to the south. Climbing one thousand feet."

My mom would load up the rest of the kids and the dog in the Suburban and drive to the airport. Once the whole family was reunited at the airport for breakfast, our conversation turned into a ground school lesson.

"What are the three most important words in aviation?" my dad would ask us.

"AIRSPEED, AIRSPEED, AIRSPEED," we three daughters would say in unison.

Listening to my dad's stories about the 82nd Airborne really kept us hanging from our seats. It was like watching a movie with our ears. It sounded exciting to jump out of airplanes, talk the way the Army guys talked ("pass the fucking salt, please"), and be an overall badass paratrooper. He jumped out of airplanes, shot machine guns, and "camped" in the woods. It all sounded like an incredible adventure. I was awestruck by my dad's experiences and told myself that someday I'd join the Army just like he had.

We spent so much time at those local airports that we knew the pilots and the maintenance guys. We learned the pilot lingo. My father instilled a "look but don't touch" policy whenever we were around airplanes and runways. This basic respect for aircraft and aviation paid off immensely when we actually became pilots.

When I was about six years old, Dad dropped me and my eleven-year-old sister Kelly off at the dock at Lake Chelan, in central Washington State, where our family often spent summer vacations. The area we were staying in was only accessible by boat or floatplane. It was windy that day and, as he flew to the south end of the lake to pick up my mom and five-year-old sister Lacey, the lake grew dangerously rough with swells so large they could swallow the plane. Oblivious to the danger, Kelly and I cheered and waved when he touched down and motored over. Only years later would we learn what skill and luck it had taken Dad to land a floatplane in such dangerous waters with his wife and youngest daughter and our black Lab, Lizzie, as passengers.

Kelly, Lacey, and I—my dad called us his piglets—grew up thinking it was perfectly normal to have an airstrip in the backyard. Ours was a 2,100-foot strip of closely trimmed grass on my family's 175-acre farm, where my parents grew and harvested alfalfa to sell as horse and cattle feed.

Our driveway was half a mile long, and we couldn't see a neighbor or hear any sign of civilization except the occasional log truck slamming on its jake brakes to go around a curve on the highway. It was our very own wilderness playground, and my sisters and I took advantage of it every day. I don't think the words "we're bored" ever came out of our mouths. We were outside causing havoc all over the farm from right after breakfast until dinnertime, which Mom would signal by ringing a huge bell on our deck.

My mom and dad taught Lacey and me how to ride four-wheelers when we were about seven and eight years old, giving us the freedom to explore the farm. Only eighteen months apart, Lacey and I were frequent partners in crime. When we got just a few years older, we rode the four-wheelers through the backwoods all over other people's property, stirring up dust and generally creating chaos wherever we went. Every once in a while a neighbor would come out on the porch and yell at us to get off their property. We would go extra fast for those drive-bys.

Aside from the freedom and the fun, we actually did work on

the farm. One of our jobs was to flip hay bales. We would drive the four-wheelers behind the tractor my dad was baling hay in. We'd jump off and flip the bale right side up so it could be picked up properly by the bale wagon. The fields were huge and there were thousands of bales to flip. Lacey and I had it down to a science: the first half I drove, she flipped; the second half we swapped.

We would much rather have been running around the farm, swimming in our pond, hiking, exploring, or getting into trouble, but helping is how we pulled our weight around the farm. One of my favorite times was when my mom would come out to meet us with a picnic lunch and we would all sit around together in the middle of the woods. We would often make a campfire and toast marshmallows.

Kelly was five years older than I was, which usually meant that I was trying to be just like her and, as a result, driving her crazy. Lacey and I idolized Kelly. We were the typical little sisters who mimicked everything their cool older sister did. In my eyes, Kelly could do no wrong.

She proved herself one day when a group of us had just finished skiing at Mount Hood Meadows, one of our favorite ski slopes. Kelly and two of her friends had the ski day planned, and her two little sisters, who were both under twelve at the time, wanted to tag along. When it was time to head home, all five of us piled in my sister's car: a 1972 Oldsmobile. It was huge, almost like a limo. And it was made of steel. We nicknamed it "The Slime" because it was painted a disgusting puke-green color. Kelly was only sixteen and my parents wanted to make sure that as a young, inexperienced driver, she was in a safe car that would protect her if she ever got into an accident.

The roads were icy and slick that day as we drove down the narrow mountain road. Out in front of us, driving in the opposite direction, a Land Rover lost traction and started sliding on the ice, putting it on a head-on collision course with The Slime. Lacey and I were completely oblivious to what was going on, but Kelly knew we were about to get in an accident.

"Prepare for impact!" Kelly yelled at us.

Dink!

The Land Rover hit us head-on and started spinning away. Kelly brought The Slime to a stop. We all looked around at each other, unfazed, but also incredibly impressed that The Slime had done what my parents had always hoped it would—protect us. It barely had a dent while the Land Rover took some serious damage.

Of everything the three of us experienced as kids growing up on the farm, the most important was that we got to experience freedom: to explore, be creative, and be wild. With that freedom came the responsibility to solve the problems we got ourselves into. It also helped develop character that led us to always push the limits. *No* wasn't in our vocabulary. We loved every wild minute of it.

From an early age I knew I wanted to be a military pilot. When I was nine, my dad bought me a model of an F-14 Tomcat fighter jet for my birthday. To me, it was the coolest thing in the world. Later, when I was in eighth grade, my parents sent me to Space Camp in Alabama for a month. Instead of the space part, I did the Aviation Challenge, which was like mini military boot camp. We marched around in formation, went to survival school, learned how to escape from a helicopter that crashed in the water, flight training, you name it. During my mock survival school at Space Camp, I had a severe allergic reaction to poison ivy. That came back to haunt me years later during real military survival school, SERE—survival, evasion, resistance, escape—when I reacted to poison ivy again so badly I had to go to the emergency room—but not until after I'd completed the course.

My obsession with flying waned during high school, when I got into competitive gymnastics. I trained hard. My mom drove three hours round trip five days a week to my gym on the outskirts of Portland, Oregon, until I was old enough to get my license and drive myself. In 1998 I became the Oregon State All-Around Gymnastic Champion for my level.

But my dream of flying was reignited when I went to the University of Washington in Seattle. I tried out for the UW Husky cheerleading team and thanks to my tumbling moves, made the team. I actually couldn't believe I made it. I didn't have an overly bubbly personality. I was used to the seriousness of competitive gymnastics. But I could do backflips, so I think that made up for me having to force a smile on my face. At the end of the 2000 football season our team made it to the Rose Bowl, so I cheered in the Rose Bowl parade and the football game, where UW won against the Purdue Boilermakers. A few weeks later our cheer team headed to Florida to compete in the national cheer competition.

But something was missing from college. Nothing I studied held my interest. The only class I got an A in was an elective about aviation. Everything else bored me to death, and as a result I put little effort into them, and bounced back and forth between what I wanted to declare as a major.

Then something happened that would change the course of my life forever, as it did for many Americans.

I was asleep in my basement room of a house I shared with a few other friends in Seattle, just a block away from campus, when my roommate came running down the stairs early one morning.

What is she doing coming down here so early? And why is she holding the phone?

"Amber, your mom's on the phone. There was a bomb or something at the World Trade Center and she wants to talk to you," she said as she handed me the phone.

Huh? I still wasn't quite awake.

"Hi, Mom," I said.

"Get in front of a TV right now," she said. The cold tone of her voice sent chills down my spine.

"Why, what's going on?" I asked.

"We were attacked," she said. "I have to go. Your dad is flying a plane home from the middle of nowhere in Montana right now and I don't even know if he knows yet. They are about to shut down all of the airspace across the country."

I turned on the TV and saw the second plane fly into the South Tower of the World Trade Center.

Everything changed in an instant. Instead of the military being something I had always thought about doing, now I wanted to join. The path I was meant to be on was now crystal clear: I wanted to join the military and fly. Now.

I immediately started looking into military flight programs and visited all the branches—Air Force, Navy, Marines—except for the Army. All of the recruiters said I needed to finish my college degree and come back and talk to them. But I didn't want to wait.

Dad told me to talk to the Army even though I had been reluctant to try them because who would have thought the Army had a flight program? I was nineteen years old and thought I knew best. But I listened to him and gave the Army a shot. I learned that the Army's aviation program was smaller than that in some of the other branches, but it seemed like the perfect fit for me. I could apply right away, without having to finish my degree. I could get college credits as I went, and the Army would even help pay for them. There was one catch, though: if I were selected, after all of the tests, interviews, and medical and physical exams, I'd be joining the Army to become a helicopter pilot, not a fixed-wing pilot.

I had never even been in a helicopter. I knew I wanted to fly, but flying helicopters had never crossed my mind. My dad always said that helicopter pilots were crazy to fly a machine that had ten thousand moving parts all working against each other. And I loved flying planes. What if I hated flying helicopters? The unknown was giving me cold feet.

Then, one weekend, I met my parents at an air show in Olympia, Washington, about an hour's drive from Seattle. The air show was offering $60 rides for a twenty-minute flight in a Robinson R22 helicopter, which looks like a life-size version of a remote-control toy. I decided to go for a ride. The pilot let me take control of the pedals and the cyclic—two of the three flight controls (the other is the collective). It was amazing. When we landed, I jumped out and ran over to my parents to tell them the good news. I couldn't stop smiling. I was hooked. Helicopters were for me.

Aside from that twenty-minute helicopter flight, all my flight time had been in fixed-wing aircraft. I had plenty of flight time in Dad's Cessna 150. Regardless of what I'd be flying in the future, having a general knowledge of aviation would be helpful. It was time to get my private pilot's license.

I spent that summer studying airspace, sectional charts, aerodynamics, and how to read weather briefs. I began flying with a flight instructor out of the Dallesport airport, about a thirty-minute drive from my house. During all of my previous flight experience, my dad had been in the cockpit with me. The responsibility had always been with my dad, not me. Now I was responsible for the decision making going on in the aircraft. And I loved that pressure.

After a handful of flights with my instructor, it was time for me to take my first solo flight. I was terrified, excited, and nervous all at the same time as my instructor and I took off in the Cessna 150 and flew in traffic pattern. But mostly I was ready. My dad had done this, my mom, my sister Kelly. Now it was my turn.

I did three takeoffs and landings with my instructor. After my third landing he said, "All right, taxi back to the passenger area."

"Why?" I asked even though I already knew the answer to my question.

"Because I am getting out. It's time for you to solo," he said.

I slowed the airplane to a stop as we pulled onto the passenger ramp.

"Fly the same way you did with me and you'll be fine. I'll be talking to you on the traffic pattern radio. Go get 'em!" he said. Then he unplugged his headset and jumped out of the airplane and ran toward the terminal. I'd never felt so alone as I did sitting by myself in that airplane.

And just like that, once my instructor was out of sight, all of my nerves were gone. It was now or never.

I pushed in the throttle and the airplane began to vibrate as it started to move forward toward the runway. As I turned the plane into position for takeoff, I went over what I had to do in my head: three takeoffs, three landings. Piece of cake.

"Dallesport traffic, Cessna Three-Five-Zero Delta Echo, taking off runway three-one, staying in the traffic pattern," I said over the air traffic radio. This airport was really small, so there was no air tower separating and controlling traffic. It was up to the pilots in this airspace to maintain communication with and separation from other air traffic.

My right hand on the throttle, my left on the yoke flight control, I pushed the throttle all the way in and the aircraft roared to life, barreling down the runway. As the needle continued to rise on my airspeed indicator, I pulled back on the yoke and felt the nose wheel of the airplane lift off the ground, followed by the trailing wheels. I was airborne! For the first time in my life I was flying solo.

As I climbed to traffic pattern altitude, the scenery below grew distant. I made a left turn to begin my traffic pattern. Takeoff was complete and successful. It was time to set up for landing. When I was halfway through the traffic pattern I made my radio call: "Dallesport traffic, Cessna Three-Five-Zero Delta Echo is downwind, turning base leg for landing runway three-one."

I needed to get this right. Takeoffs were considerably easier than landings. My dad had told me: *If things aren't right on your final approach, do a go-around. Don't ever think you are too good to do a go-around. They teach you how to do one for a reason.*

A go-around is merely aborting the landing by putting in full throttle, continuing to fly rather than descend, and climbing back up to altitude to allow yourself to set up the landing again. A pilot can do a go-around for any reason that he or she feels would make the landing unsafe, whether strong winds, overshooting the runway so there's not enough room to land, or an object on the runway.

I pulled back the throttle and began my descent toward the runway, turning the airplane to our final approach for landing.

"Three-Five-Zero Delta Echo, short final, runway three-one," I said over the radio.

I pointed the nose toward the numbers on the end of the runway, just as I'd been taught. Using my peripheral vision to assess my rate of descent as I got closer to the ground, I was lined up as I should be.

As I crossed the threshold of the runway, I pulled back the throttle to idle in order to reduce power and I pulled back on the yoke flight control to flare the airplane to level it and allow the back wheels to touch down.

Squeeealll!

When I felt my back wheels make contact with the runway, I pulled back on the yoke as far as possible to keep the nose wheel off the ground as long as possible. The plane continued rushing down the dashed centerline of the runway, and as it slowed, the nose wheel touched down on the ground.

"Nice work, Amber!" my instructor said over the radio.

I was beaming. I couldn't wait to do it again.

———

In September 2002, a few months after my solo flight, I took my private pilot's license check ride and the written, oral, and flight exams. I passed all of them. I was officially a pilot. I didn't want to wait another day. I applied for the Army Warrant Officer Flight Program.

Almost four months later, in mid-January 2003, I was on a bus with fellow recruits pulling into basic training—also known as boot camp—at Fort Jackson, outside Columbia, South Carolina. The primary basic training bases—Fort Knox, Fort Sill, and Fort Benning—were the training grounds for privates who would go on to careers in the infantry, artillery, and other combat arms jobs. Fort Jackson, or "Relaxin' Jackson," as the privates at other forts called it, was one of only three integrated boot camps, where women trained with men.

At Fort Jackson, I was beginning the first step of my training in Army aviation, the only branch of combat arms in which women were allowed then. The only reason I entered the Army was to become a combat pilot, and that's exactly where I was headed.

The bus came to a stop, the door opened, and on climbed a drill sergeant straight out of central casting—big Smokey Bear hat, rippling muscles, and a stony expression on his face.

"You have thirty seconds to get your asses off of this bus into formation!" he said. "NOW! GO! GO! *GO!*"

After we'd scrambled off the bus and milled around awkwardly to get in line, the drill sergeant chewed out the young man next to me for having a smile on his face. It was probably one of sheer terror.

"What the hell do you think you're smiling about? Wipe that smile off your face, Private!" he said about two inches from the recruit's face.

Holy shit. This guy's for real.

"Get down and give me twenty push-ups!"

We did.

"Get up! What do you think you're doing? Are you eyeballing me? Are you talking to me? You think you can talk to me? Get down!"

Oh, my God. What did I sign up for? Is this my new reality?

It was: Get up. Get down. Get up. Get down. Until we were so tired we stopped thinking and simply obeyed the barking commands. Eventually we were herded into an auditorium for the "welcome." My first day and I was already exhausted.

As we sat silently in the auditorium, drill sergeants roamed the aisles, hands clenched behind their backs, just waiting to pounce on someone who was whispering to a neighbor or not paying attention. Another drill sergeant walked onstage and looked out at us. The couple hundred terrified recruits stared back at him.

"Who wants to come up here and sing the Army song while we are waiting to begin?" he asked.

No one volunteered.

My heart started pounding. Singing in front of fellow recruits sounded worse than a couple hundred push-ups. I sank down in my seat, thankful I was on a side aisle, hoping I was out of the sergeant's line of sight.

"You," he said, pointing at a young man in one of the front rows.

The guy walked up onstage and awkwardly attempted to sing a song most of us didn't know yet.

"First to fight for the right and to build the nation's might, and the Army goes rolling along . . ."

After the song, the same drill sergeant briefed us on standard rules and what to expect over the next couple of days. No cell phones, no going anywhere alone—even to the bathroom—no fraternizing. We had to bring our canteens with us at all times and they always had to be full of water. He went over the contraband list. They specifically emphasized that Listerine mouthwash was not allowed. I knew better than to ask questions. In my two hours since I'd arrived at the base, I'd realized that the more invisible you were to the drill sergeants, the better. After the sergeant finished the brief, he looked out at us and said, "Do you miss your mom yet?"

Yes, I thought.

On the way out of the auditorium we were given paperwork, bed linens, and sleeping assignments. We didn't have uniforms yet, but we were broken down into groups and instructed to march to our barracks. I walked into my bay, which was lined with twin-size bunk beds, and set my bag on a top bunk close to the door. I assumed if I took the top bunk people would mess with my stuff less, although I didn't really have much with me anyway, just the clothes I was wearing and some toiletries. I had never traveled so light in my life.

Other women began to file in behind me and started claiming their bunks.

"Hey, can I have this one?" asked a girl who looked to be about eighteen years old.

"Sure," I said.

"I'm Courtney Young," she said, as she took the bottom bunk and set her stuff on her bed.

"It's good to meet you," I said.

She leaned in close and whispered, "I still have my cell phone if you want to use it."

"Really? Thanks!"

Later that night, Courtney gave me her cell phone and I crawled into my wall locker next to my bunk and called my mom. And I didn't get caught.

It was our little secret. Courtney and I became instant friends. She was at least five eight, a lot taller than I am at five four. She had long, dark hair and a fun, outgoing personality that always lightened our mood after we'd gotten yelled at by the drill sergeants. Courtney knew how to make our bunk beds to the drill sergeants' standard, which helped us perform better on morning inspections.

A few days later we spent an entire day in the uniform warehouse called CIF—Central Issuing Facility—where we were issued uniforms and equipment. We got our daily uniform, the green and brown "woodland" combat uniforms known as BDUs (battle dress uniforms), black lace-up combat boots, physical training uniforms (sweatshirts and sweatpants that said "Army," running shoes, hats, canteens, duffel bags, E-Tool (compact shovel), socks, sports bras, and more. We had every uniform and piece of gear for every scenario we'd face at basic training.

Almost two weeks later, on assignment day, the drill sergeants seemed to be randomly assigning us to our basic training companies. But Courtney and I cracked their code. The drill sergeants had lined us up in rows of fifty and, as they walked down each row, counted off "one," "two," "three," "four," assigning each soldier a number.

"Courtney, make sure you are in a number four spot. Make sure you get number four!" I whispered to her.

We managed to trade places with other soldiers just in time to make sure we both got assigned the number four without any of the drill sergeants noticing. We ended up being battle buddies, which meant we ended up going everywhere together.

Basic training is all about taking people from all walks of life, breaking them down, and building everyone back up to the same level. It teaches you everything. All you have to do is never quit. No matter what.

"They are always going to try and get you to quit," my dad had told me before I left for boot camp. "They want to get rid of the weak ones. If you can't make it through basic training—emphasis on the training—how do you expect to be able to fly a helicopter in combat? Always keep going. Take another step. Always keep putting one foot in front of the other. Never quit."

He was right. Every time I was exhausted, pissed, overdone, pushed to my limit, I remembered his advice. "Pain is temporary, pride is forever" became my mantra, and I repeated it to myself every time I needed a little self-motivation.

About halfway through our training, we began running obstacle courses. They're meant to instill confidence and teamwork. Mostly I thought they were fun. We crawled through mud, climbed over walls, and maneuvered across rope bridges and cargo nets.

We learned to tie a Swiss seat so that we could rappel down a forty-foot wall called Victory Tower. On Victory Tower day, our company gathered in the bleachers next to the tower for our safety brief.

"Safety comes first. No talking. The drill sergeant at the top of the tower will give you further instructions. Climb the ladder to the top only when instructed to do so," the drill sergeant said. "And now Sergeant Jackson will demonstrate rappelling the wall."

Sergeant Jackson stood at the top of the tower ready to rappel. All of a sudden, next to him a human figure came up over the top and started free-falling four stories to the ground.

Boom!

The human figure hit the ground right in front of us. People screamed. I sat there in shock.

The drill sergeant started laughing.

I made myself look at the object lying on the ground. It didn't move. Then I realized it was a dummy that we used to learn CPR on.

I had never rappelled before, had no idea what to expect, and now was recovering from the fact that I thought someone had just died right in front of my eyes. But all the drill sergeants thought it was hilarious. Almost immediately, they called on a few soldiers to get to the tower.

Then I heard, "Smith! You're up."

I ran to the wooden ladder and began the climb to the top. The higher I climbed the more nervous I got. At the top I pulled myself over the edge onto the platform where the drill sergeants were. I got in line behind a few other soldiers.

As I waited, one of the drill sergeants came up and inspected my Swiss seat harness. Then it was my turn.

I walked to the edge, looked over, and instantly regretted it. I imagined the dummy human flying through the air and the impact it made on the ground.

"I'm connecting you to the rope now," the drill sergeant said as he locked me into the harness. "Are you ready to go?"

"No, Drill Sergeant," I said honestly.

"Well, you better be," he said, laughing. "Just lean back and push off. Go."

I had to do it. If I died, I died, but I still had to try.

Pain is temporary, pride is forever.

Holding the rope, I leaned back over the edge so my legs were at a ninety-degree angle to the rest of my body and pushed off the wall. I didn't fall. The rope held me just fine. I moved my right hand that was holding the rope away from my body to give me some slack in the rope just the way the drill sergeants had taught me. I pushed my legs and began bounding down the wall, going faster and faster every time I came back to the wall. Before I knew it, I was on the ground.

I loved it.

M16 rifle training followed Victory Tower day. We had to know our weapon inside and out: all of its components, how to clear a jam, and how to shoot a target. We spent hours in safety instruction. The Army had been using the M16 since the Vietnam War, where it was highly effective in jungle warfare. Even though we were still using the M16 at basic training, once I got to my operational unit as a helicopter pilot we would have the newer variant, the M4. A shorter, lighter rifle, it had internal components that were essentially the same, which was why it was so important to learn now how the M16 worked.

On range day, it was raining. I walked past my drill sergeant on the way to my firing position and yelled, "Weapons up and downrange,

Drill Sergeant!" Each of us had to yell that to the drill sergeant every time we walked onto an active, live fire range. This meant that the barrel of my rifle was safely pointed downrange, away from people and toward the target.

The firing range had at least ten foxholes in a line facing downrange at the green plastic pop-up targets. The foxholes were about a couple feet deep and were surrounded by stacked sandbags. I walked to my firing position, set my M16 on the sandbags, and jumped down into the foxhole. The rain came right through my uniform as I propped the barrel of my M16 on a sandbag to help support it while I was firing. My Kevlar helmet was too big for my head and kept slipping down in front of my eyes. In between pushing the helmet back, I grabbed an ammo magazine that was sitting on the sandbag and slapped it into the rifle. I pulled the charging handle to the rear to put a round in the chamber.

"Fire when ready," said my range instructor.

I pushed the safety switch from safe to semi, put my face close to the rifle, and aimed the front and rear sight posts on the target. I steadied my breathing and squeezed the trigger, again and again, adjusting my aim every time before firing.

Shooting was exhilarating. I'd shot rifles before, but never an M16. The only thing I didn't like was how long it was. It doesn't have a collapsible butt stock like the M4, and my arms aren't that long, so it was a little harder for me than for bigger soldiers to keep it tucked in the pocket of my shoulder, which helps to aim accurately at the target and reach the trigger. But I made it work.

Every time we finished shooting at the range, we headed back to the barracks to deep-clean our M16s. The drill sergeants allowed us to talk while we were cleaning them, so Courtney and I always had a good chat. She and I would claim our spot on the hard floor and I'd lay out my cleaning cloth towel. I carefully dismantled all of the components of my weapon: the carrying handle, the rear sight post, the rail covers, the receiver. I grabbed my toothbrush from my cleaning kit and began brushing away any dust, dirt, or carbon that had gotten on each component since I last used it. I left for last the dismantling and cleaning of the bolt carrier, firing pin, firing retainer pin, and cam pin, because they were smaller and easier to lose. We'd been warned more than once not to lose them.

After our first day at the range and about an hour of cleaning, my M16 looked as good as new to me. I reassembled it, jumped up, and marched it over to my drill sergeant for inspection.

"My M16 is clean, Drill Sergeant," I said.

He looked at me without saying anything and grabbed my M16 out of my hands. He inspected the outside, turning it over and looking at every single crevice. He opened the lower receiver of the rifle from the upper receiver and stuck his pinkie finger in the barrel. When he pulled out his finger, it had the smallest ring of black carbon soot on it.

Damn it.

He held up his finger for me to see.

"Not good enough!" he said. "Don't bring it back to me until it's clean."

"Yes, Drill Sergeant," I said, and grabbed the rifle back from him, disappointed in myself for missing that spot. It didn't happen again.

Almost two and a half months later, in March, my entire company, called "Ridgebacks," stood outside our barracks in perfect formation, blinking into a cold afternoon drizzle. Our drill sergeant paced through this forest of stiff grunts in our standard woodland camo uniforms.

"Are you crybabies ready to act like soldiers yet?"

"*YES, DRILL SERGEANT!*" we yelled in unison.

I was three rows back, in the middle, trying to focus on the words through my exhaustion. We'd been marching for hours, carrying rucksacks full of all our gear on our aching backs.

I was so hungry for sleep, I was fantasizing about the claustrophobic military hooches we'd sleep in that night, elbow to elbow with a battle buddy in a pup tent no bigger than a twin bed on the cold, damp ground. My top bunk in the barracks now seemed like the Ritz.

A woman's blood-curdling scream brought me back to the present.

Soldiers slammed into one another all around me, scrambling to move farther back. A girl two rows in front of me dropped to her knees, screaming at the top of her lungs.

"Jesus, save me!" she screamed with her arms reaching up toward the sky.

Um, could she seriously be any more dramatic? What the hell is going on?

Then it hit me, the white smoke pouring into the formation. Suddenly my eyes, my skin, my lungs were on fire.

"Gas! Gas! Gas!" someone in the now-chaotic formation yelled.

Other soldiers were tapping their shoulders with their fingertips, the signal for a chemical attack. We'd been tear-gassed.

This feeling, however awful, was not entirely new. A few weeks earlier we had been through the "gas chamber," which every private in the Army must endure as a universally dreaded test of boot camp. Rappelling, shooting, and throwing my first grenade were the fun parts of basic. But no one likes going to the gas chamber. While standing in a single-file line and wearing a gas mask, we were ordered to do jumping jacks. The drill sergeants wanted to make sure that we were good and out of breath by the time they made us take off our gas masks and inhale. Most recruits try to fake the mandatory deep breath, but the sergeants can see right through that and make them take another. And another. Then they began to ask us questions.

"What's your Social Security number, Private?

"When's your birthday!"

Only when you answer coherently can you reseal your mask and leave.

Then the real fun begins. Your nose overflows. Your eyes gush. Your face gets slimed with more mucus than a human sinus should be able to produce. You might try to wipe it off were you not actively choking on every breath.

That drill was to prepare us for times like this, when we might encounter something unexpected, which is usually how tear gas arrives. But even with training, you never know how you'll react until it happens. Most of my company ran downwind, directly into the gas.

I walked the other way.

One hundred paces from the site of attack, comfortably out of the gas, I noticed a group of drill sergeants watching me. With a nod and a smirk, they acknowledged my ability to think beyond the lemming mentality. For a split second, at least, we had an understanding. Then they sent me back to suffer along with the others. But by then, most of the gas had dissipated.

———

A few days later my shiny black dress shoes squished in the grass as I proudly marched across the Fort Jackson parade field with hundreds of other soldiers in our Class A green uniforms. Marching in formation almost seemed natural after thirteen weeks of boot camp. I wanted to look up over my right shoulder and into the stands where all of the spectators were, but that would be breaking protocol, so I kept my eyes straight ahead at the soldier in front of me. Somewhere in the stands was my dad, who had flown all the way across the country from our home in Washington State to South Carolina, so he could watch me graduate from basic training and we could spend a few hours together.

Like most of the other soldiers, I had never been away from my home and family for so long, and I had missed them. Yet I had learned so much about myself and life during basic. It had opened my eyes to the vast world outside my little hometown, a world I now wanted to explore. But mostly I had learned about people—how young Americans can be so undeniably different yet can come together because of their own individual calling to serve their country. That common thread united us.

It had been a long couple of months. I had been tested over and over and I thought I might fail a couple of times, but I never gave up. And after working out nonstop—running, marching, push-ups, sit-ups, obstacle courses—I was in the best shape I'd been since I stopped doing gymnastics four years earlier. Waking up at 5:00 a.m. every day was the new normal for me, which is saying a lot, because I am not a morning person. Basic training wasn't the hardest stage of my Army career, but it was the initial phase of transformation from dumb kid to an adult.

Aside from a college football game, the basic training graduation ceremony was the grandest gathering I'd ever been to. Parents, sisters, brothers, aunts, uncles, girlfriends, boyfriends traveled from around the country to see their loved ones march across the parade field, having completed the first step in becoming a soldier. The bleachers were filled with cheering family members.

After graduating we were allowed to wear our respective ranks. I was an E-2 private and had one stripe on my shoulder that looked like an upside-down V. The drill sergeants called them "mosquito wings." This was a milestone for me, but I still had a long way to go.

I'd only be wearing my private rank for a few weeks until I started Warrant Officer Candidate School. After that, I'd start flight school. This would take at least another year of training, studying, and more training. It wasn't going to be easy, but I had just passed test number one and was eager for the next.

After my company completed the pass and review march in front of the crowd, we continued marching to an empty parking lot, where we were dismissed. I found my dad in the massive crowd with a huge smile on his face. I ran over to him and gave him a big hug. His middle piglet was now on her way to becoming an Army helicopter pilot.

We walked from the parking lot over to my barracks, where I'd spent countless hours with my battle buddy cleaning our M16s, cleaning the bays, beautifying the area around the buildings. I got to give him the tour.

"Here's my bunk, Puppy," I said, tapping my mattress. I had started calling my dad Puppy when I was about five years old and the nickname stuck.

"Some things never change," he said. "I'm pretty sure we had the same blankets back when I was in the Army in the sixties."

Soldiers weren't allowed to leave the base, so we went to the post exchange—or PX, the Army base version of Walmart—had some food, and got some ice cream. Courtney joined us. For those few short hours, I let my guard down for the first time since I had left home. It was so nice not to have a drill sergeant breathing down my neck every five seconds.

The visit was over before we knew it. I didn't want to say good-bye, but if all went well, I'd get to see my dad and the rest of my family at my Warrant Officer Candidate School graduation in a few months. Still in uniform, I now had to report back to basic training headquarters to catch the bus that was taking all of the soldiers to Fort Rucker, Alabama. Dad and I hugged good-bye.

And just like that I was on my own again. I picked up my body-size green duffel bag, walked over to the bus, and threw the bag in the luggage compartment. I walked up the stairs and onto the bus.

"Is this bus going to Fort Rucker?" I asked the driver.

"It sure is."

Next stop, Warrant Officer Candidate School.

3

MOTHER RUCKER

2003

Fort Rucker, Alabama, Home of Army Aviation

All Army aviators attend flight school in Fort Rucker—aka Mother Rucker—a small, isolated base in southern Alabama, which is also home to Warrant Officer Candidate School (WOCS). WOCS is sort of a continuation of basic training, only stricter and with more academics and a focus on becoming an officer. Every day we would get up at 5:00 a.m., do PT in the humid early Alabama mornings, and come back to the barracks with seven minutes to shower, brush our teeth, get dressed, and back outside in formation. This kind of schedule makes you extremely efficient at time management. Class leadership woke us up every morning by yelling in the hallway, "Good morning, candidates! Today is Tuesday, April seventh. It is zero five hundred hours. The temperature is seventy degrees. The chance of rain is sixty percent, the humidity is one hundred percent. It is now zero five . . ."

We spent most of the day in a classroom, learning how to become good warrant officers. Warrant officers are different from standard commissioned officers in the Army—lieutenants, captains, majors, etc.—who are on a leadership career path where they go on to be platoon leaders and commanders and lead soldiers. Warrant officers are known as tactical and technical experts in their field, and for the majority of warrant officers in the Army, that job was being a pilot. Commissioned officers can be pilots as well, but they focus more on leading the flight unit and planning operations and missions. There are five warrant officer ranks. The initial rank is warrant officer 1 (WO1). From there you get promoted to chief warrant officer 2 (CW2) and can progress throughout your career all the way to chief warrant officer 5 (CW5).

Our WOCS classes ranged from lectures on uniform and appearance standards and leadership style to equal opportunity policies. We weren't allowed to talk during class, but we were allowed to drink coffee—a big step in independence compared to basic training, where the only drink we usually had was water from our canteens.

The majority of candidates were former noncommissioned officers or enlisted soldiers. I was the oddball with zero Army experience other than basic training, which didn't count for much. They called people like me "high school to flight school" or "street to seat." A handful of other women were in the class, but I was the only "high school to flight schooler," which made me feel like they knew what they were doing, and I didn't.

The first week of WOCS was quite an adjustment, even after the rigors of boot camp. One predawn morning, before PT formation, the fire alarm went off at three thirty. I jumped off my top bunk bed and onto the floor as my two roommates stirred.

"Do you think we need to make our beds before we leave?" I asked them. We had been there less than a week, and the thought of leaving our room in anything but pristine condition terrified me. An unmade bed? The horror!

"No. It's a fire alarm," my roommate said.

We could hear the other candidates running down the hallway. My two roommates headed out the door before me. As I began to step out of my room, I came face-to-face with my worst fear. Standing in front of me was one of our TAC (training, advising, counseling) officers—essentially the WOCS version of a drill sergeant. I didn't say anything as I looked up at him.

"Go back in your room, candidate," he said to me, his arms folded across his chest.

"Sir, Candidate Smith, shouldn't I go downstairs with everyone else?" I asked in the formal way we have to address TAC officers.

It had to be a test. Why else would he tell me to stay in my room when everyone else was downstairs?

"No, just go back to sleep," he said in a normal human voice, not the stern, no-nonsense TAC officer tone they usually use.

"Sir, Candidate Smith, I should go be with everyone else," I said, still not giving up.

"Seriously, just go back in your room and shut the door. This isn't a test," he said.

"Sir, Candidate Smith, yes, sir," I said, and retreated back inside my room.

I was so uncomfortable I made my bed. I didn't know what else to do. I could hear the other candidates downstairs getting yelled at by the TAC officers.

"Do you have all of your people accounted for, Candidate?" I heard one of the TAC officers yell at the candidate who was in charge of ensuring accountability for all of the candidates.

"Sir, Candidate Spade, all candidates accounted for, sir!" the candidate said.

"Really? Can you even count? Is this how you are going to lead in combat? You are going to lose track of your own people and not even know it?" the TAC officer yelled. "You are missing two people!"

So that's what this was about. It *was* a test, just not for me. It was for the candidates downstairs getting grilled. I was merely selected at random to be one of the two "missing" people.

About an hour later my roommates walked back into our room. I felt so guilty.

"What happened?" I asked.

"We just got smoked a lot," she said. "Smoked" is Army lingo for having to do some kind of physical exercise, lots of push-ups, flutter kicks, or burpees, until you are "smoked."

And by then it was 5:00 a.m. Time for PT, physical training.

PT was pretty much the only thing I was good at initially. I would max the physical fitness scale but had to work hard to pass everything else. I was having to learn every rule and procedure for the very first time, whereas most of the other candidates had been in the Army for years and knew those procedures and could do them in their sleep. Learning the Army command and rank structure and policies and procedures was essentially like learning a new language in a six-week crash course. There were three categories within the rank structure for the Army: enlisted, warrant officers, and commissioned officers. Enlisted had twelve ranks, warrant five, and commissioned ten. For each rank we had to memorize their insignia, pay grade, title (verbal and written), and duty. For a newbie like me it was confusing. I couldn't wait to get to flight school, where I might actually be good at something.

One day about halfway through WOCS, I was in the chow hall and grabbed a water glass and put it up to the faucet at the same time as another candidate. Our water glasses hit.

"Sorry!" I whispered.

Out of nowhere, the biggest and most terrifying TAC officer, Mr. Lopez, was leaning down to my level, face-to-face.

"Candidate! Did you just speak?" No talking was allowed while in the chow hall. His voice echoed throughout the room.

"Sir, Candidate Smith, no, sir," I said.

Mr. Lopez's eyes narrowed. He slowly turned his gaze to the candidate standing next to me whom I had accidentally banged glasses with.

"Candidate, did she just speak to you?"

"Sir, Candidate Casey, yes, sir!" he said.

Candidate Casey looked at me with the most embarrassed and helpless expression on his face.

Mr. Lopez turned back to me.

"Candidate, you better be outside the door of my office in TAC Alley by the time I get back there after lunch," he said to me.

"Sir, Candidate Smith, yes, sir," I said.

I had done my best so far to steer clear of TAC Alley, where candidates were sent when they were in trouble. It was the hallway on the bottom floor of our barracks. I had hoped to avoid it entirely during WOCS.

I finished lunch as fast as I could, even though my appetite was gone. I was terrified. To make sure I wasn't late, I ran toward the TAC Alley entrance. Outside the entry are pull-up bars, and everyone who enters TAC Alley has to do five pull-ups. I jumped up and grabbed the bar and did my pull-ups.

I jumped down, wiped off my hands, walked up the steps, and opened the door. Halfway down the hallway, Mr. Lopez's name was next to one of the closed doors. I hesitated a second, then raised my right hand and banged on the door three times.

"Sir, Candidate Smith, reporting as ordered, sir!" I said, loudly so he could hear me through the door.

"Proceed, Candidate," Mr. Lopez said.

I walked in and stood at attention in front of his desk.

"Stand at ease, Candidate," he said.

I relaxed a bit and clasped my hands together behind my back as Mr. Lopez looked at me across his desk.

"Candidate, why did you tell me that you didn't speak to that other candidate?"

"Sir, Candidate Smith, I accidentally hit him with my glass and I unintentionally said 'Sorry!' It was just a reaction. I wasn't trying to talk to him at all, sir," I said.

Mr. Lopez sat in silence as he looked at me.

"Candidate, write me a five-hundred-word essay on leadership and turn it in to me tomorrow. And stop saying 'Sorry!'"

"Sir, Candidate Smith, yes, sir."

I couldn't believe it. I had thought he was going kick me out of WOCS.

"Dismissed," he said.

As I turned out of his office, I vowed never to do anything that would land me in TAC Alley again. And I never did.

———————

The majority of my class was headed to flight school once WOCS was completed. A few of the other candidates would go on to be "walking warrants," meaning they weren't pilots—they had other Army jobs in supply, medical, engineering, or legal. But I had begun this journey to be a pilot, and the possibility of flying an Army helicopter for the first time was finally on the horizon.

After an intense month and a half in Alabama, it was once again graduation time. My entire family flew all the way across the country to watch me take my oath of office at the ceremony at the Fort Rucker Aviation Museum and to pin my new warrant officer 1 rank on my uniform. It was a welcome reunion—strange, because I had changed in the six months I had been gone—but incredibly great to see everyone.

I had evolved into a different person, a better person. I'd experienced so much in such a short period, and seeing them again made me aware of the transformation that had taken place. I was proud to share my accomplishments with my family. After all, my parents' encouragement was the reason I was there in the first place. Our time together was too short, but I was ready to get to flight school.

———

Helicopter flight school started in July. Once there, I had a freedom that I hadn't experienced in my short time in the Army. We got to live off base, have a car, and eat wherever we wanted. In other words, we were treated like adults. Flight school was like the Army's version of college for warrant officers: more than a year of learning to fly, plus survival school and mission training, broken down into four phases—primary, instruments, mission aircraft training, and warrant officer basic course.

We had a class schedule for academics as well as a flight schedule for our time out on the flight line, where we would have our lessons in the TH-67 Army training helicopter. The TH-67 was used for basic flight training and instrument training before we moved on to get our Army mission helicopter: UH-60 Black Hawk, OH-58D Kiowa Warrior, AH-64 Apache, or CH-47 Chinook.

Helicopters were badass. Flying one was like driving a race car—exhilarating. The TH-67 was my first love; it reminded me of those little news helicopters that fly over traffic jams. There isn't much to it, just the basics. It is a Bell 206 single-engine, two-blade helicopter that has the two pilots up in the cockpit and one seat for a passenger in the back. These helicopters are painted white and orange and are called "Creeks." An older, basic helicopter, the TH-67 was perfect for beginners like us to learn to fly. It has minimal analog flight instruments, including an altimeter, airspeed indicator, vertical scale indicator, and temperature gauges. In the Army it is referred to as a "slick bird," meaning it had no mission equipment on it, no weapons, no radar or navigation equipment. We flew it with doors and enjoyed the A/C that we wouldn't have once we got to the "real" Army helicopters.

From day one of our primary flight training phase we were paired with "stick buddies," teams of two who would fly together with an instructor. I was paired with Mike Desmond, a warrant officer like me who had been in the Army for seven years. He had served as a signal intelligence staff sergeant but had decided he wanted to become a helicopter pilot. Mike and his wife had a young daughter, and they would invite me, the clueless twenty-one-year-old kid, to their house for dinner, where Mike and I would study our helicopter emergency procedures and aircraft flight limitations. We quickly became great friends; he thought it was cool that someone like me was going to become a pilot.

"Someone like you." I got that a lot. I still do. The military is full of normal women who defy whatever stereotypes other people may attribute to us. Wearing lip gloss and shooting enemies are not mutually exclusive.

Mike and I flew together and learned a lot from each other. Every time one of us made a mistake in the cockpit and was reamed by the instructor, the stick buddy in the backseat watched and listened to make sure that we didn't make the same mistake twice. Mike also helped indoctrinate me in the Army's ways; he was my go-to guy for standard Army questions, the answers to which most of my fellow pilots already knew. Mike never made me feel stupid for asking questions.

My TH-67 helicopter instructor pilot (IP), Mr. Mitchell, was a Vietnam veteran who had flown UH-1 Iroquois (mostly known as Hueys) and Cessna L-19/O-1 Bird Dog airplanes in the war. The Huey is best known from its service during the Vietnam War, it has a distinctive thumping sound from its massive two-bladed rotor system. Hueys had many mission profiles, including troop transport, medical evacuation, and resupplying troops. Some Hueys were modified with weapons systems, while others were "slicks" and only had door gunners for weapons.

The Bird Dog is a high-wing, tandem-seat airplane with a single engine and a propeller. It conducted many tasks, including reconnaissance, forward air control of other aircraft, target acquisition, and support of combat search-and-rescue missions. Mr. Mitchell and I instantly hit it off when I told him that my dad loved the L-19 Bird Dog so much that he had restored one and given it the old Vietnam paint job—olive drab with Army markings. Some of my fixed-wing flight time had been in my dad's Bird Dog. Every once in a while, when Mike and I were sitting at our table with Mr. Mitchell, he would tell us some Vietnam stories.

"I was sick of not getting any mail," Mr. Mitchell said. "The aircraft that were supposed to deliver the mail continued to come, but they just stopped bringing the mail for a couple of weeks, so one day I just decided that I was going to hop in my Bird Dog and fly to the base that has the mail and get it. And that's what I did. All by myself."

"They let you do that?" I said, shocked that he got to take matters into his own hands.

"No, they didn't let me," he said. "I didn't ask, I just did it. And then everyone back at our base was happy they finally had their mail."

Mike and I laughed. No one would get away with something like that in the Army today. They would be hung out to dry.

Like Mr. Mitchell, most of the other TH-67 flight instructors were veteran Vietnam-era pilots. They were in their midsixties, all rough and tough. They couldn't have cared less about the rules, and pretty much got away with not following them. Since they were retired, this flight school instructor job was just for fun. They only worked half days, didn't have much to lose, and liked to do things their way. And we loved them for it.

Flight instructor stories were usually the topic of conversation on the bus to and from the airfield every day. My favorite story was from a flight class that was ahead of ours. A pair of stick buddies was out flying with their instructor when midflight, he pulled out a cigarette, lit it, and smoked while critiquing the students' flight maneuvers. Not only was that against the rules, it was a huge safety risk. Smoking was strictly prohibited, just like on commercial flights. In the Army, you are not allowed to smoke within fifty feet of a helicopter. But the old Vietnam guys didn't care and neither did we. All we cared about was learning to fly.

We couldn't wait to get in the air for our first flight in the TH-67. The first flight is called the "nickel ride." The origin of the name varies depending on who you talk to, but I'd been told it came from the instructors saying, "If I had a nickel for every time one of my students did . . ."

Mike and I had been through the ground school academics portion of the TH-67 instruction and we were ready for the real deal—we were ready to fly. We grabbed our brand-new, super-clean flight bags, which contained our helmet, flight gloves, checklist, and other essentials, and reported to our instructor.

Mr. Mitchell wasn't in a rush. We walked out to our aircraft and I pulled out my checklist and opened it to the preflight page. Our checklist contained all preflight, engine start, shutdown, postflight, and emergency procedures. It was mandatory that we use our checklist during preflight and the engine start sequence. Sticking to the checklist helped prevent pilot error or accidentally skipping over simple but necessary steps for flight safety.

We went over every component in the engine and the transmission, the main rotor and the tail rotor. When we finished, Mr. Mitchell said, "Amber, give us a crew brief."

"Me? Okay," I said. I turned my checklist to the crew brief page and began at step one. I'd been over a crew brief in practice, but never for a real flight.

"I'll be flying first in the right seat. Mr. Mitchell is the IP in the left seat. Mike will be the observer in the backseat and we will switch out seats back here at the airfield when we are halfway through the flight. Mike, you will be the fire guard for the start sequence," I said.

Mike and I would both get a chance to fly on our nickel ride. I'd fly the first half of the flight, then we'd land, and Mike and I would swap seats so he could have his turn on the controls and fly for his half.

"If a real emergency occurs, Mr. Mitchell will be on the flight controls and I will back him up if necessary," I continued.

Once I finished the rest of the checklist—where we would egress in case of an emergency, how to properly transfer the controls between pilots, our scheme of maneuver and flight path, and any weather updates—Mr. Mitchell did his own crew brief to ensure we were all on the same page and that I hadn't missed anything important. I realized that he had assigned me to give the initial crew brief for practice to see how I'd do it.

Then he climbed into the left seat and Mike moved outside the rotor system to act as the fire guard. I walked around the nose of the helicopter to the right side and put on my flight vest. Butterflies danced in my stomach as I stepped up into the cockpit and sat down, but I wasn't nervous. I was excited.

I began the engine start sequence. I made sure the key was turned to the on position, then cracked the throttle on the cyclic to the idle position, and pressed the ignitor toggle switch for the required two seconds. The engine whined and the rotor blades slowly began to spin, getting faster and faster with every rotation. I gave Mike the thumbs-up sign, and he walked to the passenger door and got in the back of the helicopter.

"All right," Mr. Mitchell said. "We are ready for takeoff. Come on the flight controls with me so you can get a feel for takeoff and hovering."

There are three flight controls in a helicopter—cyclic, collective, and foot pedals (also known as antitorque pedals). There is a complete set of flight controls on both sides of the cockpit, so the two pilots can trade off flying the helicopter. The cyclic looks like a joystick and is in front of the seat between his or her legs; the pilot uses his or her right hand to fly it. The cyclic controls the roll angles of the helicopter, front, back, left, and right. It is the control input for turning the helicopter. The collective, a lever on the left side of the pilot, has a throttle at the end of it, similar to a motorcycle throttle. You twist the throttle all the way to the left to fully open it, which gives you maximum RPM (revolutions per minute) on the rotor blades. The collective also controls the pitch angle of the rotor blades, which allows you to increase or decrease power. As some instructors like to put it, "Pull collective up, trees get smaller. Push collective down, trees get bigger." The foot pedals control the yaw of the aircraft, which keeps the tail of the helicopter from wagging. Only minor pressure is necessary in forward flight, but while hovering, stronger pedal input is required to stabilize the helicopter and to turn left or right.

Flying the helicopter requires simultaneous but proportionate input from all three flight controls. If you want to increase your speed, you have to pull up on the collective to increase the pitch of the rotor blade, which increases power, and you have to proportionally push forward on the cyclic to dip the nose of the helicopter to prevent it from climbing. If you want to climb, you would do the same procedure, except you would pull back on the cyclic to allow the nose of the helicopter to pitch up to gain altitude—all while making small but constant adjustments on the foot pedals to counter the changes in power you've applied. Throughout the entire flight, you constantly maintain inputs to all three flight controls, which is exhausting, both mentally and physically.

"Roger," I said, focused and ready as I grabbed the collective with my left hand, the cyclic with my right, and put my feet on the pedals.

Mr. Mitchell lifted the helicopter up to a hover. This was it, my nickel ride. My first flight.

Mr. Mitchell leveled the helicopter out to straight and level flight. "You have the controls," he said.

I tightened my grip on the cyclic and the collective.

"Roger, I have the controls."

"Let's see some S-turns," he said.

Basically S-turns are drawing an S in the sky with a helicopter. I slowly pulled the cyclic to the right to start my right turn. Then I eased it back to the center and then to the left to start my turn to complete the S.

"Not bad at all," Mr. Mitchell said.

Right then, I knew I had made the right choice joining the Army.

I loved the hands-on flight portion of training. The classroom instruction for academics, not so much, but it was equally important because it explained all aspects of aviation and being a pilot. Every day I walked out onto the tarmac, I felt a twinge of excitement. It was a nonstop challenge. And I love a challenge, so I tackled each and every moment head on. From pre-flighting, to scraping off the Alabama "love bugs" that covered the helicopters every morning, to conducting inflight emergency procedures, traffic patterns, how to talk on the radio, and what to do if your engine quits—I learned something new every single day.

After my first few days of flying, I was still struggling with hovering. Everyone else was struggling, too, but with my aviation background and competitive nature, I wanted to be able to hover immediately.

Mr. Mitchell liked to describe hovering as an art. It requires finesse, not force, and someday it would just come to you. And the sooner the better, he made sure to mention. Hovering, like forward flight, was a blended movement of all three flight controls—collective, cyclic, and foot pedals—at the same time. It's a learned feeling to be able to control it and make an input to one flight control while reducing another. Flying in forward flight is like patting your head and rubbing your stomach while riding a bike. Hovering is like patting your head and rubbing your stomach while trying to balance on a beach ball. He called the skill the "hover button."

"One day you won't be able to hover to save your life; the next day, suddenly, you'll press your hover button and be able to do it without thinking, without really changing anything from the day before," Mr. Mitchell said.

Mr. Mitchell recommended to both Mike and me that whenever we went home after work, we should sit on the toilet and pretend to be sitting in the cockpit and mock hover while holding a broomstick as the flight controls. (Flight training is not as glamorous as they make it out to be in the movies.)

On my way home from work, I called my mom. "I'll never be able to hover. It's driving me crazy. I just can't do it," I said.

She laughed and said, "Amber, this reminds me of when you were in gymnastics and you told me time after time you'd never be able to do giants." "Giants" is a move on the uneven parallel bars where you swing all the way around the bars, 360 degrees into a handstand position. Giants were my archnemeses—until I could do them.

"Were you able to do them?" she asked.

"Ughhh, yes," I said, getting her point.

On the next flight, Mike, Mr. Mitchell, and I flew to an empty field next to the runway to practice my hovering skills. I grabbed the flight controls. Both of my feet were planted firmly on the foot pedals.

"You have the controls," Mr. Mitchell said to me over the radio through my helmet.

"Roger," I said, tightening my grip.

As he let go of his set of the flight controls, I felt the aircraft start to slide to the left. I made a flight control input correction with the cyclic and we stopped sliding. We were just sitting there about three to five feet above the ground.

I had found my hover button.

After primary, the next phase of flight school was instruments. Mike and I had to say our good-byes—we were only stick buddies for primary. We still saw each other in passing, but that was really it. The instrument phase was boring without Mike, and I didn't take to it the same way I had to primary. It was challenging, monotonous, and slow-paced. For the first half of the course we flew in a Huey simulator for half the day. The second half of the day we spent in the classroom, where we studied instrument rules and procedures.

For the second part of the course, we got back in the TH-67 to fly instruments in the clouds. I hated flying a single-engine aircraft in the clouds. It was essentially flying blind—you could only see what your instruments were telling you. You had zero visual references, making it that much harder to fly. It felt like playing a video game, and I had always hated video games. You know who did well in instruments? People who played video games. Luckily for me, instruments lasted only a couple of months.

Following instruments, we had to rank our aircraft preference, one through three. It was probably the most anxious time of flight school, aside from the final check-ride for graduation. Being new to the Army and not having any battlefield experience, I had a hard time choosing what I wanted. There was so much more that went into flying Army helicopters than just wiggling the sticks. Each aircraft had its own unique mission that was essential on the battlefield.

The CH-47 Chinook is a huge workhorse (we called it the flying school bus) that transports troops and supplies. It was not really appealing to me. The AH-64 Apache was a gunship, the helicopter all the guys with big egos seemed to want to fly, so I steered clear of that one, too.

Then there was the UH-60 Black Hawk, which was the most popular. Everyone wanted to fly a Black Hawk, a Hollywood fan favorite that always got the most attention. Its mission was troop transport, air assaults, and medevac—medical evacuation flight. I thought it would be fun to fly, but I was attracted to the Kiowa Warriors. I loved flying the TH-67, and the OH-58 Kiowa Warrior resembled it—in body style. But I wasn't exactly sure about its mission.

I spoke with a former infantry soldier turned pilot who was picking Kiowas because the mission is "badass." Kiowas help the ground guys, and having been out on the battlefield, he appreciated all that the Kiowas did.

Kiowa Warriors have a singular role in military aviation: they are basically infantry in the air. A small, two-seater helicopter, the Kiowa functions as a scout. The scout mission is to provide light attack and low-level reconnaissance direct support for troops on the ground. Ground guys love the Kiowa because it is the only military aircraft that "thinks" like an extension of the troops on the ground. And that airborne extension of the team is what made the Kiowa so successful in the war on terror in multiple theaters of operation.

The Kiowa has three different weapons systems options and can carry two weapons at a time: a .50-caliber machine gun, a rocket pod that holds seven 2.75-inch high-explosive (HE) rockets, and a Hellfire missile rack that holds two missiles. The standard configuration was the .50-cal and the rocket pod.

The Kiowa's unique mission can change from day to day or hour to hour, so Kiowa crews have to have multiple skills. One day the mission requires the crew to conduct reconnaissance for IEDs during convoy security. The next day they might respond to a troops-in-contact (TIC) with the enemy request for a close-combat attack, and engage the enemy with their weapons system. Another day they might search for enemy activity in a known hot spot, or observe and adjust artillery fire. Then they might have to call in a medevac or coordinate with fighter jets to drop bombs.

Kiowas are able to navigate narrow canyons and crest mountaintops, flying so close to the ground that a pilot can identify, with his or her bare eyes, the curved magazine of an AK-47. But what truly separates the Kiowa is that it breeds a different type of pilot. Kiowa pilots are in the cavalry and have a reputation Army-wide. Kiowa pilots are the wild child, the cowboys.

I was sold on Kiowas. Plus if I got selected to fly the Kiowa, I got to do Flight School XXI, a new, more advanced type of flight school that none of the other aircraft had yet.

And then the results came out: I got Black Hawks. I was devastated, but there was nothing I could do. So I talked myself into thinking my new aircraft was the greatest thing in the world.

My first day of Black Hawk ground school was in a part of Fort Rucker that I had never visited. At last, I was no longer the immediate newbie. I felt like I was finally moving up in the world.

I walked into the classroom, recognized a few familiar faces from the primary and instruments phases of flight school, and sat down at one of the high school–style desks that filled the room, putting my notebook on the arm of the desk. The chatter died down as the instructor walked to the front of the room.

"Welcome to day one of your Black Hawk Advanced Aircraft Qualification course," the instructor said. Then the door of the classroom swung open. We all turned our heads to see who was the unfortunate soul who was late to the first day of class.

A second lieutenant appeared in the doorway.

"Can I help you, sir?" the instructor asked him. They exchanged a few words that none of us could hear.

"Is Ms. Smith in here?"

Noooooo. What am I getting in trouble for?

"Yes, sir. I'm Amber Smith."

"Grab your stuff and come with me," the lieutenant said. *Holy shit. Why am I getting kicked out of the first day of Black Hawk flight school? I haven't even had a flight yet!*

I stood, grabbed my backpack, and headed for the door. The lieutenant followed me out and the door slammed behind us. Once we were in the hallway, he looked at me and smiled.

"You're not going to be a Black Hawk pilot. You're going to be a Kiowa pilot."

"What? When?" I had already talked myself into being a gung-ho Black Hawk pilot and wasn't sure what to make of this new news.

"Right now. My instructions are to come get you. One of the guys who got a Kiowa slot for this class had a medical emergency. You're next on the list for Kiowas and are going to take his place. You need to get to Kiowa Flight School Twenty-One, now. You'll be joining Quicksilver flight class."

Great; now *I* was going to be the student who was late to the first day of class.

I made my way to the other side of the base to where Kiowa training took place, found the classroom, opened the door, and walked in. A dozen or so men sitting around study tables turned around and looked at me.

"Is this Quicksilver flight?" I asked.

———

Day one in our classroom at the flight line, instructors overwhelmed us with information, tests, and procedures. Stressful but necessary, flooding students with all of that information is part of weeding out people who wouldn't be able to handle the pressure of combat. Our lead instructor pilot, Andy Miller, was a chief warrant 3. Every day at the beginning of class, he went over the objectives of the day and called on a few students to answer questions and recite certain procedures.

"Ms. Smith," Mr. Miller said one day early in the training, "what are your engine oil limitations and emergency procedures?"

I stood up, my heart pounding. I completely blanked out. I had nothing. I had been studying with the other students, but I hadn't prepared to get up and explain answers to my instructors.

"Um, I don't know," I said, embarrassed. The classroom was silent, all eyes on me.

"Um, you don't know? Sit down."

I sat down in my seat next to my stick buddy. Sitting across our table, my personal instructor pilot, CW2 Ellington, glared in my direction.

"Don't you *ever* embarrass me like that again. I am really disappointed."

"Yes, sir."

I was mortified. The basic training of flight school had been relatively easy, but I was now in the advanced part of aircraft qualification, and my cockiness about my aviation background had caught up with me. If I wanted to succeed now, I would have to work my ass off for it like everyone else. Right then and there, I decided I was never going to be unprepared again.

The next day was our first "5&9" test on the limitations and emergency procedures chapters of our aircraft manual. The answers on the test were not negotiable. You had to get every single answer right and it had to be verbatim. You either got 100 percent or you failed.

Motivated by my failure the day before, I memorized every single limit and emergency procedure. I studied all night long. I went over and over my flash cards at least a hundred times.

The day after the test, Mr. Ellington walked into our classroom. With a strange look on his face, he handed me my scored test.

"I'm pleasantly surprised," he said.

I looked at the paper lying on the desk in front of me: 100 percent. Only one other student besides me had passed.

———

When it was time to get out of the classroom and move to the flight line, I'd be flying with Mr. Ellington. Unlike the TH-67, there was only room for the two of us in the Kiowa—the pilot in command and the copilot—so my stick buddy had to wait on the ground while I flew until it was his turn to fly. Mr. Ellington and I would land and my stick buddy and I would swap out.

I'd never seen a Kiowa up close and personal before, and as I approached it on the tarmac, I could see that my earlier comparison of the Kiowa to the TH-67 was way off. Their airframe structure may resemble each other slightly, but that's about it. The Kiowa has four rotor blades, sits much lower to the ground, and has many more components, including weapons systems.

Compared to the slick helicopter I was used to, the Kiowa cockpit was incredibly busy. And it was awesome. It had a glass cockpit (all digital flight displays), like that of an airliner. Everything was digital except for the analog standby instruments: airspeed indicator, altimeter, and attitude indicator. The dash had two multifunctional displays (MFDs), one in front of each seat, which looked like TV or computer screens with square buttons on either side to make selections from the screen. The MFD controlled most of the systems: navigation, weapons, communications, mast mounted sight (MMS) system, maintenance features, historical engine data, and digital flight instruments. Between the two MFDs were the analog standby flight instruments, the remote frequency display (RFD) and RPM percentages, and the torque and turbine gas temperature indicators. The RFD was the display for our five radios. You could select which radio you wanted to talk on from a shortcut button on the right side pilot collective. Below the standby instruments was a digital panel with more engine indicators, and below the main dashboard was the keyboard. That was also where the master arm switch was located, which allowed you to arm the weapons systems, a common occurrence while deployed. The .50-cal machine gun arm, re-cock, and safe switches are there, too. The windshield above the dash and the chin bubble below were made of Plexiglas. Above the pilots' heads were more Plexiglas windows, and between them was the circuit breaker panel. There were so many circuit breakers.

On the copilot's side, the MMS control panel sat to the left of the MFD. The copilot operated the MMS, which looked like a round bubble on top of the helicopter, above the rotor system. With both thermal and video imagery, the MMS allowed the pilots to remain concealed behind terrain but still be able to search for and acquire targets in the distance. The system also had laser capabilities to designate targets. It was essentially a recordable video camera with a really large zoom.

The Kiowa's fuel tank held 110 gallons of usable JP-8 jet fuel. When Kiowas flew on missions in combat and were carrying a standard weapons configuration of .50-cal and rockets, their on-station time was usually about 1.5 hours before they would have to stop what they were doing and break station to head to FARP for refuel. Once refuel was complete the Kiowa team would return to their mission and could fly until they needed to refuel again. In a standard mission, Kiowa teams go into refuel multiple times.

I had a lot of studying to do.

I had memorized the different buttons' names and functions, but that was different from being able to apply them practically and swiftly while flying, talking on the radio, and understanding the developing situation on the ground below us. But I worked hard every single day. I made mistakes on every flight, but I learned from my screwups. Slowly but surely things started to flow. My muscle memory kicked in and instead of searching for different switches, my hand just reached for them. Instead of having a death grip on the cyclic when I flew (because I was concentrating so hard), I began to relax in the cockpit. I flew better when I wasn't so rigid.

The Kiowa and I were a perfect match. I enjoyed flight school, challenging though it was. I was now twenty-two, and life was good. I was thinking very little about the gravity of my new career path after flight school.

But Mr. Miller didn't hesitate to let us students know what we would be getting into once we graduated and went out into the real-world Army. One day, he began the class a little differently than usual.

"I want to share an email with you from one of my former students who is deployed in Iraq right now," he said.

We fell silent. We all knew we were headed to Iraq; we just didn't know when. The war had been going on for more than a year now. Going into combat was inevitable.

"'I engaged the enemy in an open field,'" he read. "'I shot a man with fifty-cal machine gun. It blew his arm off. Shooting someone didn't have the effect on me that I assumed it would.'"

We all just sat there, not sure how to respond.

"What you are learning here today," Mr. Miller said, "you will likely have to use some day in the very near future in combat. The war is real. So look to your left and your right. Some of you are going to make it. Some of you are not. That's the reality of the job."

Quicksilver flight was headed to Molinelli Aerial Gunnery Range, on the outskirts of Fort Rucker. It was something we'd been waiting for:

to shoot live ammo from the .50-cal machine gun and rockets from our helicopter.

I was flying with Mr. Royce, one of Quicksilver flight's IPs. The first stop at the range was at the FARP, where we loaded up the aircraft with .50-cal bullets for the machine gun and the 2.75-inch rockets. First was a familiarization flight. Mr. Royce would be shooting in the right seat and I'd be observing in the left. In a Kiowa, the only trigger for the weapons system is on the right-side cyclic, so whoever is sitting in the right seat is the one who pulls the trigger.

As Mr. Royce pulled the helicopter up to a hover and took off toward the range, I glanced to my left out the open door at the .50-cal machine gun barrel, which was no more than a foot and a half from my seat. My excitement suddenly turned to nerves. I had no idea what to expect when it was fired.

"How loud is it?" I asked Mr. Royce through my radio.

"It's loud," he said.

"Are you going to tell me before you pull the trigger?" I asked.

"Yes," he said. "Just be ready for it. I can't really describe it, you just have to experience it for yourself."

"Roger," I said, though I was still uncertain.

He banked the aircraft to the right, so our weapons systems were pointed downrange at the targets on the ground.

"All right, are you ready?" he asked, as if I had much of a choice. "Inbound hot."

I held my breath.

Dat! Dat! Dat! Dat! Dat!

I felt the pressure of every single bullet beneath my body armor as he fired the .50-cal. My brain rattled. My teeth rattled. My eyeballs rattled. I felt completely disjointed once he stopped pulling the trigger. I waited for my vision to readjust and for my ears to stop ringing, which didn't happen. I felt like I had just been thrown against a wall. I hoped that was the closest I'd ever be to getting shot.

"Outbound cold," Mr. Royce said as he turned the Kiowa 180 degrees back toward the beginning of the range, indicating that the weapons systems were in the safe position. "How was it?"

"That was so awesome," I said as we turned inbound toward the target for another gun run.

———

A few days later I was back at the range with Mr. Royce, but we were flying at night. We had to learn to shoot under night vision goggles. And this time, I was in the right seat pulling the trigger.

Shooting from the Kiowa was more fun than I had imagined. After my familiarization flight, I learned to clench my teeth before the gun went off, which prevented me from biting my tongue. I got used to the .50-cal pretty quickly, especially after I realized that the anticipation of the gun going off was the worst part. And being in the right seat when the .50-cal went off wasn't nearly as bad as being in the left seat.

Once our weapons were loaded with ammo, I picked the helicopter up to a hover and departed the FARP for the range. Our cockpit instrument panel was nearly blacked out, because when flying under NVGs any white light made it difficult to see.

I turned the helicopter to the right to put us in position to shoot downrange.

"Let's start with rockets," Mr. Royce said.

"Roger," I said. "Inbound hot, rockets."

I pointed the Kiowa toward the target and aimed. I lifted the trigger guard with my thumb and pressed the trigger.

Shunt. Shunt.

Two rockets sailed through the air toward the target. Firing rockets didn't have anywhere near the effect on the pilots as the .50-cal did. Shooting rockets was relatively quiet.

"Outbound cold," I said as I turned the Kiowa and began a "race-track" pattern to set us up for another engagement. Tactical attack aviation units use the term "racetrack" patterns because the engagement profile literally follows the pattern of a racetrack. When you are inbound, your weapons are armed, pointed at the target, and ready to engage. When you turn outbound, you do a left or right 180-degree turn to fly back to your starting point. Once you get to the starting point, you do another 180-degree turn and fly back toward the target, ready to engage again. The outbound part of the flight gives the crew a couple of seconds to readjust for the next inbound attack engagement.

"Switching to fifty-cal," I said as I turned inbound.

"Roger," Mr. Royce said.

"Inbound hot," I said.

I put my sights on the target. I held down the trigger.

Dat! Dat! Dat! Dat! Dat!

A row of .50-cal tracer fire lit up the night sky.

Boom!

A loud bang filled the cockpit. Unnaturally loud, it almost sounded like we'd hit something and now were dragging it. I took my thumb off the trigger and my heart skipped a few beats.

"I have the controls," Mr. Royce said.

Did the engine just quit? Did something happen to the transmission? Did we hit something?

We had zero warning indications in the cockpit that something was wrong. All gauges and levels read normal. Yet the sound continued.

"Do you know what side that boom sound came from?" Mr. Royce asked, urgency in his voice.

"I couldn't tell," I said. "It was hard to pinpoint."

He slowed the helicopter airspeed, and the sound almost went away. I was thoroughly confused at this point, but Mr. Royce suddenly laughed.

"Take out your flashlight and point it at my foot pedals," Mr. Royce said. All the tension in his voice was gone.

I grabbed my flashlight, flipped up my NVGs, and pointed the light at his feet. As my eyes adjusted to the bright light, I saw that most of the chin bubble, the curved window down by our feet, was missing. Made of Plexiglas, the chin bubble starts just below the dash and goes all the way to the foot pedals, which helps with visibility because Kiowa pilots make steep banking angles while flying mission.

"The chin bubble is gone," I said.

"Just what I thought," Mr. Royce said. "The pressure from the fifty-cal shattered it."

I still wasn't laughing, but I was relieved.

The initial boom had been the chin bubble shattering. The loud sound following the boom was made by the wind coming through the hole, which is why the sound lessened when we decreased the airspeed.

"I guess we're done shooting for the night," Mr. Royce said. "Let's head back to the house."

It was my first real in-flight emergency, and while I was relieved that we weren't going to crash into the trees, I couldn't unclench every muscle in my body until I felt the skids of the Kiowa safely touch down at the airfield.

———————

After six months of living and breathing everything Kiowa Warrior—180-degree autorotations, emergency procedures, memorizing security and reconnaissance procedures, learning to operate the imagery technology, crew coordination, navigation—day, night, and NVG—learning how to shoot a .50-cal machine gun and rockets, Hellfire missiles, and Stinger missiles from the air—I took my final check ride and became a Kiowa Warrior helicopter pilot. It was by far my best day in the Army to date.

While the flight portion of flight school was over, I still had to complete the last few courses—survival school, water survival training ("dunker"), and warrant officer basic course.

In dunker, we learned how to get out of a helicopter if it crashed in the water. We performed mock helicopter dunkings, for which we were strapped into the cockpit, which was then raised in the air by a cable attached to the top of a building, and dropped into a swimming pool. The "cockpit" flipped over, and we had to try to get out without drowning—over and over, until our muscle memory kicked in so we could get out properly. I'm not going to lie: it was miserable, and I definitely thought at least once that I was going to drown.

After that was SERE, also known as survival school. We pilots trained to know what to do if we crashed or were shot down behind enemy lines. I spent days navigating through the thick, spider-infested Alabama jungle. We crawled through swamps. We didn't eat for days. We drank swamp water full of algae, slime, dirt, and sand—which was kind of like eating rather than drinking.

I survived survival school, but I didn't come out unscathed. I had poison ivy all over—face, legs, hands, everywhere—and had to go to the emergency room for oral steroids to tame the allergic reaction.

But the hard part was behind me.

During the final week of flight school, a senior warrant officer from Army headquarters came to talk to the entire class of about forty-five newly trained pilots about our duty assignments. Six of us were Kiowa pilots.

"Who among you is going to Two-Seventeen CAV at Fort Campbell, Kentucky?" he asked.

Fort Campbell is the home of the 101st Airborne Division,

Screaming Eagles. This massive airborne division has a historic legacy dating back to World War II.

I raised my hand along with one other pilot.

The senior warrant officer zeroed in on me.

"YOU are going to Two-Seventeen CAV?" he asked, with a look of incredulity on his face.

"Yes, sir," I said.

"Well," he said, "you are going to quite the prestigious unit."

4

SINK OR SWIM

August 2004

2-17 CAV, Fort Campbell, Kentucky

The 101st Airborne Division, Screaming Eagles, is a legendary unit. Nonetheless, my dad was quick to call me a puking buzzard, since the Screaming Eagles were the friendly rival to my dad's unit, the 82nd Airborne, stationed at Fort Bragg, North Carolina. During World War II, the heroic 101st had been among the brave who stormed the beaches of Normandy, France, on D-day, and clashed with the Germans in the Battle of the Bulge at Bastogne. The division also fought in Vietnam, the first Iraq war, and Operation Desert Storm, as well as post-9/11 Afghanistan and Iraq. When the 101st was activated in 1942, Major General William C. Lee, its first commander, famously said that the 101st "has no history, but it has a rendezvous with destiny." Seven decades later, the 101st is the premier air assault division in the world.

My sister Lacey came to Alabama from Phoenix, Arizona, to help me pack my household items, and together we filled my gray Ford Mustang and began the six-hour trip north to Clarksville, Tennessee, a small Army base town just outside of Fort Campbell. I was glad to have my sister with me for the trip. She had recently applied to the same warrant officer flight program I had just completed and was waiting to hear back from the Army to see if she had been selected.

I couldn't wait to leave Alabama. It represented being young and new and inexperienced. It had been a year and a half of nonstop training, getting yelled at, struggling, studying, getting knocked down, and getting back up. I was ready to get to Fort Campbell and settle down. I was tired of the constant rat race of training. Life would be simpler once I got to 2-17 CAV—short for cavalry. We'd all be on the same playing field and work wouldn't be as hectic or as tough. Or at least that's what I hoped.

My new unit, 2-17 CAV, was a squadron in the 101st Combat Aviation Brigade and had been on the mission in 2003 that killed Saddam Hussein's sons, Uday and Qusay, in Mosul, Iraq. Their mission had also become legend at Fort Rucker among all of the flight school students. Uday and Qusay had been numbers two and three on the U.S. Central Command's Most Wanted List from the Saddam regime. During the operation, the ground commanders from the 2nd Brigade Combat Team, 101st Airborne Division, called in the OH-58D Kiowa Warrior helicopters, with their .50-cal machine guns and 2.75 rockets, to engage the building in which the Husseins were hiding. The successful operation signaled the beginning of the huge influence that the Kiowa Warrior would have throughout the Iraq war.

I was assigned to Alpha Troop—which I immediately dubbed as the best troop in 2-17 CAV. Alpha Troop was also known as the Annihilators. My hopes for normality went out the window, though. I was not like everyone else. I was a warrant officer junior grade. No one liked the WOJGs. We were the new guys. We hadn't proven ourselves yet, which meant we weren't part of the team. We were viewed as annoyances, liabilities. Similar to what is also known as an FNG—fucking new guy. And being the only female WOJG in our troop meant I got even more scrutiny.

WOJGs got all of the good jobs, such as cleaning the office and bathroom, sweeping and mopping the floors, taking out the trash, and taking everyone's shit. It was like going back to basic training, CAV style. Oh, and I got to be the "fridge bitch," too. That task, reserved for the newest WOJG of the troop, was to always ensure that our refrigerator in the office was stocked with every Coke product known to man and the freezer with every type of frozen pizza, White Castle hamburger, and ice cream bars. It really was the easiest job to have, but also the most demeaning.

In the early days, when cavalry soldiers rode into battle on horseback, they wore Stetsons—cowboy hats—which became icons of the cavalry. Today, our horses are Kiowa helicopters. We still honor our roots with a tradition called "breaking in your Stetson" at "hail and farewell" banquets, which happen a couple of times a year. This is when officers and NCOs gather to welcome the newbies and say farewell to outgoing members of the troop who are moving to other units.

My welcome "hail and farewell" occurred about a month after arriving at 2-17 CAV. I still didn't really know anyone very well in my troop. They kept me at quite a distance. Partly it was because, until you went through the break-in rituals, you were basically an outcast. At the banquet, the commander of each troop got up and "roasted" each new person before moving on to the serious good-byes for the people leaving.

"And next we have WO1 Amber Smith," my commander said at the podium. "Amber, where are you? Stand up."

I stood up, all eyes on me.

"Sit down!" everyone yelled in unison.

I sat down.

"Stand up!" they yelled again.

I smiled and stood back up.

"Amber just joined us from straight out of flight school at Fort Rucker. She's from White Salmon, Washington, has two sisters, loves bulldogs, long walks on the beach, and doesn't have any kids—that she knows of," he said.

The room broke out in laughter.

Luckily there were a couple of other newbies to get to, so they didn't focus on me for too long. WO1 Jason Arrowood was one of them. When I arrived at Alpha Troop I'd recognized him from flight school. He was tall and blond and had been in the class in front of mine at Fort Rucker. From the short time I'd known him I'd discovered that he had a great sense of humor and was really smart about everything Kiowa.

Once the official part of the dinner was over, we moved outdoors for the less formal and messier part: breaking in our Stetsons. All the pilots who had already been to Iraq had dusty, dirty Stetsons. We had to buy our own Stetsons—they're not issued by the Army—and were not allowed to wear them until they were officially broken in.

Soldiers and pilots wearing broken-in Stetsons lined up, and all of us newbies stood in line facing them. One by one, the guys moved through the line pouring a little something into each of our Stetsons. There's alcohol of every kind—tequila, beer, a shit ton of moonshine—and things of nauseating viscosity. In addition to alcohol, my Stetson was bequeathed mashed potatoes, Worcestershire sauce, and canned corn. It's a suicide on steroids.

I uneasily looked to my left and right at Jason and the other newbies holding their Stetsons. *Are we really going to have to consume this?* Their eyes seemed to share my concern.

And then we got our orders:

"Drink!"

I held my Stetson up in front of my face and tilted it to my mouth. A lot of it sloshed down the front of my shirt. What made it in tasted approximately like vomit. It was chunky and slimy, like the swamp water from survival school back at Fort Rucker. Then the guys came forward and shoved what was left in our Stetsons in our faces. Voilà! My Stetson was broken in.

My eyes burned. So much alcohol had mixed into my hat that it ate through the leather straps. Afterward I had to pull out the disintegrated straps and jerry-rig the hat with 550 cord—Army-issued parachute cord that is extraordinarily strong and useful (rated to hold up to 550 pounds). Even after the disgusting stuff that was poured into mine, my Stetson was still very clean. Clean was not the desired look—yes, I had broken in my Stetson in the traditional sense, but the real break-in would occur when I took it to war with me.

Back at the office, nothing much changed after the ceremony. Breaking in my Stetson didn't carry as much weight as I'd hoped. And there would be other initiation rites during that first year of training for deployment.

One day, a junior warrant officer, Mike Smith (everyone called us brother and sister), came up to me and said, "Hey, Amber. I need you to go to Sergeant Muller and get some rotor wash. It comes in five-gallon containers. We have to wash the aircraft." Warrant officers were fairly informal, and it was customary for warrant officers of all ranks to call each other by their first names.

I marched myself over to Sergeant Muller—one of our platoon sergeants—and asked for the rotor wash.

"Hmm," he said. "Let me go look for it."

He walked off to look, leaving me behind with some of the crew chiefs. I was still getting the "new girl" looks from people, like I was this mythical unicorn that didn't belong in the hangar in a flight suit.

"Ma'am," one of the crew chiefs said, "someone's fucking with you."

"No," I insisted, "it comes in a five-gallon container and it's specifically for the aircraft."

Sergeant Muller came back, looking genuinely puzzled.

"I can't find any," he said. "You need to go check with the parts guys."

So I went over to the Quality Control office, where extra aircraft parts and larger maintenance actions were managed. I asked the guys over there. Their faces shifted in an odd way. Then they smiled, and said, "You've been fucked with."

I realized I'd been had.

There is no such thing as "rotor wash," other than the kind that is created from the wind that passes through the blades of the helicopter while they are spinning. You wash the helicopter with soap.

As I walked back into the pilots' office—without any rotor wash— all of the pilots folded over in laughter. I laughed with them even though I was embarrassed that I had been such a dumbass.

———————

After a couple of weeks in Alpha Troop, I still hadn't gone on a single flight. I finally got the chance when one of our maintenance test pilots, Justin Reagan, was going on a test flight and needed someone to go with him.

Justin was a senior warrant officer and had been to combat. I was more than a little intimidated by him. We hadn't said more than two words to each other in the two weeks I'd been there, so I was actually surprised that he even knew I was in the troop. This was my first chance to fly in the Kiowa outside of flight school, and I was ecstatic to get back in the air.

"Yes!" I said when he asked me to go, and jumped out of my chair. The other WOJGs whined under their breath that they were missing out on a flight.

"Well, grab your shit, let's go," he said. "I'll meet you at the aircraft. We're in 518."

I ran out of the office and into the hangar to my pilot locker, which housed all of my flight gear. I grabbed my helmet, my flight bag and checklist, my flight vest with my radio, first-aid pouch, tourniquet, and other survival equipment. I also grabbed my body armor. Now that I was in an operational unit, we had to fly with body armor on every flight, to ensure that we were used to flying with it when we got to combat.

Train as you fight.

I threw my body armor and vest over my shoulder and lugged the rest of my gear through the big hangar doors and out to the flight line. Thirty Kiowas were parked in three rows. Alpha Troop's Kiowas were in the first row, and Justin was already at our helicopter. I picked up the pace. I wanted to make sure I did my part with preflight.

I dropped my stuff on the left side of the aircraft and began my preflight duties. I walked back to the tail of the aircraft with my checklist and began the inspection. The tail rotor looked good. I ran my hand along the smooth tail boom toward the engine and opened the cowling that covered the engine. I grabbed the tail rotor drive shaft inside the engine compartment and gave it a firm shake to make sure nothing felt loose. After all of my engine checks, I closed the cowling and stepped up on top of the .50-cal machine gun mount, which was attached to the aircraft at its center, to climb on top of the helicopter so I could inspect the main rotor system. I grabbed the top of the rotor mast to pull myself up the rest of the way and inspected each rotor blade for any signs of damage or excessive wear and tear. It all looked good to me. I hopped down to the ground.

"Everything look good?" Justin asked me as he walked by.

"Yep, no issues on my side," I said.

Justin continued to the back of the aircraft and did a full walk-around inspection of the Kiowa. He was the pilot in command of this aircraft for this flight, and it was his responsibility to make sure everything was good to go.

I leaned in to the left side of the cockpit and reached down to the foot pedals to adjust them so my feet could reach them. Since I'm only five four, I had gotten used to rolling them all the way in so they were closest to my seat. The seats in the Kiowa are fixed, so the only adjustments you can make in the cockpit are to the pedals.

"All right, let's strap in," Justin said.

I climbed into the seat and began to put my four-strap shoulder harness seat belt on as fast as I could. Justin climbed in, strapped in, and was halfway through the start sequence by the time I finished buckling in.

Wow, I need to get faster at all of this, I thought as Justin picked up the Kiowa to a hover and made the radio call to the air traffic control tower for our departure to the test flight area. Since I'd never flown at Fort Campbell before, I had no local-area orientation, so I was basically useless as a copilot for this flight. But it wasn't an issue. As a maintenance test pilot (MTP) Justin could fly alone for certain flights. Sometimes an MTP would take up a maintenance crew chief for a flight so the crew could see what it was like to fly a Kiowa.

The helicopter began to shudder as we took off from our departure point at the end of Destiny parking ramp—where 2-17 CAV parked our helicopters on the airfield—and headed west. The altimeter read 500 feet as we leveled off. As the terrain below me grew distant, I took a quick second to take it all in. This was what I loved: being up in the sky, flying the Kiowa.

"Have you ever done a CCA before?" Justin asked.

A CCA—close combat attack—is a flight maneuver where the Kiowa engages a target with its weapons systems, normally within close proximity to friendly forces. The pilot usually flies toward the target low and fast, then pitches the nose of the Kiowa up for a quick rise in altitude—we call it the "bump"—then pushes the cyclic forward. This points the Kiowa and its weapons at the target, creating a steep angle that stabilizes the helicopter during the engagement and sets the pilot up for an easy shot. The altitude and pitch angles change abruptly at a high rate of speed.

"Just in flight school," I said.

"Okay, I'm going to show you a real one," Justin said.

We didn't have any ammo, and we weren't actually shooting. Justin was just going to demonstrate the maneuver to me.

"Roger," I said.

"Just don't touch anything or freak out, okay?" Justin said. "See that cluster of trees at twelve o'clock? That's my target."

"Roger," I said, thinking, *Why would I freak out?*

The aircraft jerked up and threw my head back against the seat, but I kept my eyes on the altimeter to see how high we pitched up. Three seconds later Justin pushed the cyclic over to level out the aircraft and set us up for our angle of attack. He continued to push the cyclic forward, angling the nose of the Kiowa toward the ground. I put my hand reactively on the dash to keep me from falling forward. I'd never seen the ground from such a steep angle before. It looked and felt as if we were in a nosedive. I felt my butt start to lift out of my seat.

"Engaging with fifty-cal," Justin said, pretending to pull the trigger. "Breaking right."

He pushed the cyclic right, whipping the Kiowa away from the target. My body slammed to the back of the seat once again.

"Did you get all of that?" Justin asked once we were out of the maneuver. "Did you see what I did?"

"Roger, you mean how we went past thirty degrees nose down?" I asked. Thirty degrees up and down was the Kiowa pitch angle limitations, meaning you can't exceed thirty degrees during any maneuver, like we just did.

"Uh, um, yeah, don't repeat that to anyone," Justin said. He clearly hadn't expected me to be watching the flight instruments during the maneuver.

"Roger," I said.

"Do you want to try one?"

"Yes!" I replied with a huge grin.

"You have the controls," Justin said as I grabbed the flight controls.

After I'd completed the maneuver, we landed and went through the procedures that finished our mission. I grabbed my gear and headed back into the hangar to put it away. I was walking on air. Flying always brought a smile to my face. A pilot in our troop was waiting for me at my locker.

"Did you puke?" he asked.

"What? No. Why would I puke?" I asked, annoyed.

He laughed.

"Well, a few of us were just making bets on how long you'd last. You know, before you puked," he said.

I loved this stuff, I wasn't scared of it. And it never made me sick. "Sorry to disappoint, but you all lost," I said.

Our days as newbie warrant officer pilots began with PT at about 6:30 a.m. If you scored high enough on your PT test, you didn't have to go to organized PT with the rest of the troop. So since I'd aced the test, I went to work at 9:00 a.m. Then I studied. Airspace, aerodynamics, 5&9—aircraft limitations and emergency procedures, parts and pieces of the aircraft. Sometimes all of the new pilots—because there's strength in numbers—went out in the hangar and worked with the MTPs. They knew the Kiowa inside and out and they always taught us stuff we'd never learn in a classroom, invaluable knowledge about the aircraft.

After maintenance procedures, we'd start up the helicopter to make sure everything was functioning properly after the work that had been done on it. Also, we swept the floors, took out the trash, and—still—stocked the fridge, because we were the FNGs. We also worked on additional duties, such as key control (organizing the keys that belong to the troop for buildings, containers, etc.), physical security, or night vision goggle maintenance. We didn't get to go home until we were released and, as the new WOJG, it was asking for trouble not to be around constantly. For some reason, people always noticed if I wasn't there. I guess it was to be expected, as I was one of only two female pilots in the forty-person troop.

Every once in a while I was lucky enough to get put on the flight schedule and actually fly. On those days, I did all of my usual tasks but added flight planning to my to-do list: got the weather brief, went through the preflight routine, did a logbook inspection, filed a flight plan, ensured we had scheduled fuel stops and that our weather brief was within our weather limitations, and developed a scheme of maneuver for our flight. These were all standard procedures to ensure that the Kiowa was safe for flight. And I had to constantly make sure I didn't mess any of it up.

I started my flight progression about a month after arriving at 2-17 CAV. Flight progression was basically a continuation of everything we had learned in flight school crammed into a handful of flights with our IPs. After graduating from flight school, moving to Fort Campbell, getting settled into my new troop, and having not flown for a few months, I found it challenging once I got back in the cockpit. I was still a brand-new pilot and flying was still a perishable skill—without practice, I got worse. Even more challenging was remembering all of the things I had studied in flight school—different mission procedures, tasks, techniques, and tactics. I was no longer working with a bunch of other clueless flight-school students; I was working with combat veterans who had been to Iraq and done the real deal—so I looked like an overwhelmed idiot when I first started flying with them. Every flight was difficult—every flight gave me something new to react to and learn.

The pilots who had deployed to Iraq before saw every task we performed from a different perspective. We had gotten word that 2-17

CAV would be headed back to Iraq sometime within the coming year, so I needed to learn as much as I could from them in a short time. I always knew I'd deploy sometime in my Army career; I just never assumed it would be within a year of getting to my unit.

On word of our impending deployment, our commanders and operations planning cells crammed our schedules with every possible training opportunity: training flights, mock deployments, and helicopter gunnery, among other things. I was barely keeping my head above water. Flight school had nothing on my first year in 2-17 CAV.

One morning, I opened the door to the Alpha Troop office in our hangar at Campbell Army Airfield a little before 9:00 a.m. I always made sure I was a few minutes early. Sitting at a table in the pilots' office was a tall guy with super-short blond hair and wearing a green one-piece flight suit called a pickle suit. On his shoulders was CW3 rank, but he looked too young to be a CW3. As I walked past him into the office and set my backpack down on my desk, he stood up and stuck out his hand.

"I'm Chris Rowley," he said. "I'm your new IP. Good to meet you."

And so I began flying with Chris for the rest of my flight progression. He was an excellent instructor pilot and taught me real-world flying skills that I'd need when we deployed. Chris had transferred here from 3-7 CAV, and had been to Iraq with 3rd Infantry Division during the invasion in 2003. His combat stories were mind-boggling: shooting at the enemy, getting shot at, flying over the ground guys.

"That's great that you can make that approach into that little confined space. But what are you going to do if you start taking fire from your nine o'clock?" Chris would ask. He was always pushing me to think outside the box, to think ahead of the aircraft, to be aware of my surroundings and be prepared for every scenario that could—and likely would—happen in combat.

In addition to the normal flights we made out of Campbell Army

Airfield, we did simulated training in the field—what is known as "going to the field"—four times in my first year. They were meant to train up the unit for combat. We had to pack our rucksack—the Army's version of an enormous hiking backpack—with all of our gear, even gear we didn't need for our flight missions. In addition, we had to take all of our chemical protective gear, gas mask, canteens (even though we drank out of CamelBaks), wet weather gear, and an E-Tool. We stayed in old-school, Vietnam-era tents. We slept on cots and used Porta Potties. We had to wear our Kevlar helmets everywhere, "in case we got attacked."

We called the whole experience "embracing the suck."

During my first field experience with 2-17, we slept on cots under tents in the mud as snow fell outside. We had to wear chemical boots— the big rubber boots almost reached my knees—or we'd be covered in mud. Potbellied stoves were the only things that kept us warm. Everyone got to fly once during the training, but as a WOJG, my primary mission was to pull CP (command post) guard for Alpha Troop, on the graveyard shift, while everyone else was sleeping.

We had such an influx of new pilots from flight school that it was hard to get everyone on the flight schedule, so we waited—trying not to grow too frustrated. While on guard/radio/coffee duty, I would see the four-man flight teams come in to the CP to get their flight gear and get some coffee before their flight brief at the TOC—tactical operations center. I wished I was on their team and was getting to go flying instead of walking back and forth the length of the tent to stay awake.

One time one of the pilots told me I made good coffee. Success.

By early 2005 we had our deployment orders: we were headed to Iraq in early September. This date put us on the schedule for the Joint Readiness Training Center (JRTC), where units play war games once a year at Fort Polk, near Alexandria, Louisiana. It is a simulated deployment with an area of operations, friendly forces, and enemy forces who can try to slip into the camps at night and attack. Each unit has an assigned mission. Ours consisted of convoy security for ground forces, aerial security during ground assaults, and IED reconnaissance. And throughout it all, the unit was being watched and graded by trainers stationed at JRTC. The Kiowa pilots had another helicopter follow us throughout our flight and watch our every move. After the mission was over and we were back at the TOC, the pilots from that helicopter would debrief us and gives us pointers on what we did well as a team, what we did wrong, and ways to improve.

This first trip to JRTC was a lesson in patience. Throughout my four weeks at JRTC I didn't learn much about war. It was more of "hurry up and wait." A few of us would try to pass the time by going running on one of the perimeter roads around our camp. Mike Slebodnik—a warrant officer and instructor pilot (IP)—would often join us for a jog. He was in his midthirties, shaved his head, and always had a smile. Mike had joined Alpha Troop at about the same time I did, so he was still fairly new to the troop, although his transition into the unit as an IP went a whole lot smoother than it did for me as a WOJG. But Mike was respectful and fair and always helped me with my flight progression. I always knew I could go to Mike if I had a "dumb" question and he wouldn't completely destroy me for it.

During operations at JRTC, I flew only once—with a staff officer whom I'd never met before and who basically used me as a weight bag in the left seat. But I did take out the trash a lot and I also became well versed in making hourly radio check-in calls to the squadron TOC while on radio guard all night. All part of earning my keep in the troop. JRTC unified us as a unit. Like it or not, we were going to war together.

Still, some of the pilots just didn't like me. I have always been a people pleaser, and so the fact that some people did not care to have me in the troop, for no particular reason, bothered me. No one really—aside from the other newbies—wanted anything to do with me. I was the oddball.

This reality was a punch in the face. I'd been naïve to think that Alpha Troop would be easier than flight school. I guess I hadn't taken it seriously when people said, "The Army isn't a job, it's a lifestyle." I was going to have to adapt even more than I already had as an FNG if I was going to survive and advance in this demanding, unforgiving environment.

The first thing I learned was to shut my mouth, to never say something without thinking first, and to always consider my audience. The less I talked, the less unwanted attention I'd receive. For a woman in the Army, any type of attention drawn to you—good or bad—was bad. The less I stood out, the better. I had learned at boot camp that being invisible was a good thing, and it still applied at my unit. Standing out results in getting in trouble, extra work, looking like an idiot in front of everyone.

CW3 Lori Hill, the only other woman in my troop, was everything I wanted to be—strong, independent, well respected, fun, and an amazing pilot. The guys wasted no time telling me that if I wanted to succeed in Alpha Troop, I needed to look no farther than Lori. She had red hair, was super fit, and a great runner. Flawless, she made me all too aware of my newbie awkwardness. Unfortunately, I couldn't seem to crack the code. Why didn't the guys seem to like me the way they liked her?

Lori had been in the Army since 1987 and was two ranks above me. She had been in Desert Storm and had been stationed in South Korea. She had been a TAC officer at WOCS at Fort Rucker, which intimidated almost everyone. TAC officers are worse than drill sergeants. Even after I graduated from WOCS, if I saw a TAC officer at Fort Rucker I walked the other way. The fact that a former TAC officer was in the same troop as me was a little tough to get used to, but Lori was indifferent to there being another girl in the troop, which was a good thing. I had a lot of hard work ahead of me, but the reality was that everyone went through some rite of passage in the unit. I made mistakes; I learned from them; I changed.

Saying it was a lot of work is an understatement. It was exhausting. It was twenty-four hours, seven days a week of nonstop stress, testing, and being under the microscope.

Still, I kept putting one foot in front of the other. I had a choice: I could either sink or swim. I just didn't know how long I would be treading water before I could swim.

5

HURRY UP AND WAIT

September 2005

Kuwait

My entire Kiowa squadron, about three hundred people, dressed in digital camo Army combat uniforms (ACUs), snaked around a Kuwait-bound plane on the tarmac at Fort Campbell, waiting to board. A big D-10, it was a civilian-contracted plane, like a commercial jet you'd board at the airport. We each held a lot: our Stetson, Kevlar (helmet), body armor, and a carry-on bag that was bursting at the seams. Oh, yeah, and our M4 rifles. As we made our way onto the plane, it felt strange carrying a large weapon down the aisle of a commercial jet and stowing it under our seats. Thank goodness we didn't have the M16s we used in boot camp—they are as long as broomsticks.

Other equipment had left for Iraq two months earlier on a container ship. In the belly of the plane, my rucksack and duffel bag had everything else—two months' worth of shampoo, soft floral bedsheets, flight suits, ChapStick, PT clothes, extra boots. Everything we brought, we had to be able to carry.

The seventeen-hour flight would stop in North Carolina, then Germany, and continue on to Kuwait. I sat in an aisle seat next to Lori.

We'd both brought a bunch of fashion and workout magazines to keep our minds off the obvious. But mostly we slept. The flight docs gave us Ambien, which helped knock us out for most of the flight. I felt a vague fear of the unknown, but excitement kicked in as we made our final descent into Kuwait International Airport, just outside Kuwait City. As the wheels of the plane touched down on the runway, I looked out the window and saw nothing but glowing lights in the night sky. This was the first stop on our year-long deployment. After most of my unit disembarked, I walked up the aisle of the DC-10, trying to prevent my M4 rifle from banging the back of each seat I passed.

At the door of the plane, the desert night air blasted my face with the heat of an open oven. *So this was what the guys who had been here before had been talking about.* I was groggy, but we still had a bus ride through the desert to Camp Udairi, a staging base for inbound and outbound aviation units near the Iraqi border. (It was later named Camp Buehring, after Lieutenant Colonel Charles H. Buehring, who was killed in Baghdad in 2003.) There, we would spend about two weeks conducting "environmentals"—practice flights to get used to flying and shooting in the desert.

On the bus, I sat by a window, next to Mike Slebodnik, the IP I'd flown with through my progression as a pilot in Alpha Troop. As our bus convoy left Kuwait City and headed into the desert, the windows of the buses were covered with dark curtains to conceal that we were uniformed U.S. soldiers. I parted the curtains slightly for a peek outside. One of our armed Kuwaiti military escorts—a tan Humvee with a machine gun mounted on the back—drove past the bus. Driving on the opposite side of the highway were BMWs and Mercedes-Benzes, luxury cars, the only other vehicles on the road. I guess it was a sign of oil money.

Camp Udairi was in the middle of nowhere, the Udairi Range Complex, a sea of sand uninhabited except for some Bedouin tribes herding goats, sheep, and camels. Surrounded by desert in the north-western corner of Kuwait, it's almost halfway between the Persian Gulf to the east and the Iraqi border to the northwest. The base is a complex of huge white tents with concrete floors that look like green-houses. It has a defac—dining facility, also known as the chow hall—a makeshift gym, sleeping quarters, and a paved runway. And lots of sand, everywhere: up my nose, in my eyes, in my teeth, in my ears. I was constantly getting sandblasted by the wind. My ChapStick addiction didn't help. Every time I put it on, it acted like a magnetic force, attracting sand and dirt to my lips. Regardless, I made sure that my ChapStick was always easily accessible. I had a ChapStick cap with a D-ring on it, which was always attached to my belt loop, and I always kept one D-ringed to my flight body armor, too. Quite handy, if you ask me.

I was eager to see for myself what war was like. My imagination ran wild with the intense, thrilling stories from the pilots who had been to Iraq in 2003. One pilot told me that he had deployed late to northern Iraq and had to meet his troop in Mosul. They were short on body armor and weapons, so he had had to make the trip without either, including while riding in the convoy ride from Mosul to his base. I was thankful for the body armor and my M4, even though I had to haul them around everywhere with me. Another pilot told me they used to have to sleep in the open desert next to their Kiowas because no U.S. bases were set up yet for them. They had to lay out their sleeping bags on the ground next to the aircraft skids. He said the sandstorms were the worst.

After preparing for this moment for two and a half years, I was relieved I was finally here. I wondered how I'd do.

My first lesson in going to war was mildly disappointing: hurry up and wait. This is one of the Army's standard operating procedures—urgency followed by indefinite waiting with little or no information. My entire troop was restless with questions. *When are we flying into Iraq? Where will they send us? What is going on with the war?* This would be the theme of our three-week stopover at Camp Udairi. And because we were still in transient mode, we would only fly a couple of times at Udairi, to knock out our required flights of environments and gunnery. Other than that, we found any activity we could to pass the time: going to the gym, eating, watching movies.

We had no TV and very limited Internet access, mostly reserved for emailing our families to tell them we had arrived. To get access we had to go to the USO centers, put our names on a waiting list, and hope to get to use one of the five computers with Internet access. More than once I got halfway through sending a detailed email to my family, only to have the Internet momentarily shut down, deleting all of my content, and using up my allotted time for the computer.

People started to bicker over nothing. I guess it was the anticipation. We felt like racehorses in the starting gate, waiting for the gun. Prolonged boredom allows your imagination to run wild. Every day there was a new rumor about when we were leaving for Iraq and where we'd be headed. I tried not to get wrapped up in rumors because that's all they were. One of these days we'd get the real deal.

We were so restless that our superiors suggested organized PT, which struck me as odd. On deployments, we had the freedom to exercise on our own schedules, so garrison training in a war zone was odd. Besides, most of us were already working out a couple of times a day, just to stave off the boredom.

I learned that embracing the suck was not solely reserved for field exercises.

Without moonlight, the desert was impossibly dark. It was almost a cave-like darkness, both flat and infinite, where you can't see your hand in front of you and you lose all points of reference. Darkness can be both your friend and your foe. It can help make you invisible to the enemy, but it can also be a danger. On my first night environmental, I would learn exactly how.

"Clear up left?" I said to my IP, Chris Rowley, who was sitting in the left seat next to me in our Kiowa. We were on the tarmac, ready to go.

"Clear up left," he said, indicating it was safe to bring the helicopter up to a hover.

I felt the skids get light beneath me as I increased the collective, and we lifted into the night sky above Kuwait. As we gained altitude, I sensed the desolation of the desert—a big dark canvas with no city lights. Aside from a few stars in the sky, it was pitch black.

Through my old-school NVGs, which have lousy resolution and contrast, the desert floor beneath us flickered in different shades of green, pixelated and grainy. New NVGs feel almost like you're flying during the day.

"Watch your altitude," Chris said.

"What?" I was "outside" at the moment, meaning my vision was focused outside the aircraft. Based on what I could see of the world around me, I thought I was at a hundred feet. I came "inside" for a moment and glanced at the altimeter.

Three hundred feet. In seconds, we had tripled our altitude.

"Whoa! How did that happen?" I said, stunned.

"That's the desert," Chris said. "Flying under NVGs. It'll trick you."

When it's that dark, spatial disorientation can become a major hazard. Your depth perception goes straight to hell. People who fly over the ocean or the desert can see the lights of a distant city and become rapidly disoriented. They can mistake the city lights for stars and fly right into the ground.

I remembered the instructor pilot in flight school who had

warned me, "The desert floor is like the ocean. It has no depth. You can't tell if you're two hundred feet off the ground or about to smack right into it."

A veteran of the Gulf War, he had flown over the deserts of Iraq. Back then he didn't fly with a copilot; his left seater was just an observer. One time flying over Iraq, he was cruising over the desert when he felt an alarming shudder. His skids were nearly bouncing off the desert floor. His depth perception had been so compromised that he had nearly flown into the desert floor while still thinking he had plenty of altitude. He quickly realized he was unable to trust what his eyes outside were telling him. He had to force himself back inside to look at the altimeter and pull up.

"Always trust your instruments," he told me. "Don't believe your eyes." Sometimes it's not the enemy trying to kill you, but the desert.

After my own experience of this optical illusion, I increased my visual scan from the instrument panel in the cockpit and out to the terrain below, a constant situational awareness to maintain the correct altitude.

We had one other task to finish before our mission was complete and we could return to base: a brownout landing under NVGs.

Brownout landings are a common problem in the desert. As you land, the force of the air from the rotor blades stirs up a bowl of dust—the actual rotor wash, as opposed to the soap that doesn't exist—and this mini dust storm makes nearby objects invisible, including the ground. It's like flying into the clouds. It's a bigger problem for the larger helicopters, which have bigger rotors and stir up more dust. It's not too often that we have to set down our aircraft outside the wire—outside our base—but sometimes it's necessary, so pilots have to be familiar with the dangers of landing in the desert.

"See that tumbleweed?" Chris said to me over the radio. "Land abeam it."

"Roger," I said, as I reduced the collective to put us on glide slope—the path the aircraft follows to make the desired landing position.

"Come in steep with a swift glide path, keep your angle, and commit to the ground," he said.

I brought in more power as our altitude decreased. The dust cloud got larger as we got closer to the ground. But the skids made contact with the ground before it was too bad. Under NVGs, the dust cloud didn't seem as thick as it actually was.

"So now you know how to do a real brownout landing," Chris said.

We were mission complete and environmental complete, so we lifted off and headed back toward the faint lights of Camp Udairi in the distance. When we landed and I took off my helmet, my face was covered with a significant layer of sludge—sand and dirt. It was everywhere. Layers of dust had stuck to my lips, too. Sandy ChapStick was an excellent, yet disgusting, exfoliator. I needed to get a scarf to fly with to cover my nose and mouth, stat. Because soon enough combat would be our reality and I wouldn't have time to care about the sand in my face.

———

It was time to test fire our personal M9 handguns and M4 rifles.

My M9 was jamming every time I fired it. That wasn't completely out of the ordinary in the desert, where sand and dirt can get into the components. If you don't keep both the weapon and the ammo magazine clean, the weapon might fail on you when you need it most. But that wasn't my problem. My gun was clean. My armament officer looked at it, and after firing it himself, suspected that a component had actually failed or broken. He promised we'd try to get it fixed once we got to Iraq. So that meant I'd be flying into Iraq with an M9 that would jam every time I fired it. Great.

After three weeks in limbo, we had watched all of our movies, and had moved on to borrowing from each other. We'd shopped at the local trinket shops just to fend off the boredom. It was: Eat. Movies. Gym. Eat. Work. Movies. Gym. Eat. Repeat.

Then we got the call. Alpha Troop gathered around our commander, who was sitting on a green standard-issue Army cot in our greenhouse tent. He had just gotten back from a briefing for all of the commanders on our insertion plan. He was looking down at his bright green notebook. We stood silently in a circle around his cot. He looked up.

"Tomorrow night is the night," he said, looking at each of us in turn. "We are going to Camp McKenzie, near Balad, about sixty miles north of Baghdad."

This is what we had been waiting for. We were going to war.

At Balad Air Base, Iraq, strapping into the aircraft prior to a mission in 2005. (Photograph by Ed Dalsey)

In our "greenhouse" tent at Camp Udairi, Kuwait, after packing up our gear to head into Iraq, September 2005.

Alpha Troop photo taken at Camp Udairi, Kuwait, before moving into Iraq for our deployment, including myself, Lori Hill, Mike Slebodnik, Jason Arrowood, Frank Villanueva, Chris Rowley, Mike Smith, Ed Dalsey, Mike Hambrecht, and Blane Hepfner, September 2005.

Filling out the logbook after a mission in our AO near Camp McKenzie, Iraq, before taking most of my gear off, October 2005.

Watching the sunrise on an early-morning flight in Diyala Province, Iraq, December 2005. (Photograph by Mike Hambrecht)

Lori Hill and me outside our CHUs at Balad Air Base, Iraq, January 2006. A rare day off together!

Loading high-explosive rockets into the rocket pod prior to a mission at Balad Air Base, 2006.

Chris Rowley and me after the night mission when our aircraft got shot up by an AK-47 between Baqubah and FOB Normandy near Miqdadiyah, Iraq, January 2006.

With my Kiowa on the parking ramp in Kirkuk, Iraq, June 2006.

Flying with Chris Rowley, who is waving at the ground unit we are providing aerial security for in Kirkuk AO, 2006.

07.16.2006

08.13.2006

Chris Rowley, Jason Arrowood, me, and Frank Villanueva. Our Kiowa flight team before one of our last missions of the deployment in Kirkuk AO, Iraq, August 2006.

Hanging outside our command post (CP) in my Stetson at Balad Air Base, 2006.

08.22.2

Last flight in Iraq, flying over the open desert, August 2006. Flying from Kirkuk, Iraq, to the port in Kuwait.

Family photo: my mom, Betsy; me; my sisters, Lacey and Kelly; and my dad, Lane, at Fort Rucker, Alabama, at Lacey's Warrant Officer Candidate School (WOCS) graduation. (Photograph by Betsy Smith)

This photo was taken just south of Fort Campbell, Kentucky, on a cross-country to JRTC in Louisiana.

With Deidra Adams and a local Afghan who owned the Jingle truck we were standing in front of. Local nationals (as we called the Afghans) often worked on the U.S. bases. We had just arrived in Jalalabad and were still intrigued by the decorative nature of the Jingle trucks (military slang for those types of trucks in Afghanistan).

Flying with Chris Cook in Afghanistan, 2008.

Ready to strap into the Kiowa for a night mission with all of my gear on (including my ChapStick) in Jalalabad, Afghanistan, 2008.

Taking off out of FOB Blessing in eastern Afghanistan in 2008. (Photograph by Deidra DeJiacomo)

Conducting preflight with Chris Cook prior to a mission in Jalalabad, Afghanistan, FOB Fenty, 2008. I'm doing the math for our weight-and-balance form to see how much fuel and ammo we can carry.

Conducting an air-to-ground integration brief with the French ground forces at FOB Morales-Fraiser, just outside the Tagab River Valley, fall 2008. Toby Long is briefing them and I am holding a 2.75-foot high-explosive rocket to show what we carry on the Kiowa.

6

WELCOME TO IRAQ

September 2005

Camp McKenzie, Iraq

We roared down the runway in a giant turboprop C-130 Hercules, a flying warhorse big enough to hold several helicopters. My body armor vibrated against the seat as we ascended into the Kuwaiti night sky. Our destination was Balad, where we would then board a Chinook helicopter that would take us to Camp McKenzie, our new home in Iraq.

Sooner or later, my older sister, Kelly, who was currently in C-130 flight school in Little Rock, Arkansas, training to be a Hercules pilot, would be deploying, too. She'd fly missions like this one, transporting troops and essential supplies of food, ammo, and weapons. It gave me hope that our time in the desert would overlap.

As one of ten Kiowa pilots on board alongside other members of our squadron, I was slightly annoyed that I had not gotten to fly a Kiowa in Iraq, but I was low enough on the totem pole that it wasn't surprising. I knew I'd get my fair share of flying soon enough.

As we crossed the border, the butterflies in my stomach rose. Somewhere down below us a war was going on. *Holy shit, I'm now in a war zone. What if the aircraft we're in takes fire? How will I react?*

Why was I nervous now? One of my fellow Kiowa pilots sitting across from me flashed a smile, as if my nerves were visible for all to see. That snapped me out of it. The last thing I needed was to freak myself out before anything happened. I had to have my head in the game.

There was no interior lighting, and the only window was a small circular one on the side door where the paratroopers jump out. The aircraft began to descend, and we made our approach into Balad Air Base. As the aircraft banked left, a flash of light caught my eye. We made a steep enough turn that I could see the little village lights below. My first view of Iraq.

Upon landing, the plane taxied to the transient-passengers terminal, where we exited the plane. The sun began to creep above the horizon as we made our way to the terminal, which was nothing more than a plywood shack surrounded by large concrete barriers covered with desert-colored camo netting. The area under the camo net was packed with other soldiers waiting to get a flight to wherever they were going in Iraq. Our flight north to Camp McKenzie would be a quick ten to fifteen minutes, but our Chinook helicopter wasn't picking us up until that night, so we had some time to kill. We claimed a vacant area under the camo net and set down our gear.

Boom! Boom!

A massive explosion shook the ground beneath my feet. No one around me did anything except look around.

"What was that?" I asked one of the guys I was traveling with.

"Probably an enemy rocket or a mortar," he said. "Happens all the time. But we're surrounded by concrete barriers so we should be good."

My worst nightmare about going to war was a rocket or mortar round flying through the air toward our base without our knowing it had been launched or where it would land until it exploded on the ground. We'd have zero warning and no sort of precautionary measure to take, because the sirens usually went off after the rocket or mortar had detonated. As a pilot I knew there was a chance I could crash, get shot, or possibly even die every time I took off on a mission. It was almost expected. But when you are on the ground within the safe confinement of an FOB, getting mortared is, or at least was, not expected. I didn't remember hearing about this from my guys who had already been to Iraq.

"If you hear the explosion, you know you are safe," one guy said. "If you hear a high-pitched whistle or scream, that's when you know you're in trouble. You only hear the whistle if it's pretty close to you."

I hoped the mortars and rockets would not be as bad at Camp McKenzie. I was ready to get there, start flying, and take out some of the enemy who were firing at us.

After two weeks at Camp McKenzie, I still wasn't on the flight schedule. I had the feeling my commander and my senior warrant officer didn't think I could handle it. Other newbie pilots were flying, most of them former enlisted soldiers, many of whom had been to Iraq before as aviation mechanics, crew chiefs, or infantrymen. I was an outsider; they didn't know if they could trust me in the air in this environment. Even though I'd learned to fit in better with my unit, sometimes I still smiled too much. I definitely didn't attempt to act like a badass. I didn't know there was anything wrong with that, but there was. I didn't fit the mold.

While the others flew, I stewed on base and tried to keep myself busy. I swept the floor. I filled the refrigerator with soda, like a good fridge bitch. I did aircraft run-ups after maintenance was completed. I waited. And waited. And the more I waited, the angrier I got.

Every time I asked why I wasn't on the flight schedule, I got the same answer: "Oh, the referendum is coming. We don't have time to give you your local area orientation flight."

My superiors kept promising I would fly *after* the referendum—the day Iraqis would be voting on their Constitution—and the most anticipated day for enemy activity since we had been in Iraq. There were hundreds of polling stations across the country, and they were vulnerable to attacks by insurgents hoping to interfere with the vote.

Then, the night before the referendum, one of our IPs came into the pilots' office and said, "Amber, you're up. Go get your shit ready for tomorrow—we need you to fly."

I looked up at the IP with suspicion. They'd used the referendum as an excuse for me not to fly, so I didn't really buy it.

Is he messing with me?

When I saw no trace of humor, I jumped up and ran to gather my flight gear, helmet, and flight bag. It was a suboptimal situation. I was to fly with an MTP who wasn't in my troop. For my first flight in country, I would be paired with a pilot I'd never flown with before and had only met in passing. But at least I was going to fly.

I started the trek back to my CHU—the container housing unit, what we called home in Iraq—to get some sleep for my early wake-up for my flight the next morning. On the way, I nearly bumped into Katie Gallagher, one of the new warrant officer pilots. She had to work in a staff position at the headquarters unit—a position no warrant officer wants to be in—because there was no more room in the line unit for additional pilots. Katie had enlisted as an intelligence soldier, but she wanted to fly, so she put her flight packet in and was accepted into the warrant officer flight program. She had gone through flight school about six months behind me, so I hadn't met her aside from passing in the hallways at Fort Campbell. I didn't really know her, but she was slotted to come to Alpha Troop once there was room for another pilot. She was absolutely gorgeous, with long black hair and a beautiful complexion. I was happy to welcome another woman who understood the crazy dynamic of being in a troop full of guys on a deployment.

"I finally get to fly tomorrow," I said to Katie.

"Good luck and fly safe. Looking forward to the day I get to fly," she said.

"You'll be up soon, too. I'll let you know how it goes," I said.

As I continued walking back to my CHU, I looked up and saw the constellation Orion shining brightly in the dark sky. I instantly thought of my family. Orion was our constellation. In the 1960s, when my dad was a celestial navigator for Pan Am World Airways, he had to commit the star constellations to memory. He literally flew around the world by navigating the stars. When my parents got married and moved to the farm I grew up on, the rural night sky was perfect for stargazing, and Orion was a favorite. We always said that no matter where we were in the world, no matter how far apart, when we saw Orion, it connected us. I smiled at the thought. But I barely slept that night.

———

I was the first to arrive at the TOC for our mission briefing the next morning. The enemy had been threatening to attack Iraqis in an attempt to prevent them from going to the polls. Saddam Hussein's trial in Baghdad was set to begin in a few days. The enemy was constantly knocking out power grids, citywide, to cause unrest among the residents. Dead Iraqis were often found in ditches with their hands tied behind their backs and a bullet hole in their heads, execution style. The enemy would try anything to prevent a successful referendum. Which was all the more reason it was essential for Kiowas to be in the air that day. Our mission was to escort the Iraqi army convoy that would transport the people's votes to their army compound to be counted. As part of our duty, we would be scouting ahead of the convoy's path and around the neighborhoods it would be traveling through.

My PC for the flight, Brad Andrews, and I headed out to the aircraft without saying much. We did our preflight check and I strapped into the left seat of the Kiowa, ready—*finally!*—to fly in combat. I did all of my copilot tasks—setting up comms, the nav system, and the weapons—as Brad started up the aircraft. The rotors chattered beautifully as we climbed to about a hundred feet and crossed over the wire of the base. I saw Iraq for the first time from a Kiowa.

I put my left hand up to grip the open door frame of the aircraft, only my thumb inside, as I usually did when copiloting. It had always been comfortable before, but now that we were in enemy territory, I felt a strange sensation knowing that we were a prime target for the enemy. I brought my hand back inside where it was (sort of) protected by the armament side panel, a piece of steel that covers most of the side of the copilot's body—except for the head. Without that armor, we would have been exposed.

Iraq looked different than I had imagined. It had more vegetation, and anywhere near a water source, the land was covered in palm trees. Those palm groves were a natural safe haven for the enemy. Their lush canopy was so thick that we couldn't see through it from the air, but the enemy could easily shoot an AK-47 or machine gun at us without giving away their position. It was a win-win for the enemy, so we avoided flying over palm groves if at all possible.

Because it was daylight, we flew low and fast, from 50 to 150 feet above the ground. We also had to fly erratically—up, down, left, right—to avoid staying in the crosshairs of an enemy weapon. We were like bumblebees in a garden—all over the place.

It was a rush, like driving a race car that could zip around the sky. Even with all the training I'd done over the past two years, I'd never experienced flying like this.

"Wires, twelve o'clock," I said to my PC in the right seat of the Kiowa.

"Roger," he said.

There is always something trying to bring down an aircraft, and it's not always the enemy. One threat we constantly faced in the air were wires of all kinds, including high-tension power lines and telephone wires, as well as towers, and pig stickers—the razor-thin antennas that stuck up over houses and mud huts everywhere. When we flew low at about eighty knots, or followed cars driving along the road, it was almost impossible to see wires. We could never stop our scan for them, or they would sneak up on us. Many of those towers and wires had taken the lives of Kiowa pilots in Iraq.

Kites were a hazard as well. Iraqis flew kites all the time—they were as common as pig stickers over the populated areas and also extremely hard to see. Depending on the size and strength of the rope they were attached to, kites could do significant damage to a helicopter if the cords got wrapped around the rotor system. After a mission, we often got back to base to find all sorts of colorful cords tangled into the rotor system, like ribbons on a birthday present.

Whenever we flew over people, they stopped what they were doing and looked up at us. Some jumped up and down and waved with excitement. Others just glanced up and went back to what they were doing. Some threw rocks at us.

We flew for hours escorting the convoys to and from the polls and conducting route reconnaissance. I was doing my best to stay on top of my left-seater/copilot duties—managing the nav system, talking on the radio, conducting recon looking for IEDs and signs of suspicious activity, taking down notes—but at first I was a little overwhelmed, task-saturated, and in awe of my surroundings. Thankfully, my PC was a seasoned pilot and extremely patient. He knew it was my first flight in-country. After an hour or so, I settled in to it.

Whenever we bumped the aircraft up to clear a set of high-tension wires, we got a visual on our convoy on the road beneath us. The Iraqi army drove these little white Toyota-like pickup trucks, usually with large machine guns mounted in the rear bed. They sped down the paved road, which was littered with potholes, trash, dead animals, and IED holes. Civilian vehicles pulled over to make way for the armed convoy.

Our aircraft followed the lead, but we also had to push out far-ther along the road to conduct reconnaissance. The two aircraft stayed together, and we checked all along the route for IEDs, any sign of an ambush, or anything else suspicious. The trick was to get far enough in front of the convoy to conduct reconnaissance properly, but not too far away in case the convoy came under fire or hit an IED and needed our help immediately.

We didn't encounter any of the dangers that we'd been briefed about, even after several intense hours of flying, until the end of our mission. As we approached one of the convoy's destinations, a heavily guarded and secure Iraqi army compound, we suddenly heard,

Dat! Dat! Dat! Dat! Dat!

The rapid fire of a machine gun was so close it sounded like it came right out my left door. *Had we just taken fire?* My PC banked the aircraft hard left as we flew over the convoy's trail gun truck. Out my door, I saw the Iraqi gunner in the truck firing warning shots behind them at a civilian vehicle that was speeding up toward the convoy. The car screeched to a stop.

So that's what a machine gun firing on the ground sounded like from a hundred feet up. I'd heard machine gun fire before, but usually from another Kiowa—and I'd usually known it was coming. This time I'd been caught off guard. Those rounds sounded close.

Beneath us, the convoy slowed as it drove through the gates of the Iraqi army compound. We had safely escorted the convoy to its destination, and all of those brave Iraqi men and women who had gone to the polls in the midst of the terrorist threats of violence would have their ballots counted.

We headed back to base. By the time we landed, we'd flown for seven hours on my first combat mission. Nothing like getting thrown right into the war to get you going.

That night back at the base, I slept like a baby.

7

BETTER SAFE THAN SORRY

December 2005–January 2006

Balad Air Base, Iraq

Within a month of my first flight in-country, we moved from Camp McKenzie to Balad Air Base. Our area of operation (AO) was the same, though, so thankfully I didn't have to learn a new one. I was happy about the move because the bigger bases always had better food, but I was not happy about the rocket and mortar situation. Balad was like a magnet for them, and the base got pummeled daily. I never got used to that.

Missions were steady and frequent. After flying for a few months, we got to know the ins and outs of our AO, which made navigating easier. Regardless of what our specific mission was, it seemed like we were continually getting diverted to respond to TICs—troops in contact.

One early frigid morning, our team took off at four from Balad. We flew east of the airfield to our designated test-fire area—an island in the middle of the Tigris River. I was flying in the left seat, with CW3 Mike Hambrecht in the right. Mike was a maintenance test pilot in Alpha Troop and we flew together occasionally.

Dat! Dat! Dat!

The .50-cal rounds rattled my brain as Mike fired the machine gun. The bullets rained down on the target—a single black rubber car tire. The island was usually deserted, and this early even the duty donkeys weren't there. They had grown so immune to our test firing that they didn't even move when they heard our guns go off.

As we flew away from the island, I tuned up the ground unit's frequency to let them know we were on the way to conduct reconnaissance and security in their AO.

"Bayonet, Bayonet. This is Annihilator Eight-One, flight of two Kiowas, six hundred rounds of fifty-cal, eight rockets, one and a half hours on station. Let us know if you need anything," I said over the radio.

"Roger, Annihilator. We've got a couple of friendly convoys in the AO. We'll let you know if we need you."

Mike turned the Kiowa down Route Crystal, an east-to-west road. Our mission was to conduct reconnaissance, so I leaned out my door to look for any evidence that IEDs might be concealed in the debris scattered along the road. People were just starting to stir and come out of their homes to go about their lives.

"Annihilator Eight-One! This is Bayonet One-Six, a convoy of four Humvees on Route Trigger. We've got a TIC. One of our vehicles just hit an IED. Need you on station *now*!" a voice shouted over the radio.

"Roger, Bayonet," I said. "We're en route. Should be there in a couple of minutes. Do you need a medevac? What's the status of your guys?"

I punched in the grid coordinates to Bayonet's location on my keyboard into the nav system so Mike could fly directly there.

Mike banked the Kiowa left to head north toward the TIC.

"Negative, Annihilator. Luckily, we're all okay," Bayonet replied.

In the distance I could make out the stalled convoy on the outskirts of a village.

"Bayonet, it's Annihilator, we've got you in sight."

"We need you to find the triggerman who blew the IED. Pretty sure it was detonated remotely," Bayonet replied.

Mike flew low and fast over the convoy and banked left. Something caught my eye. Two military-age males on the west side of the road in a farm field.

"Coming around left," Mike said. "What are these guys doing?"

I looked down and saw a man standing close to the road and another who was farther away from it, farming in the dirt field. The man near the road broke out in a full-on sprint toward the actual farmer. Once he reached the other man, he awkwardly stood next to him in an attempt to appear as though he were with the farmer. Except the real farmer wanted nothing to do with him. He started to walk away from the other guy, except every time he moved, the other guy followed.

"Bayonet, I think we have a suspected triggerman," I said. "Single military-age male was near the road when we arrived on station and once he saw us he ran to a farmer and pretended to farm with him. They are now a couple hundred meters from your location in the farm field."

"Roger, Annihilator, we've got them in sight."

I watched one of the Humvees from the convoy start to drive down the small dirt path toward their location. Mike set up an orbit around their location that put us in a position where we could provide cover fire for the ground guys in case the suspected triggerman had any weapons on him.

The Humvee came to a halt, and the ground guys jumped out of the vehicle with their M4s drawn on the men in the field. The men in the field immediately put their hands up. The Iraqi interpreter began yelling at the two men and motioned for them to come over to the vehicle. They complied.

I looked at my watch. We needed to head to a follow-on mission.

"Bayonet, looks like you've got it under control," I said. "We've got to break station and head to another mission, since this is no longer an active TIC. We'll still be in the AO, so give us a call if you need us."

"Roger, Annihilator. We're good here. Thanks for your help," Bayonet said.

Mike broke right out of our orbit and headed north. The only break we got during our missions was the flight time en route from one ground unit location to the next. During the en route time we had to ensure that we were prepared for our next mission. I punched the grid coordinates into our nav system and tuned up the new frequencies for our next mission.

We were linking up with Punisher 6, a ground unit that was conducting a cordon and search of a nearby village. Our mission was to provide perimeter security of the village to ensure that no one left the cordon. Punisher was embedded with an Iraqi army unit and they were going house to house in search of the enemy and weapons caches.

"Punisher Six, this is Annihilator Eight-One, flight of two Kiowas, six hundred rounds of fifty-cal and eight rockets, about one hour on station time," I said.

"Roger, Annihilator. Currently friendlies have cleared the east side of the village and are moving west. Request aerial security to prevent cordon breach," Punisher said.

Mike flew the Kiowa in a larger counterclockwise orbit so the village would be out my door and I would have a good vantage point for reconnaissance to find anyone trying to flee the village. We had good situational awareness of the ground guys' location as well as the road that served as the western border of the cordon. I spotted a group of men gathered near a building on the edge of town.

"We've got a cluster of three or four males in the northwest corner trying to flee," I said to Mike.

"Roger, eyes on," Mike replied.

Mike flew the Kiowa low and slow next to their location and they all looked up.

I stuck my arm out the door of the Kiowa and pointed my finger at them, then pointed back to the village. I did this a couple of times, and they caught on to what I was doing and quickly complied. A year ago I never would have guessed that hand and arm signals would come in so handy for a Kiowa pilot in combat.

We continued our reconnaissance around the village. As Mike flew on the northern side of the village and began to turn south, I caught a glimpse of two objects moving in the open desert a couple of hundred meters southwest of the city.

"Mike, I've got two more guys headed away from the city at our twelve o'clock."

"Roger, I've got them," Mike said as he flew toward them.

Mike flew the Kiowa fast and low right next to the two men. They stopped and looked at us and began walking again.

"Definitely military-age," I said. "And they definitely came from the village."

I switched back to radio the ground guys. "Punisher, we've got two military-age males in the desert a couple hundred meters southwest of the city," I said.

"Annihilator, we need you stop them," Punisher replied.

"Roger, Punisher."

Mike flew by them again, low and slow. I attempted to use my hand and arm signals to communicate to them to head back into the village. No luck this time.

The men stopped and one looked up at the helicopter. Another waved his hand up at us as if he were trying to shoo away a fly. Then they continued walking.

"Guess these guys are trying to be tough," I said to Mike.

"Let's see how tough they are when you put your M4 in their face," Mike replied.

I reached onto the dash, unhooked my M4, and pointed it out the door. A round was already loaded in the chamber. Mike started another slow-and-low pass. I looked down the sight of my M4 at the two men. They looked up at us and saw my M4 pointed at them. They stopped walking away from the cordon. I pointed the rifle toward the town. The two men turned around and began walking toward the town quickly.

Well, that was easier than expected, I thought.

Mike laughed. "I bet they don't like it that a girl is pointing a gun at them."

One of the men looked up at the helicopter and flipped us off.

"Punisher, the two men are headed back toward the town," I said.

"Roger, we've got them in sight."

We flew orbits around them until they were close to the edge of the village, where the Iraqi army was waiting for them. Once they were in the custody of the Iraqi army we continued our mission. But by then, word had gotten out that no one was going to have any luck attempting to flee, and the rest of the mission was quiet.

———

It was my last day to wake up at 3:00 a.m. for the early-morning shift. At least for a couple of weeks. Today we were flying a reconnaissance and security mission around our AO. I was flying with CW2 Scott Cotriss as my PC, but I was flying in the right seat and he was in the left. CW3 Ed Dalsey was our AMC in the trail Kiowa.

We took off shortly after sunrise and began flying around the Balad airfield, looking for any signs of suspicious activity, especially any rocket or mortar launch sights. It was nice to fly in the right seat and be the primary person on the flight controls, instead of always running the nav, comms, MMS, and weapons systems, as you do when you are in the left seat.

"Annihilator Two-Three, this is Yankee. We've got a mission change for you. We got a report that a Raven crashed somewhere on the south side of the airfield. We need you to find it," the battle captain said over the radio.

"Roger, we'll take a look."

A Raven is a small drone or unmanned aerial vehicle often used by ground units. It actually looks like a white model airplane a kid might have, but is bigger, a bit over a yard long and with more than a yard-long wingspan. You launch it by hand like you would those small balsam planes that kids get.

We had a large area to search and not much time. We needed to find it before it fell into the hands of anyone outside the U.S. military.

South of the airfield were a bunch of open farm fields scattered with clusters of mud huts. I flew the Kiowa in a methodical flight path to ensure we didn't miss anything. Back and forth. With the trash all over the place, and all over Iraq, everything seemed to resemble a Raven. And we had no idea if the device were intact or in pieces.

"Somebody probably already picked it up," I said after scanning for about twenty minutes.

"That's a good possibility," Scott said.

I flew toward another group of mud huts surrounded by farm fields.

"I've got it!" Scott said.

I couldn't believe it. Scott wrote down the grid coordinates.

"Yankee, we've located the Raven and are going to land and pick up. Will call when we're en route back to the airfield," Scott said.

I slowed back and looked for a place to land. I didn't want to blow the Raven away or damage it further, but I didn't want Scott to have to walk too far to get to it and have him exposed away from the Kiowa. I found a bare patch of dirt, north of the mud huts but south of the farm fields. It put the Raven behind us, but that was the best we could do.

"I've got a good overwatch for you guys," Ed said from the trail Kiowa. His Kiowa was in a position to shoot anyone who tried to threaten us while we were on the ground.

I pointed the nose of the Kiowa toward the dirt patch and descended as fast as I could. We would be a target as soon as we came in to land, and we'd be a target sitting on the ground. We were just going to have to make this happen as fast as possible. I felt the skids of the aircraft touch the dirt, and I continued to lower the collective until we were firmly on the ground.

"All right, I'll be back in a minute," Scott said as he unbuckled his seat belt.

"I'll be here," I said as I watched Scott walk away until he was out of view.

It was weird and uncomfortable being in a Kiowa sitting outside the wire, alone. Eerie. The mud huts were behind me, so I had no way of knowing if someone were to sneak up on me. Luckily, our guys in the trail aircraft would radio me. But I pulled out my M9 from my leg holster and set it on my thigh, just in case.

A few minutes passed. No activity. It seemed to be taking Scott a while.

Then I saw Scott appear with his arms full of pieces of the Raven. He set them all down in his seat, and, piece by piece, shoved each bit into any available empty space in the aircraft. Somehow it all fit. I put my M9 back in my leg holster.

"You guys have a gathering of kids behind the tail of your aircraft," said Ed, who was still in his overwatch position in the air. "They are getting kind of close to the tail rotor."

"Scott is getting strapped back in now and then we'll be taking off. Let us know if they get any closer," I replied.

"Ready to go," Scott said.

"Roger, clear your side for me to make sure those kids are out of the way," I said.

"Yep, you're good," he said.

I pulled up on the collective and took off straight ahead. I banked the aircraft to the right and headed straight for the airfield.

"Yankee, Annihilator Two-Three, we've got the Raven on board and are inbound for Balad now," Scott said.

"Roger, Annihilator. There's already someone at the FARP waiting to pick it up. Thanks for your help."

"You got it. Anytime."

After we dropped off what was left of the Raven at the FARP and parted ways with the broken bird, we continued our mission in the AO. We started route reconnaissance for a convoy that was passing through the area. I flew ahead of the lead vehicle, scouting for any possible IEDs, to ensure that, if we spotted a suspicious area, the convoy would have enough time to stop before hitting it. It was a huge responsibility. We wanted to make sure the convoy got to wherever it was going safely.

"Scott, do you see that?" I asked. About three hundred meters ahead of the convoy was an IED hole in the middle of the road with an object in it. But I couldn't make out what it was because there was trash surrounding it.

"Roger, I've got eyes on it," Scott said. "Definitely suspicious."

"Jaguar Two-Six, Annihilator Two-Three, we got a possible IED about three hundred meters in front of your lead vehicle. Previous IED hole with an unidentified object inside," Scott said to the convoy.

"Roger, Annihilator," Jaguar replied.

I banked the Kiowa right and turned back toward the convoy. All of the vehicles had come to a stop.

"Annihilator, this is Jaguar. We called EOD [explosive ordnance disposal] to come clear it for us. Can you pull aerial security for us while we wait?"

Every ground unit reacted differently when we would report suspicious objects on the road or possible IEDs. Some would say "thanks for the heads up" and drive right on by whatever we thought looked suspicious, while others said "thanks" but stopped the convoy and would wait to get it cleared by EOD before proceeding. Regardless, we reported anything out of the ordinary and allowed them to decide. Sometimes it turned out to be an IED, other times it didn't. Better safe than sorry, I believed.

"Roger, no problem," Scott replied.

We began flying a wide orbit around the convoy. Civilian car traffic started to line up behind the convoy. People were getting out of their cars and waving their hands around, clearly pissed about the traffic jam.

After flying around for an hour with nothing going on and the convoy still stopped, we were growing restless.

"Jaguar, what's EOD's status? The civilian traffic behind you is getting pretty bad," Scott said.

"Roger, we see it. EOD is en route."

Something familiar in the distance down the route caught my eye. It was coming toward the parked convoy we were covering. I flew the aircraft down the route away from the front of the convoy.

"There's a U.S. convoy on the opposite side of the road speeding toward the IED," I said over our team radio frequency.

"Shit," Scott replied.

"Anyone tracking this unknown convoy? Or have a frequency to contact them on?" I asked.

Silence.

Time was running out as they continued barreling down the road.

I flew the Kiowa straight toward the convoy and buzzed its lead vehicle. But we didn't have comms with it, so we weren't able to persuade it to stop. We attempted some hand and arm signals with no luck.

This is not happening, I thought.

I cringed as the lead vehicle approached the suspected IED location, fully expecting to see and hear an explosion at any time. The lead vehicle slowed as it approached the stopped U.S. convoy, and came to a full stop right next to the suspected IED.

Nothing exploded.

"You've got to be kidding me," I said to Scott. "What are the chances of that happening?"

"Jaguar, it's Annihilator. I'm sure you've got eyes on the convoy that stopped next to the IED by now, but if you have comms with them can you relay the sitrep [situational report]?"

"Roger, Annihilator. And EOD is here."

After an hour and a half of flying in circles, no injuries, a random convoy, and lots of angry Iraqis trapped in the traffic jam, EOD cleared the suspicious object. It turned out to be nothing. I still say it's better to be safe than sorry. Sometimes it seemed like our job description was to merely survive a complete shit show. Today was no exception.

8

BINGO

January 2006

Miqdadiyah, Iraq

We were flying blacked out, invisible from the ground. Through my NVGs, the desert skimming two hundred feet beneath the skids flickered in shades of green. We were headed east, hunting the enemy. It was a cold January night, and the chill cut through the fire-retardant long underwear I wore beneath my tan flight suit. My fingers were stiff and numb inside my gloves as I gripped the cyclic with my right hand and the collective with my left. My helmet and goggles provided some protection from the wind, but my face stung with cold every time I pulled my neck gaiter down to talk into the mic.

"Hope this night picks up," I radioed to my trail aircraft. So far, a couple of hours in, it was looking slow. I was on the flight controls in the right seat, with Chris in the left. We were flying lead for our Kiowa team.

Ahead of us I could see a settlement of mud huts clustered on either side of the road. Faint lights flickered outside the boxy beige homes, which blended in with the washed-out hues of the desert. To the north, a small river snaked its way toward Baghdad, outlined by wisps of vegetation that stood in stark contrast to the vast emptiness of the desert.

This was a routine reconnaissance mission between Baqubah, an al-Qaeda hot spot, and Miqdadiyah (Mook-a-dee-ya), a small town toward the border of Iran. The route between them was a literal mine-field for American convoys: IEDs came in many clever disguises and were hard to spot—packed into potholes, hidden in trash, rigged in abandoned roadside vehicles, even planted in the carcasses of donkeys and dogs. Some were detonated by pressure plates, triggered by the weight of a tire. Others were set off remotely, from a cell phone or walkie-talkie. Sometimes they were linked together in a deadly web called a daisy chain.

Flying combat reconnaissance missions had become second nature. No more feeling vulnerable with my hand sticking out the door of the Kiowa. No more nervousness from the newness of the war. On every flight I had been faced with a new scenario, which required me to constantly make new decisions and rapidly gain knowledge and expe-rience. I had fine-tuned my left-seater skills and become comfortable and skilled as a copilot. Pilot-in-command training was in full effect, and I had my sights on making PC sometime in the near future.

"Coming around left," I said on the radio, telling the trail aircraft to move into an overwatch position as we moved closer to the ground.

"Roger," said the trail PC. "Picking up an outer."

I eased the cyclic to the right, and the helicopter banked tightly into a hairpin turn, allowing us to get a closer look at a suspicious-looking pothole filled with trash, a common cover for IEDs. Chris dropped a waypoint on the grid to mark the location as I peered out of the doorless cockpit.

"We're good," Chris said. "Just some trash. Nothing suspicious."

"All right, it was nothing," I said to trail. "Continuing."

"Roger. We're with you."

We resumed as lead aircraft, and the trail fell into our standard flight formation, flying slightly above and behind us.

Chris pushed up his NVGs to look at the MMS screen in the cockpit, which he had skewed to the route of our recon mission. While Chris trained his attention on the screen, I scanned outside for any signs of trouble. One pair of eyes inside the cockpit, one pair of eyes looking out.

"I've got contact," Chris said abruptly, keying the mic so that the trail aircraft could hear. "Three guys with shovels on the road up ahead—couple hundred meters."

On the MMS, three figures glowed hot white against the blackness onscreen. They were bending over a hole in the ground, placing something large inside.

"Amber, come left, I don't want to lose these guys," Chris said. "Let's get into a figure-eight pattern so I can keep the MMS on them."

I flew in an infinity pattern, allowing Chris to keep the enemy in sight on the MMS. They would hear the rotors any minute. We had seconds to develop the situation that was going on below us and set up a course of action.

"That's a fucking round," Chris said. "Does that look like a round to you?"

"Yep," I said. "That's definitely a round."

Three guys digging a hole in the road in the middle of night was more than suspicious activity. These definitely weren't local dirt farmers, which is what we called locals who went through the motions of farming with no visible green results.

We were confined in tight airspace, framed by FOB Normandy (a tiny base on the outskirts of Miqdadiyah), by the enemy, and by tall power lines on our left, so I didn't have much room to maneuver. NVGs mess with your depth perception, too, and if our rotor so much as clipped a wire, it would roll the helicopter into a ball, like twine, and we would go down in a flaming mess.

"I've got the wires," I told Chris, who startled every time he looked up from the MMS at power lines in his face.

The strong winter winds buffeted the helicopter, gusting us dangerously close to the wires. Maintaining the figure-eight pattern in these suboptimal conditions was a difficult, draining maneuver. And we had to keep a safe distance from the enemy, in case they pulled out an AK-47 or an RPG. There were a lot of factors to process at once.

By catching these guys in the act, we had gained positive identification, one of the requirements to fire. Once you lose it, it can be hard to reestablish. We didn't want to lose sight of them.

We were running out of time. The enemy would hear us any second now, and we had blown through our bingo fuel level—the point at which it is required to return to base and refuel. Our flight regulation mandated us to land with a twenty-minute fuel reserve—about 100 pounds.

"What's your fuel?" I radioed to trail. "We are about one hundred and sixty pounds."

"Roger, we're at one hundred and fifty pounds."

A hundred fifty pounds of JP8 fuel gave us no more than thirty minutes before we would run out of gas and the engine would quit. And we were nowhere near a FARP—forward, arming, and refueling point—for refuel.

"All right, let's just keep an eye on the fuel," Chris barked over the radio. "We don't have time to fuck around, so let's set this up."

Before we could pull the trigger, we had to develop the situation, report it up to headquarters, and coordinate with the ground unit at the base. We had to set up a gun run for the engagement, and the air mission commander—AMC—had to make the decision to shoot. Only then could we pull the trigger.

While Chris kept the enemy on our MMS, trail called up the

ground forces at FOB Normandy, less than a mile away. The situation report was curt and tense:

Three enemy, emplacing an IED on a road. We'll be engaging. Need a clearance of fire.

The radio operator at FOB Normandy said that all U.S. troops were accounted for and inside the wire—no convoys or patrols were off the FOB that night. But they had to go up the chain of command for a clearance of fire approval. Who knew how long that could take?

The fuel gauge blinked yellow. We were now flying on our reserve fuel.

As soon as we arrived on station, the enemy heard the rotors. We had blown our cover. They dropped the IED and ran to the nearest ditch on the other side of the road. They lay down in it, frozen like rabbits, believing perhaps that in the darkness we could not see them. But there's no hiding from a Kiowa. Once we have you on the MMS, especially at night, there is no escape.

In accordance with our rules of engagement, we had legal authority to fire on the enemy. Positive enemy target ID. Hostile intent. Hostile action. The area was clear of friendlies, and all U.S. forces in our area of operation were accounted for. All our ducks were in a row.

But our hands were tied. We could not fire without the approval of the AMC, who was in the trail aircraft. He was stalling, waiting to hear back from Normandy for an authorization to fire.

"Hey, what are we doing?" Chris said with a growl at trail. "I need an answer *now*."

"Two more minutes," the AMC said.

The fuel gauge ticked down. Our window was closing.

"What the fuck are they doing back there?" Chris said.

Chris keyed the mic over our internal frequency so only I could hear. "Amber, we are out of here in two minutes, with or without trail," he said. "If they want to stay here and fuck around because they can't make a decision and have a flameout, that's on them. We're going to get gas."

"Roger."

One minute passed and I watched the blinking yellow "Chiclets" of the fuel gauge continue to drop. I'd never seen it down this low, this far away from a fueling station. Now we were just praying not to flame out.

"Chris."

I didn't have to say anything else.

"GO!"

I banked the aircraft right and south, breaking contact and heading straight toward FOB Caldwell, the nearest fuel depot. It would be about a ten-minute flight. Could we make it? I wasn't sure. I had never heard of a pilot running out of fuel. It just didn't happen. Not only would it ball up an aircraft, but if you were lucky enough to walk away from the crash, you would probably never fly again. This was grounds for losing your wings.

But if we had to crash, this was the place to do it. Our flight would take us over a rural stretch of desert, a flat and sandy emptiness devoid of people and obstacles—about the best of a worst-case scenario. If we ran out of gas and the engine flamed out, I knew what to do, at least in theory. Since the Kiowa is a single-engine aircraft, if the engine quits, the only option is to autorotate—that is, make a controlled crash.

This is how you do it: You disengage the rotor from the drive train—like putting a car in neutral—so that it spins freely after the engine has quit. If you don't, you're dead as dust because the helicopter will drop out of the sky like a rock. You must drop the collective flight control immediately once the engine quits to keep the rotor blades' RPM as high as possible. Once the collective is down and you are autorotating, the air passing through the blades keeps them spinning as you fall, like a child blowing into a pinwheel, and this slows your descent. You maintain a glide path with a survivable rate of descent, and aim for a flat place with no obstacles—what better place than the open desert?

Chris put in a direct waypoint in the nav system that gave us the fastest route to FOB Caldwell, and I steered the aircraft to follow the arrow on the display. The fuel gauge lost another yellow Chiclet. We were getting closer to the red. There weren't many red Chiclets.

"Hey, we broke station," Chris radioed to trail. "We're headed to Caldwell and hope we make it."

"Roger. We did, too. We've got you in sight."

The ten minutes felt like an hour as we watched the fuel gauge creep lower and lower.

"Chris, that was stupid," I said. "We shouldn't have pressed it this far."

"I know," he said. "That was really dumb."

"And what the hell? We had them. Trail blew it."

Why was trail waiting for clearance of fire? We didn't need it. And besides, clearance of fire doesn't mean you are cleared to engage, it's not a weapons release authority; it just means that all friendlies in the area are accounted for. As a crew, we had been confident that we could successfully engage with little to no collateral damage, with zero risk to friendly forces. We'd had a clear shot.

The chance of our finding them again after refueling was slim to none. And even if we could, it wouldn't be as simple as pulling the trigger. Once you break contact, you have to reestablish positive ID and hostile intent. If they dropped the IED and ran away, it would be virtually impossible to catch them in the act again. They wouldn't make the same mistake twice.

Bong! Bong! Bong!

The warning alarm indicated we were critically low on fuel.

"I have the controls," Chris said. "If we flame out, I want it to be my fault, not yours."

I felt the cyclic shake, his cue to me that he had the controls. We flew on in silence.

At last, we saw the faint lights of Caldwell glowing in the distance. There were no other lights. Chris banked left.

Bong! Bong! Bong!

Nineteen pounds. We were flying on fumes. The fuel-boost pump had failed, and the engine was being starved.

As soon as the skids scraped the concrete helipad, Chris rolled the throttle down to idle to conserve any remaining fuel. The trail aircraft hovered over the pad to our left. We had made it.

One breath of relief was all we could afford. We had to refuel quickly and get back on scene. There was still a chance—unlikely, but possible—to reacquire the enemy. I gave the refueler a thumbs-up and tapped my watch to let him know we were in a hurry.

After refueling, we sped back to the last known enemy location on the route we had found them on. As we suspected, the insurgents were long gone. The hole was empty. We had lost our chance. But we had learned a valuable lesson: indecision is a decision. We were lucky, and we knew it. We had to call it a draw.

The enemy lived to see another day.

But then, so had we.

9

TROOPS IN CONTACT

February 2006

Balad Air Base, Iraq

"All right, let's RTB"—return to base—Tim Janson said over the radio. He was sitting next to me in the right seat of our Kiowa as the PC and AMC of our night flight. We were just outside of Balad airspace and could see the lights of the enormous air base as we approached the runway.

"Roger," said CW3 Ed Dalsey, the pilot from the lead aircraft.

We were mission complete after an NVG flight that seemed to keep us out all night in the bitter winter air. In the open-air cockpit, the cold burned our noses and cheeks, but we didn't mind because it kept us awake and sharp. My hands and feet were always colder than the rest of me, and my flight gloves didn't help much. It was often so frigid that my PC and I would have to take turns on the flight controls so the other could sit on his hands to warm them up so they were operable again. Of course, we only had this luxury when nothing else was going on and we had the time to do so. Even in combat, there were nights when there wasn't much happening, and routine reconnaissance flights could get a little boring. Those were the nights when you couldn't stop thinking about your warm bed back at the base.

Kiowa pilots often developed close relationships with the ground guys we worked with on missions in our AO. The more we worked with them, the more we got to know them, but only by our call signs. We rarely got to meet the ground troops in person or learn their real names, but we wore the same uniform, wore the same flag on our right shoulders, and were fighting the same enemy for the country we loved. They were the ones in the thick of the fight, day in and day out. They lived in tiny outposts away from the big bases with little protection from the enemy. We were their protectors when we were covering them. That was our job, why we were out there flying in the middle of the night, why we carried weapons, why we dropped everything to fly to a troops-in-contact call. We felt responsible for their safety. They trusted us to be there to help them when they needed it most, and that was a responsibility we didn't take lightly.

Tim flipped the toggle switch on the dashboard that "safed" our weapons systems and completed the before-landing check prior to touching down at the refuel pads.

"Annihilator Three-Two, Saber TOC, what's your position?" a voice said over our headquarters radio frequency. It was the battle captain.

"Saber TOC," Tim answered, "we are in refuel, headed for parking. We are end of mission."

"We've got an active TIC going on in Ad Duliyah that needs your team on station now," the TOC said. "Contact Reaper One-Six on secure radio for an updated sitrep. They are on Route Garfield and were on their way back to their base when they were ambushed with IEDs and small-arms fire. One of their Bradleys got hit and there are wounded. The medevac aircraft is being spun up now. Expedite to their location."

We needed to get to Reaper's location *now*. Tim put the location of the friendly forces in our nav system. It showed that they were about fifteen minutes away if we flew there directly.

"I'll contact tower for an immediate departure direct to Reaper's location," Ed said in the lead aircraft over the radio to Tim.

"No, let's set down in parking. I want to get more information before we head out there. I don't think we'll get there in time to do anything."

"We just got called to a TIC, we need to go," Ed said over the radio. He was clearly frustrated at Tim.

"Stand by," Tim replied curtly.

What the hell is he doing? We have a fifteen-minute flight to develop the situation en route to their location. There are U.S. guys under fire that are wounded out there all alone. This is what we do . . . LET'S GO!

My blood was starting to boil. What was Tim doing? When the ground guys are under fire, they call us because they know we will always come. It didn't matter if the enemy was gone by the time we arrived and the firefight was over. We had to at least try. Our guys were still stranded on a road in enemy territory, under attack. At a minimum, if we fly to their location, they could talk to us over the radio and hear our rotor blades, so they'd know we were there for them. I'd had ground guys come up to me after other missions to tell me how much it meant to them to have us overhead and to hear our rotors, that it made all the difference. That thought kept running through my head. *They need us now.*

But there was nothing I could do. Tim was in charge, he outranked me, and he made all the decisions in our flight and mission. It was his call.

"We are fifteen minutes away from their location. Can you relay that to them? We probably won't be able to get there in time," Tim said to the TOC. He was coming up with every excuse not to go back out.

"Understood," the TOC said. "We already told them that and they don't care. They still want you. Head out there now."

Tim continued arguing with the battle captain in the TOC. "It's too far away. We're already in parking. There's probably another aircraft already out there that's closer." I was mortified. I was furious that I was helpless. Every minute wasted arguing with the TOC was a minute we wouldn't be on station with Reaper. If an aircraft gets shot down, the first thing we expect as pilots is for the infantry soldiers to drop everything and come get us. And they expect the same out of us when they get into trouble and call in a TIC.

"We are ready for takeoff," Ed radioed, reading my mind. "Can we do this while we are in the air?"

"I'm handling it. Stand by!" Tim growled over internal before turning back to the TOC. "We are outside of our time block. We are done with our mission. By the time we get there, we won't be able to do anything."

Tim finally wore down the TOC.

"Fine, shut down," the battle captain said.

"Shut down," Tim said to me, like he had just won this argument. "We couldn't have done anything. I don't know why she was trying to make us go out there." He sounded like he was trying to convince himself that he made the right call.

When I got back to the crew chief shack—where we kept our flight gear and filled out the logbooks—I saw Ed, who was clearly as disgusted and angry as I was.

"What just happened is not okay," Ed said.

We went to the pilots' office, found some of our IPs, and relayed the events that just took place. They were shocked at first, then pissed. The incident had been so far out of our standard operating procedures. They decided to call a warrant officer meeting the following day to discuss how unacceptable this was.

I walked back into my CHU and fell into bed. Emotionally drained and exhausted from the flight and the drama, I tossed and turned. I couldn't sleep and kept replaying the events in my head. Were the guys okay? Had help arrived? Had they made it out of there alive? I kept imagining them screaming over the radio. The unknown haunted me.

In the morning, someone told me the terrible news: Two soldiers in the Bradley that hit the IED had been trapped inside and died from the blast. Another soldier was able to get out of the vehicle but was severely wounded and died on the medevac flight to Balad.

I couldn't eat. I couldn't think of anything except what had happened. Those guys were sons, husbands, fathers, and brothers. It wasn't the first time our guys had been killed. And it most certainly wouldn't be the last, but it never got any easier.

All the available warrant officers who weren't flying or on a different shift piled in the pilots' office for the briefing. A few IPs stood against the wall, their steely glare moving slowly from pilot to pilot as we got lectured.

"It's been brought to our attention that some people think they can override a battle captain's order to respond to a TIC. Let me remind you why we Kiowa pilots are different. Why the ground guys always ask for us first when the shit hits the fan. Because when they need us we drop everything to be there for them when they need us most. It doesn't matter how intense it is, how much enemy fire there is, what time of day, or what time it is. We come running. The Kiowa community has proven this battle after battle, conflict after conflict, war after war, which is why we have maintained our outstanding reputation among ground forces."

We all knew that. And that's how we all operated. I'd never seen otherwise until my flight with Tim the night before.

Beyond the reprimand we all received, Tim was otherwise not disciplined, but after that he wasn't on the flight schedule as much as he used to be.

10

FRIENDLY FIRE

February 2006
Balad Air Base, Iraq

The constant demand for Kiowas in our AO kept the op-tempo high. Kiowa coverage in our AO was twenty-four hours a day. Pilots were flying mission after mission. No amount of sleep ever seemed to be enough. I was mentally, physically, and emotionally fatigued. Aside from the combat, everything else in the war had become monotonous: the food, the gym, the people, the movies, the Iraqi bazaars. All of us were sick of each other and in bad moods. We were together 24/7, and everyone's behavior was getting on my nerves. And we still had seven months left in this godforsaken country.

The increased amount of flight time in a Kiowa cockpit takes its toll. The cockpit is cramped, the seats like rocks, and our spine position takes the shape of the letter C throughout the flight. The more I flew, the worse my posture got. I felt like the Hunchback of Balad at the age of twenty-four.

To add to the misery, we wore heavy body armor, with Kevlar plates in front and back. Strapped to those were medical pouches, tourniquets, a radio, survival essentials, an M9 handgun, a CamelBak full of water, and anything else we felt we might need if our aircraft went down and we needed to use our survival skills and E&E (escape and evade from the enemy). It was a load. We also wore a flight helmet day and night. When the sun went down, we added NVGs and a weight bag to balance the front and back of the helmet. It added a lot of weight on my neck for hours on end, but I got used to the pain. It was all part of the job description of being a Kiowa pilot.

On one mission with Blane Hepfner, conducting a recon and security mission, escorting a convoy to base, we were responding to an IED call when I whipped my head around to the left, looking for a possible triggerman in the palm groves below.

Shit!

When I tried to look to the left again, the pain shot right down my spine.

Um, this is not good.

"Hey, there's something going on with my neck," I said to Blane over our internal radio, making sure I didn't look to talk to him in the seat next to me.

"Great," he said. "All of our pilots are breaking."

Chris Rowley, my stick buddy and IP, had severe neck pain that had landed him in the hospital the week prior, and he was now on massive amounts of painkillers and grounded while recovering.

I was relieved when the EOD team had arrived at the location of the IED to dispose of the device. The EOD robot, operated by one of the EOD soldiers using a remote control, moved toward the IED hole. Most EOD robots are on a tracked wheel system, the same way a tank is, allowing them to move fairly quickly. The robot has a camera and movable arms, so that soldiers can work a safe distance from the bomb while still being able to see it up close.

We continued our aerial orbit as the robot approached the IED. A few minutes later the EOD soldiers called "all clear" over the radio and we saw the robot heading back toward the soldiers.

After the all clear, our recon mission returned to being routine. We escorted the convoy back to the base, so we weren't out there much longer. I suffered through the rest of the flight and hoped the pain in my neck would go away.

It didn't. Upon landing I was ordered by Ed Dalsey to get my neck checked out at the field medical center. I walked stiffly into the aid station and was seen by one of the flight docs right away. My neck had completely seized up and my entire body had to move in whatever direction I needed to turn my head.

"I'm going to try to move your neck," the doc said. He grabbed my head and pushed it down toward my chest and then back up.

Excruciating pain shot down my spine.

"That really hurts."

His eyes widened and his face was intense. "Are you allergic to anything?"

"No. What's wrong? Why are you looking at me like that?"

"You just broke out in hives or some kind of rash all over your neck and chest."

I attempted to look down at my shirt as far as my neck would let me.

"You need to get over to the hospital right away and get a blood test. I'm kind of nervous about meningococcal meningitis," he said. Meningococcal meningitis is a bacterial infection that causes inflammation of the membranes that surround the spinal cord and brain, and in some cases it can cause death. The symptoms can develop in hours and include a stiff neck and skin rash.

Oh, great.

After getting tested at the hospital, I was told not to be in a confined space with other people to avoid infecting them as I waited for the results. But the only place available was in my CHU. Lori didn't mind. We were at war, getting shot at all the time, so what's one more risk? I couldn't do anything but lie there in pain anyway. Thankfully the test showed no meningitis, but the pain was still there. I couldn't fly for a week while the doctors tried to figure out what was wrong, but they never did. They were suspicious of a slipped or ruptured disc, degenerative disc disease, and all sorts of other things I had never heard of before. They gave me some Valium muscle relaxers and a down slip—meaning I couldn't fly while I was on the medication.

The rest and medication helped. The pain became moderately manageable, and I got a medical up slip from my doctor so I could fly again, but the pain never fully went away. Chris called it "sympathy pain" for him because we were crewed together.

Once I got my up slip, I was back on the flight schedule nonstop. I jumped right back into missions, right back into PC training. And every time I flew, Chris quizzed me. The nonstop eyes on my every move in the cockpit was exhausting and getting old, but as usual, I couldn't show annoyance.

Amber, there are reports of enemy activity with RPGs and AK-47s down there. How should we approach the target?

Lead aircraft just took fire from that group of people on the road. Do you lay down suppressive fire in self-defense? What about collateral damage? Would you pull the trigger? You thought for two seconds too long. Lead just got shot down. You have a stuck left pedal on your flight controls. What is your immediate emergency procedure?

My mind was always racing. Applying judgment and intuition and my training and experience to the rules and regulations all in a split second put me constantly in overload mode. But this was how they trained new pilots to become pilots in command. If you couldn't handle the stress as a copilot, you'd never handle the stress as a PC.

When I flew with a senior pilot who had been to war before, it was easy to rely on his expertise and experience. Other senior pilots would also ask me what I would do in certain scenarios, how I would respond if our team got shot at, how I would set up our scheme of maneuver, when I would trade fuel for ammo, and vice versa. I always knew that if I made a bad decision they would correct it before it would become too serious. My PC would explain why he would make a different decision. It was excellent practice, but it wasn't a good substitute for doing, living, and learning, which was what I got when I flew with brand-new PCs. They were only a little less clueless than I was, so when we went out on a mission together it felt like it was just the two of us all alone out there in the Iraqi sky—but it felt good to have that responsibility. It made me analyze my strategy and options before deciding about what was best for our team and mission. Most of all, it boosted my confidence as a pilot.

As my dad always told his daughters, "Once you make PC, that's when the learning really starts."

———————

We had nonstop air mission requests from ground forces. It didn't seem like there were enough Kiowas to go around. We would arrive at one location and, soon after, get called to another. We barely had enough pilots to fill the missions we were tasked with, so we were all getting plenty of time to see Iraq from a hundred feet in the air.

I was thinking ahead of the aircraft and being proactive in the cockpit. Still, I couldn't shake the fact that it seemed like some of my guys in my troop were waiting for me to reach my breaking point and lose it on them or break down crying. I wasn't only having to prove myself in the cockpit—that was the easy part. I could fly and it was only a matter of time before all of my guys would see that firsthand in the cockpit. But having to prove myself as a member of Alpha Troop was another story.

I felt like a new calf surrounded by a pack of wolves waiting for me to fall behind so they could pounce. They were looking for weakness, and I was doing my best not to show any. I was an easy target, and some of the guys loved to take advantage of it. Most of them did it in good fun, some left me alone, and others ignored me completely. But a few went out of their way to bully me and loved watching me squirm. Being able to stand up for myself as one of the few women in a predominantly male unit and knowing when to tell my guys to fuck off when they'd crossed a line was an intricate part of survival. I hadn't quite figured it out yet, but I was paying close attention. I kept my eyes and ears open.

On my closet in my CHU, I had pinned up an image that kept me motivated. I'd also had it at home in Tennessee, where it had hung on my refrigerator. My dad used to carry it with him in his flight bag when he flew for Pan Am. It was an 8½x11, black-and-white photocopy of a drawing of a heron that was attempting to swallow a frog. Although the frog was halfway in the heron's mouth, it had its front feet wrapped around the heron's neck, strangling it. At the bottom of the paper, it read: Never Ever Give Up. Whenever I was frustrated, that image put things into perspective and reminded me to stand strong. I often tapped it before I left my room to head out to fly a mission.

I had settled into the rhythm of the deployment with my flight team. I flew combat missions with three other pilots: Chris Rowley, Frank Villanueva, and Jason Arrowood. Each time we got ready to fly we'd do a crew brief in the pilots' office. Sometimes, a handful of other pilots from the previous shift would be present for the briefs, so I knew I'd have an audience. Some pilots provided honest and useful feedback to help me improve; others just liked the sound of their own voices.

One day, Jake Sommers happened to be in the pilots' office. He was the self-appointed bully in our troop and a real asshole. An instigator, he loved to pick fights, and for whatever reason, he seemed to have it out for me. In his eyes, I didn't belong there. Somehow, my presence in the troop diminished his self-worth as a badass. If I opened my mouth or even smiled, he found a reason to go off on me. Other pilots rarely put him in his place, and the more he got away with it, the more freedom he thought he had to be an asshole. I had had about enough of him.

That particular day, before the brief, I had gone to grab our team's NVGs out of the goggle room and M4 rifles out of the armory. Back in the pilots' office with all of our equipment, the team had gathered around the briefing maps. I put our stuff down and foolishly sat next to Jake, who was only sitting in on our crew brief to be obnoxious.

"Why are you sitting next to me?" Jake said. "Did I say you could sit here?"

"Because I feel like it," I said, feeling my blood pressure rise. This was going to go bad quickly. Usually when someone got in Jake's crosshairs, it was best either to leave or to hope someone else came along so he could "adjust fire" and go after them.

"What makes you think you can talk to me like that? I outrank you. You have to do what I say. In fact, stand at the position of attention when you are talking to me!"

We were the same rank—CW2. He was senior to me within the rank of CW2, but under the rules of the Army, we had the same authority, and none over each other. It really got under his skin that some high-school-to-flight-school girl like me could be the same rank he was and fly the same aircraft he could.

"Um, no," I said.

He got in my face. "You think I'm too scared to hit a girl? I'll hit a girl in the face!" Veins were popping out on his forehead, and his face turned red.

"Ha!" I could not help but let that laugh slip out. It was a half-nervous reaction, half "you've got to be kidding me" type laugh. I couldn't believe he had just threatened to hit me, but I refused to give him the satisfaction of thinking he had gotten through to me. I didn't move from my spot on the bench. I just sat there with my best "unimpressed" face on, waiting for his next move and to see if he was actually going to hit me.

All operations inside the pilots' office had ceased. All eyes were on us.

"I don't know, Jake," Chris said with a smirk, trying not to laugh. "I think she could take you."

The entire room erupted in laughter, which infuriated Jake even more. He grabbed his bag and stormed out of the office, slamming the door behind him.

"All right, moving on," Chris said, as though nothing had happened. "Are you ready to brief?"

In that moment, something shifted. I had gained some respect. I felt like I had just conquered Rome.

11

WHAT LIES BENEATH

March 2006

Iraq and Arizona

Dat! Dat! Dat!

The gunfire was too close for comfort. I knew the enemy was stalking me and getting closer to my location. I had survived a crash, but I was all alone in enemy territory and they wanted to capture me alive. There were ground forces on the dirt road over by the wadi that we had been supporting. If I could get to them, I would be safe. But I couldn't find them in the palm groves, which were like a maze of mud trails in the darkness. I couldn't use a light or I'd lead the enemy right to me. My own heartbeat was deafening. I could hear the enemy rapidly gaining ground on me as I ran blindly through the brush.

Dat! Dat! Dat!

The sound of the banging on my door jolted me from my sleep and I shot straight up in bed. I looked around in the darkness to find my bearings. I'd had the stress dream again, the one where my aircraft was shot down over the palm groves by Baqubah, one of the hot spots in our area of operation.

My breathing slowed as I lay back down and closed my eyes. I was okay. It was just a dream, but I think it made me more tired than if I'd not slept at all. By now, I had developed my own personal "don't answer the door" policy on my day off. I had been woken up one too many times to be asked by one of my fellow pilots if they could browse through my DVD collection. Although I was thankful whoever was banging on the door had woken me from my horrible dream, if they really needed me or if it was something important, they would knock again.

Bang. Bang. Bang.

Damn it. I walked like a zombie through the darkness toward the only crack of light at the door frame, trying to be quiet because my roommate, Lori, was asleep on the other side of the room. I opened the door about an inch and peered out into the glaring light. When my eyes adjusted, I saw Chris looking back at me.

"Lori's been shot," he said. "She's in a medevac and they're flying her to the hospital at Balad right now."

I stepped through the door frame and shut the door behind me. The hospital was on the other side of the airfield, on the Air Force side of our base. I couldn't believe what he was telling me. Lori had been on the early-morning shift, but she was back already.

"Chris, what are you talking about?" I said, still half asleep. "Lori is sleeping in her bed right now. She came in after her flight a few hours ago."

"Huh?"

I opened the door of my CHU to prove to him Lori was inside. I switched the light on, knowing I was going to wake up Lori and she would be pissed.

"See?" I said. But there was her bed, perfectly made. No Lori. My heart dropped.

"Come on. Let's go," Chris said. "I've got the Humvee right now. If we hurry, we can make it to the hospital in time to meet the medevac."

I threw on my uniform, laced up my boots, and grabbed my M4, ran out the door, and jumped in the Humvee. We drove around the perimeter of the airfield in silence, the bumpy dirt road jarring my neck and bringing back the stabbing pain. We pulled into the gravel parking lot of the hospital and ran inside. A soldier with a clipboard who appeared to be in charge was in the waiting area.

"Did the medevac with CW3 Lori Hill arrive yet?" I said.

He looked up at me slowly, "No. We don't have any medevacs inbound at this time."

"When did the last one land? There should have been a medevac from FOB Normandy carrying a warrant officer pilot who's been shot."

"Sorry, ma'am. I don't know what to tell you. I don't have anyone inbound, and I don't show that a CW3 Hill came through here."

Where was she?

We jogged to the Humvee and headed back around the airfield to our pilots' office. Maybe someone there knew what the hell was going on.

I ran up the steps and pulled open the door. Lori was sitting with her bandaged foot propped up on a chair. I had never been so ecstatic to see someone in my entire life.

"We have been all over Balad looking for you!" I said. "The hospital told us you hadn't come through yet." A lump started to grow in my throat.

Knock it off. Lori seemed to be holding it together, so I wasn't going to be the one to lose it.

Lori's husband, Dennis, who was also a Kiowa pilot in our unit, but stationed in Kirkuk, about two hours north of Balad, was next to her. He had flown down as soon as he heard the news.

"How are you so calm right now?" I asked her.

She laughed (she was on some major painkillers). "I know, that was close." Lori explained that her team had taken small-arms fire in a complex attack from the enemy near Miqdadiyah, just down the road from where Chris and I had been hit with AK-47 fire a month and a half earlier. Both aircraft in Lori's team were riddled with AK-47 rounds. When Lori's Kiowa had been hit, the helicopter had lost hydraulic power, making it extremely difficult to move the flight controls. Sometimes the flight controls can become so stiff that both pilots have to be on the controls at the same time to work them or they can seize altogether.

One AK-47 round had punctured the cockpit floor and hit Lori in the ankle. She had had to make an emergency run on landing at FOB Normandy, which didn't even have a runway, just a pothole-ridden strip of old asphalt that was used for a refuel area. It was like landing on skis and hopefully sliding to a stop without hitting anything because there were no brakes. Lori had managed to do this in a confined space on an unapproved landing area. She had slowed the airspeed, avoided the Hesco baskets (the defense barriers that line the perimeter of the base), trees, and other obstacles on her landing path, and had touched down without any further damage to the aircraft.

Everything that could have gone wrong had, and Lori had reacted perfectly after being shot, saving both her copilot and herself. She was one hell of a pilot.

"They are sending me home. I have to go pack up my stuff out of our room to take with me. My toiletries and stuff," Lori said.

I headed back to our CHU to help her. As I packed her some Q-tips—she could never be without them—it started to sink in. Lori was lucky to be alive and was now leaving. How was I going to survive the rest of this deployment without her? She had been my roommate for the past seven months. She was my friend, my mentor, and we had almost lost her.

When Lori got back to our room, I had to ask her a question.

"What did it feel like?" I asked.

"Like a Major League Baseball player throwing a baseball really hard from close proximity right into my ankle," she said.

That had never happened to anyone I knew, either, but I tried to imagine it.

A few hours later, she was gone.

My CHU seemed emptier, even though most of Lori's stuff was still in our room. We were going to pack it up later in tough boxes and store it in our unit's containers until we all headed home for good.

The realities of war were hitting home. My roommate had been shot and was now headed back to the States. In January a Kiowa from another unit had taken enemy fire and crashed north of us in Mosul—both pilots killed. My aircraft had been shot up a few months earlier. And we still had more than five months left of combat.

———

I was scheduled to go on R&R in April, a little after Lori shipped out. It meant going home for fifteen days plus travel time back through Kuwait and to the States.

Home. It now had a new meaning to me. It seemed part of my old life. I told myself that if I made it home, that would be enough. But America seemed so far away from the reality I was living in. How were these two places in the same world?

As I boarded the plane to start my break, I looked at the flight attendants with envy. They were clean, their hair looked nice, they had on makeup, and they were wearing earrings. They looked happy. I longed to be a girl again. After nearly eight months in Iraq, I felt disgusting. My hair was gross, I was chronically fatigued, and I had eight months' worth of Iraqi sand packed into my sinuses. The other soldiers flirted with the flight attendants. They hadn't been around girls—other than ones like me—in the past year.

I expected to feel on the flight like it was Christmas morning when I was five years old, but I didn't. I didn't feel much of anything. I wanted to be excited and squirming in my seat for the entire flight, but I wasn't.

We landed at Dallas/Fort Worth International Airport, where we received a heroes' welcome—the fire department had parked a fire truck on either side of the aircraft and hosed it down as it passed through the waterfall. Everyone clapped.

When I got off the plane and walked out of the restricted area, I found myself surrounded by a crowd of appreciative Americans clapping, giving us high fives, and saying, "Thank you for your service!" People were waving flags and handing us welcome bags. I was so thankful, proud, and humbled, and a little overwhelmed. It all seemed surreal to me to be back on American soil.

Three hours later I landed in Phoenix, where my parents were picking me up. As I made my way off the plane, a new, weird sense of excitement and anxiety suddenly hit me. As I walked out of the jetway, I scanned the waiting area for my parents, who had the biggest smiles on their faces I'd ever seen. My dad was holding a single yellow rose.

Without saying a word, I hugged them. A few tears ran down my cheeks. It was the happiest moment in my life and the first time I was speechless. I had made it home.

Even after a few minutes, all I could muster was "Hi." I must've smelled great after sitting in a transient tent in Kuwait for three days before my sixteen-hour plane ride, but my parents didn't seem to mind.

The America I came home to was different, not because America had changed, but because I had. When I overheard average Americans having a conversation, I was often annoyed. In contrast to the people who welcomed us home from Iraq, most people I encountered seemed oblivious to what was happening elsewhere in the world. It seemed like no one knew there was a war going on. Or worse, that they didn't care.

The two weeks of R&R flew by. We went shopping, hiking, ate

at great restaurants, but mostly I just had a wonderful time being home with family. The flowers smelled better. The sun shone brighter. The food tasted better. I appreciated everything more than I ever had before. I loved having clean laundry that didn't smell like feet, even after it was washed. I loved taking a shower without wearing flip-flops. And I loved having a bathroom within ten feet of my bed. I loved feeling almost safe.

But I had brought part of Iraq home with me. I hated driving. I was constantly on the lookout for IEDs on the roads. I cringed at every pothole, every piece of trash, every dead animal. Every parked car was a possible VBIED—vehicle-borne IED. I hated being without my M9, after eight months of having it attached to my body 24/7. Every so often I'd slip into a panic and frantically search for it before remembering I didn't have it with me. It was a strange new form of torment.

Even though I had a great time, I knew it was fake. My real world was back in Iraq. Before I knew it, I was packing my bags and putting on my uniform to head back to the place where I had all the clarity in the world and only one thing mattered: your survival and the survival of your buddies. It was where I belonged.

I wanted to go back to Iraq.

12

ANNIHILATOR 24

June 2006

Kirkuk, Iraq

It was summertime in Kirkuk. A few months earlier, in April, our troop had moved from Balad to FOB Warrior to join the rest of our squadron in Kirkuk in northern Iraq. When the sun hit high noon, the aircraft skids would melt into the asphalt where they were parked on the flight line. Flying in that heat felt as if we were melting, too. I would carry an extra water bottle with me just to pour down the front of my shirt to cool me off a bit when the wind would come in the cockpit. We could drink as much water as we wanted during those day flights. All of the FARPs we stopped at for fuel had Porta Potties, but we usually didn't even have to pee because we would sweat it all out.

As miserable as the heat was, I would choose to fly in the heat over the cold any day. During day missions, when the heat was the worst, the temperature gauge on the aircraft often maxed out with the needle pointing past 50 degrees Celsius—more than 122 degrees Fahrenheit. We had to pay extra attention to our oil and engine operating temperatures to ensure that we didn't ruin the aircraft by overheating the engine. And we had to keep in mind the different times it takes for the engine to overheat at different temperatures.

On one flight, the heat was so bad that our turbine gas temperature (TGT)—the heat inside the engine—gauge on the instrument panel reached the red line. If I increased the collective to give us more power to fly over the wires we had to cross, we would exceed the TGT limitation and "burn up the engine." But desperate times call for desperate measures. Instead of flying perpendicular to the wires to cross them, I flew the Kiowa parallel to the wires at about 80 knots to give us enough airspeed to be able to bump the Kiowa up by pulling back on the cyclic, giving us altitude without increasing power. It worked. We got enough altitude to reach the top of the wires, safely tilt the cyclic right, do a ninety-degree right turn over the wires, then swoop back down close to the ground at our normal flight altitude. We were still nearly redlining, but hadn't exceeded any limitations. It wasn't pretty, but we made it work, and were able to continue the mission.

The heat also brought out the camel spiders, creatures that look like a hybrid of a scorpion and a spider and can be as big as a human hand. They are not venomous; they kill things by biting them with their big-ass jaws. A bite to a human would be painful but not poisonous. Regardless, I was terrified of these sci-fi creatures. As a child, I used to pay my little sister Lacey to kill spiders for me.

The camel spiders loved hiding under our aircraft on the parking ramp. The aircraft provided shade, and our parking spot was right next to a desert field of yellow brush and tumbleweeds, home to a plethora of camel spiders. Whenever we conducted a preflight check on the Kiowa, it was standard to stage our gear—body armor, M4 rifles, NVGs—in or near the aircraft so we would be ready to go after we completed our mission brief. One day I picked up my body armor to put it on, and this huge brownish-yellow spider ran out from under it, right toward my boot, the only thing standing between it and the brush field. I shot about four feet in the air. Once it disappeared into the brush, I shook out my body armor, hoping there weren't any more camel spiders or eggs in there. I cringed as I put it on, got in the helicopter, and started it up. I never left my body armor on the ground again after that.

———

Making pilot in command, PC, was the goal I had been working toward since I'd gotten to Iraq ten months earlier. Chris had pushed me hard from day one, putting me in scenarios I wasn't sure I was ready for, putting me in charge of the aircraft and communications. He had a do-or-die approach and would pull circuit breakers in flight to see how I would react. In the middle of escorting a convoy, he would fold his arms across his chest and say, "I am a new copilot that has no idea what to do and am completely overwhelmed. What are you going to do?" He was testing me to see how I handled things under pressure and to be sure I could make command decisions.

On one flight when I was flying lead in the right seat, with Chris next to me in the left seat acting as my copilot, I saw him lift his right arm to do something on the ceiling circuit breaker board panel between our seats.

Bong!

The alarm went off through my radio in my helmet and the warning message flashed on the right MFD screen on the dashboard: EGI FAIL.

EGI: embedded global positioning system/inertial navigation system. It is the internal computer that runs our navigation system. When it fails, the movable maps on the MFD screen are no longer accurate or reliable, meaning we are unable to get an immediate grid location to send to the ground guys or up to our higher headquarters. The movable maps are extremely helpful on combat missions, as they reduce both pilots' workload and help increase situational awareness. Without the EGI, we would have to rely on old-school paper maps (which we always have in the cockpit just in case this happens).

"We've got an EGI fail," I said.

"Roger. What are you going to do?"

"Let's reset the EGI DC circuit breaker and see if we can get it back online and pick up some satellites," I said, going through the steps of the emergency procedure. "Input our last known location so we can execute a manual EGI alignment."

The emergency procedure states that if the EGI doesn't reengage, we should pull the circuit breaker out and land as soon as practical. Losing the EGI isn't an immediate danger, since we can still fly using our standby flight instruments.

"Roger. I just reset it. It doesn't seem to be responding," Chris said, still role-playing.

Bong!

The alarm went off again and I saw SCAS FAIL on my MFD. When you lose the EGI, the SCAS—stability and control augmentation system—fails as well. The SCAS needs those gyros to provide stability and control to the flight controls. Without the SCAS the aircraft becomes increasingly hard to manage as the flight controls are less responsive.

"Just lost SCAS, too. Attempting to reengage," I said as I pushed the SCAS toggle switch up to turn it back on, even though I knew it wouldn't work while we had an EGI failure.

"Roger," Chris said. I saw his right arm move to the same position on the panel and push the circuit breaker back in. The EGI FAIL SCAS FAIL warning disappeared from the MFD.

"Oh, look at that, the EGI reset itself and we're back online," I said. We continued the mission.

Chris was never shy about telling me when I didn't meet his

standard for everything from my style of reconnaissance to the way I maneuvered the Kiowa to cover the lead aircraft. But I appreciated the constructive criticism. Thanks to his tough-love coaching and the experiences we'd faced in combat, I was geared up for the responsibilities that came with being a PC.

Once I made it, every decision in my aircraft would start and stop with me. I'd be calling the shots and I'd face all the consequences that went with that. Including pulling the trigger.

I was ready.

The final test that stood between me and PC was my check ride. Kyle Brown, a warrant officer in Alpha Troop, liked me about as much as Jake Sommers did. He'd never threatened to hit me, as Jake had, but his disdain for my presence in the troop had been obvious since day one. He was the top IP in our troop and had significant influence on whether I was recommended to take my PC ride. In his forties, he was the oldest guy in our troop and already a crusty senior warrant officer—set in his ways and cranky as hell. He usually ignored my existence except to make some snide remark about me. If he was having a bad day, we all were. Nothing helps a bad mood like spreading it around.

It was clear that Kyle did not want me as a PC. I had flown with him as a baby warrant officer when I got to the unit at Fort Campbell straight out of flight school and I'd been green, but he hadn't cared to keep up with my progress since then. Rumor had it that he had begun to get questioned as to why I hadn't been recommended for PC yet. I had flown multiple times with his boss, who believed I was ready and needed to take the check ride.

My normal flight team—Chris, Jason, Frank, and I—were sitting in the pilots' office, preparing for our flight. Kyle had been working in his IP area and gathered up his stuff and walked out of the office. Five seconds later, the door swung open and Kyle poked his head in.

"Amber, your PC ride is set for June tenth," he said, not looking at me but more shouting into the room at large.

"Okay, thanks," I said, not sure if I should believe him.

The door slammed.

Chris gave me a devious smile.

Then reality set in. I couldn't mess this up.

Kyle scheduled me for a preevaluation flight with him—a prep ride for the real check ride. He ran me through the gauntlet. He grilled me on every single emergency procedure, task, and limit. Spontaneous full authority digital electronics control (FADEC) failure, inadvertent instrument meteorological condition (IIMC) procedures, spouting off oral knowledge while flying the aircraft and conducting different flight tasks.

Everything he threw my way, I nailed. It was nerve-racking, but I was prepared. About halfway through the flight Kyle's tone changed. He finally saw with his own eyes that my skills had evolved and that I had transformed from the twenty-two-year-old kid straight out of flight school to a war-tested PC candidate. I even got a few "not bads" out of him.

When we landed and I began shutting down the aircraft, Kyle said, "If you fly like you did today, you'll be fine. Don't screw this up."

Coming from Kyle, it was as if I had just won a gold medal.

But his parting shot was serious: if I messed up even one emergency procedure, remembered one limitation incorrectly, or did not stay within a standard, I would fail the check ride. Everything was weighing on this check ride—my future as a pilot, my standing in the troop, and proving to my guys that I belonged there with them. I felt the pressure, but that's when I did my best.

The night before my PC ride, my mind was racing through every possible question I might be asked, every scenario I might get confronted with. My flight would be evaluated by the top squadron pilot,

CW4 Brian Stoner, the head IP of our entire squadron. I'd flown with Brian a few times, so I knew he was fair and professional and a great pilot. I learned something from him every time I went out with him. He would be as tough and thorough as Kyle, so the prep ride had been the perfect dress rehearsal.

The following morning, when I got into work at our pilots' office, Chris gave me my final pep talk. "Don't do anything different. Just fly like you always do with me. You'll be fine."

Chris affirmed—I could do this.

The check ride began. I conducted the mission and crew brief to our flight team. I organized our scheme of maneuver, downed aircraft procedures, weather and fuel considerations, enemy and friendly situations. I conducted all of our premission and preflight duties. When we were getting ready to take off, Brian walked around the aircraft, quizzing me on its parts and pieces—what they were, how they worked mechanically and aerodynamically, and what the emergency procedures were if a particular component failed.

"What is this tube?" Brian asked. "Where does it go? What happens if it fails? What indication will you get in the cockpit? What do you do?" Every question I answered led to another question. But I knew the answers.

Phase one was over. Now we began the combat mission—basically an evaluation of the mission we conduct daily. This was the most comfortable part of the test for me, because this is what I did every single day I flew. Brian acted as my copilot. I had been warned by other pilots that if our combat mission was slow and there wasn't much going on, Brian would likely give different mock "aircraft failures" in the cockpit to test my ability to react to different emergency procedures.

Toward the end of our mission time block, Brian said, "All right, let's head back." He'd already turned off several systems in the cockpit, usually while I was preoccupied with something else, to see how I would handle multiple system failures while on a combat mission.

"Roger."

"Annihilator One-One, it's Saber One-One," I radioed to Chris in the lead aircraft. "We're done back here. Ready to head back to base."

Silence.

I gave it a couple of seconds.

"One-One, it's One-One," I radioed again. "How do you hear me?"

Nothing.

"What the hell are they doing up there?" I said.

I looked over and saw Brian squinting, looking out the windshield. I looked straight ahead. I saw nothing out of the ordinary. Then I saw the faintest flicker of light on either side of the horizontal stabilizer, the fin that intersects the tail of the helicopter. Then I saw it again.

Are they . . .

"I think lead has lost comms," I said to Brian, realizing this was a precoordinated part of the test.

"Roger," Brian said.

I began the lost communication procedures with the lead aircraft. I had to fly the Kiowa up alongside the lead to get their attention visually.

As I began to get close, Brian said, "I've lost sight with the ground; we just punched into the clouds."

Another part of the test.

In Army aviation, it's known as inadvertent instrument meteorological conditions (IIMC), where you accidentally fly into bad weather and have zero visual reference to the ground. It's incredibly dangerous, and plenty of helicopter pilots have been killed because of weather conditions like this. The Kiowa is not an instrument-rated helicopter, meaning it doesn't have special instrument equipment in the cockpit that allows us to fly in the clouds. If we go IIMC, it's an emergency. We have a limited instrument procedure, our only option to get us safely out of the clouds. Kiowa pilots are not as proficient as other helicopter pilots who fly instrument-rated helicopters, just because we rarely ever practice it. But this procedure is a requirement for the check ride, so I knew what to do.

"Roger. We are IIMC, starting to climb to six thousand feet," I said into the radio, so the other aircraft flying with us could hear. They knew this meant their part of the mission was over, and they could return to base while I finished the rest of my check ride.

"Roger," Chris said, understanding that the "lost comms" role-playing was over.

As I leveled the angle of the helicopter, I began a gradual climb to get us to a safe altitude above any unseen obstacles, such as a tower, wires, or a mountain.

"Pull up our emergency instrument approach into Kirkuk airfield and read off our waypoints on the nav system," I said to Brian.

I continued to follow the approach into the airfield. When we got close, Brian said, "I have a visual on the ground."

"Roger." The instrument approach part of the check ride was complete. But the check ride wasn't.

I flew us back to the refuel pads and set the helicopter down for a welcome two-minute break while the armament soldiers unloaded our .50-cal machine gun ammo and rockets. Next we were going to do autorotations and other emergency procedures that do not allow live ammo on the aircraft.

An autorotation—or auto—is the emergency procedure to perform if we have an engine failure. It is the only option for a Kiowa because it is a single-engine aircraft—we don't have another engine to rely on if it fails. We also did run-on landings and simulated "stuck pedal" procedures, where the IP simulates one of the flight control foot pedals is stuck in its current position, making the helicopter fly almost sideways, depending how far the pedal is stuck. I had to compensate by controlling the power input with the collective, which helped lessen the severity of the stuck pedal, so you could land safely. Stuck pedal was not my favorite emergency procedure, since we rarely practiced it. But these were all forms of emergency procedures to get the helicopter back on the ground safely—and I completed them.

Afterward, we shut down the aircraft in parking and headed back to the pilots' office, where Brian gave me the mandatory oral exam. This was the part I was dreading most. I'd always been better at flying than memorizing information from books. Brian's quiz seemed to go on forever. And we still had to get back in the aircraft and finish the exam with night tasks and evaluations, which were essentially the same as the day check ride, but conducted under NVGs. To be a Kiowa PC in 2-17 CAV, you have to be approved for day, night, and NVG flight. Other units would sign pilots off as "day" PCs, but not 2-17 CAV. Our pilots were ready to go in all three, or in none at all.

Brian and I got back in the aircraft, and he put me through the night tasks. Then he said, "Let's head back to the house."

"Roger," I said, hoping he would give me some sign of how I'd done.

As I hovered back to the parking pad, Brian keyed the mic.

"What is your call sign going to be?" he asked.

That meant I had passed. I was now a PC. I smiled as I felt the payoff of years of training and hard work.

"Annihilator Two-Four," I said.

13

FLYING BLIND

July 2006
Kirkuk, Iraq

As we took off into the night sky, the smell of kerosene filled my nose. Through my NVGs, the oil refinery on the west side of the Kirkuk airfield looked like a smoldering green fire that lit up the sky. I had gotten used to the smell, but the stagnant summer heat seemed thick in the air, making it harder to breathe. The refinery was a significant piece of infrastructure in Kirkuk, which made it a target for the enemy. Their mission was to blow up or sabotage different parts of the refinery, and so on every mission we provided reconnaissance and security for it. We would fly low and slow to see if there were any signs of suspicious activity around the fence or the pipeline or random Iraqis who weren't supposed to be there. But it wasn't always the enemy who was trying to cause problems. Sometimes the locals were trying to steal the oil. Usually there was nothing significant to report; the Iraqis provided good enough security for the perimeter, since it was right on the outskirts of Kirkuk; we just provided an extra aerial eye for security purposes.

"This is going to be a long night," I said to my copilot, CW2 Frank Villanueva, who was sitting in the left seat in the cockpit. We were both new PCs and still had a lot to learn.

We were on the middle-of-the-night shift, which was not my favorite, but the trade-off was that we got some relief from the brutal sun. That said, trying to sleep during the day in the Iraqi summer heat was a challenge. The pseudo swamp cooler I had in my CHU was no match for the smoldering sun. The device either stopped working or started shooting out ice chunks, creating an awful racket and flooding my floor. I had many sleepless "nights," and required lots of caffeine to get through those middle-of-the-night flights. We usually briefed at about midnight, took off into the night sky for a few hours, and got to see the sunrise before our mission block was complete.

Frank had joined the Army at seventeen and deployed to Iraq with 2-17 CAV in 2003 during the invasion, so he'd gotten to enjoy the suck twice now. When we first met, he wasn't too impressed with having me in the same unit, let alone in the same cockpit. But as we flew together in Iraq, and after hours upon hours in a cockpit no wider than the width of your arms, on both monotonous flights and intense combat flights, we got to know each other. At this point in the deployment, our team was so in sync, we could finish each other's sentences.

"You've really changed my perception of women pilots in the Army," Frank said one day out of the blue as we were flying over the desert. "You can do it just like *we* can. You're actually a pretty badass pilot, and not a bad shot, either. You think ahead of the aircraft, are able to handle doing everything at once in the cockpit, and you have good judgment. I've been paying attention when we fly together."

Earning my guys' trust was huge for me. But I couldn't show how much it meant. Thankfully, he couldn't see my facial expression, since we were sitting side by side in the cockpit. Minimal emotion had gotten me this far, and I wasn't about to change that.

"You're not too bad yourself, Four," I said. Since my call sign was Annihilator 24 and Frank's was 14, we had started calling each other by our shared digit.

Tonight we were headed toward Tal Afar, a city that sits along the main highway between Syria and Iraq's second-largest city, Mosul. Tal Afar is more than two hundred miles north of Iraq's capital city, Baghdad, and had been largely taken over by al-Qaeda as a training ground for insurgents. The terrorists often indiscriminately fired mortar and rocket rounds into the city to cause havoc and spread fear among civilians. It was well out of our normal area of operation, in the northwestern sector of Iraq, and a place I had never been before. Our mission was to link up with a ground convoy and provide it with aerial security as it traveled along an infamous route that was often littered with IEDs. But first we were headed to FOB Al-Qayyarah West—or Q-West, as the American soldiers called it—an airfield on the south side of Mosul, about halfway to Tal Afar, to refuel before we linked up with the convoy.

We had just enough gas to get there. Given my previous experience nearly flaming out, I was not about to make the same mistake twice.

As we continued to fly northwest, with the glare of the refinery behind us, I noticed a haze under my goggles, a mist forming in the night sky. Our weather brief had forecast a light fog expected to break after sunrise, nothing too out of the ordinary. We still had at least an hour before dawn.

Under NVGs, there is always a stark contrast between the night sky and the ground. My goggles were getting noisy—thousands of little sparkles dancing in my imagery—and the sky looked grainy in the poor light conditions. That meant the weather was deteriorating.

During the first part of my deployment, I had hated flying under NVGs because they limited my vision and messed up my depth perception, screwing with my rate of descent when landing. It was like trying to fly a helicopter with horse blinders on. I had to be that much more alert and work that much harder to fly the aircraft. But after months of night shifts, I was more comfortable flying with horse blinders, and by the time I made PC, flying at night felt like second nature.

Leading the way, we were cruising at about three hundred feet at eighty knots (ninety-two miles per hour), with Chris flying closely behind us. Now that I was a PC, I had shifted from flying with Chris in the same aircraft to being his flight lead. But even though I was leading the team, Chris was always testing me. It was in his nature—he was an IP.

In January 2004, only a year and a half prior, one of our own 2-17 CAV pilots had encountered some bad weather flying south of Mosul, and he and his copilot were killed when their Kiowa crashed as they were returning to base. I pushed that thought to the back of my mind.

"How about that weather brief?" I said over the radio to Chris.

The haze was growing thicker by the mile.

"Yeah, this isn't looking so good," Chris said. "What do you think?"

I looked at our fuel gauge. We were nearing our halfway point, so I had to decide whether we would continue. We had to factor in the deteriorating weather conditions and our limited flexibility on fuel. If we flew past our halfway mark, then we wouldn't have enough gas to turn around and make it back to Kirkuk. The only thing worse than punching into the clouds is punching into the clouds with low fuel. Options get limited quickly. If the weather worsened and we couldn't continue toward Q-West, and we didn't have enough gas to fly back to Kirkuk, we had two options: land in enemy territory or crash when the aircraft ran out of gas. I'd take my chances on the ground with the enemy over a crash. But being on the ground behind enemy lines was definitely at the top of my "I hope I never have to do" list. The entire focus of SERE school had been learning to resist capture and evade the enemy. I hoped that I would never have to use those skills in the real world.

Luckily for us, FOB McHenry, a tiny infantry base just south of Hawija, was about halfway between our location over the Tigris River and our home base in Kirkuk. Hawija was a known hot spot for enemy activity, and the roads leading into and out of the city were always littered with IEDs and complex, coordinated attacks. If we had to turn around and set our Kiowas down, hopefully we could get to McHenry so we'd be among friendly forces. But we had no way of knowing if they were socked in as well.

I continued to hope that we'd get a break through the increasingly dense fog and link up with the convoy we were supposed to escort. The window to turn around was rapidly closing.

Out the right side of my doorless cockpit and on the ground below us, vegetation surrounded the recently churned farm fields and created a nice contrast through my NVGs. Objects were clearer and more defined; they also had a halo around them. We were losing visibility rapidly.

"I think it's getting worse. I'm going to slow back a bit and keep an eye on it," I said to Chris over the radio.

"Are you good?" I asked Frank. "What do you think?"

"If you're good, I'm good. I trust you," Frank said.

"Okay, I'm going to tighten up a bit behind you," Chris said over the radio. "I don't want to lose a visual on you."

If two helicopters go into the clouds at the same time, it increases the chance of a midair collision.

I didn't want to lose those ground guys in the convoy and leave them alone out there in enemy territory.

As we crossed the Tigris River, the terrain straight ahead was mostly desert, reaching to a distant mountain ridge. There was no longer the contrast of the farm fields, and it was that much harder to tell the difference between the ground and the sky.

Suddenly we were flying blind in a sea of lime green. For that mere second, I could not see the ground, other aircraft, or wires that could bring us down. The hairs rose on the back of my neck.

"Coming around right!" I said to Chris over the radio. "We lost all contrast with the ground for a second. We need to get out of this now."

It happened so quickly. One second we could see the ground, the next we couldn't.

"Roger, I've still got you and am with you," Chris said.

I pulled a tight 180-degree right turn and headed back in the direction we had just come from. Usually making that tight a turn in bad weather conditions would be frowned upon, since you can quickly become spatially disoriented, but I could not have cared less about official procedure at that point. I cared about not being 100 percent submerged in the increasingly dense fog or flying into the side of a mountain, the ground, or having a midair.

"Watch your altitude," Chris said.

Frank had been watching our radar altimeter and called out any significant altitude deviations, while I was focused on flying. In poor weather conditions, it is critical to maintain a constant scan across your instruments in the cockpit and back to the outside. It reminded me of when I flew my environmentals with Chris in Kuwait ten months earlier, when he had demonstrated just how easy it was to become spatially disoriented and why it is so critical to rely on your radar altimeter. You can't always trust your eyes—they can play tricks on you, especially under NVGs—but you must always trust your instruments.

"Three hundred feet," Frank said, reading out the altitude.

Three hundred feet was good for now. It kept us high enough that we wouldn't fly into any wires or towers that we couldn't see, but low enough that we were able to keep a visual with the ground. We needed that option in case we needed to land right away.

Other than Frank's altitude readings, the cockpit was quiet. We were too nervous to talk. I was thankful that Frank and I had a positive crew coordination. It minimized any chance of one of us becoming disoriented. We were both doing our best to get us out of there alive.

"Are you guys still back there?" I asked Chris. I didn't like the silence and wanted to make sure we hadn't lost them.

"Yep, right behind you," Chris said.

The contrast with the ground and other obstacles began to increase. And then, just like that, the sun popped up on the horizon.

Daybreak. The sun had saved us. My muscles relaxed a bit as we flew out of the fog.

"It's never been so nice to see the sun or the Iraqi ground," I said over internal as I flipped up my NVGs. I wanted to kiss the ground, but flying in the safety of the sunlight was enough for me.

Chris laughed into the mic. "You guys good up there?" he said.

"We are now," Frank said.

I banked the helicopter to the left to take a look back at where we had just come from. I saw a solid white wall of impermeable fog from the ground to the top of the endless sky. It appeared to be an ominous blanket of death that had been thrown over the Tigris River that early morning—just waiting to devour its next victim. Today that wasn't going to be us.

14

ONE LAST MISSION

July–August 2006

Kirkuk AO, Iraq

We had mere weeks left before the deployment was over and we could head home. We still had plenty of missions to complete between now and then. I was on days for the remainder of my time in Iraq, so the heat would be my constant companion. Every morning I headed to Green Beans Coffee with Chris and Frank—it was the Iraq version of Starbucks, or at least we pretended it was. They used shelf-life milk that didn't need refrigeration, but we got used to it and learned to like it. (I still crave Green Beans vanilla chai latte.) Once we got our caffeine fix, we headed to our mission brief at headquarters.

That morning, the TOC was already buzzing about our mission, which was to be an enormous multifaceted air assault with a combination of Iraqi army soldiers and U.S. forces. Soldiers would be flown in on Black Hawks and Chinook helicopters and inserted into the town of Hawija and neighboring Riyadh in search of al-Qaeda terrorists who had holed up there. Both cities would be cordoned off, no one in or out. Our troops would then go door to door in search of terrorists. We'd provided air cover for the ground guys on many of these types of missions, but never before on this scale.

Once we'd gotten our mission tasks and gone over our scheme of maneuver, our team headed out to the aircraft, conducted preflight, and was ready to go. I climbed into the cockpit and started the helicopter.

"Annihilator Two-Four, this is One-One. How do you hear me?" Chris asked over the radio.

"Lickin' chicken," I said, which meant "loud and clear."

"Roger, have you the same. Let's take off a little early," Chris said over the radio. "I want to head out to test fire and make sure both of our guns are working. If one of them jams or is broken, I want to have time to come back here and switch aircraft."

"Sounds good to me. Ready when you are," I said. "Kirkuk tower, Annihilator Two-Four, flight of two, requesting direct departure to the west," I radioed to the tower.

"You are cleared for takeoff, Annihilator," the tower said.

"Coming up," I radioed to Chris. "Headed to test fire."

The words "test fire" reminded me of a troubling moment from a recent flight with Chris. He had listed me as flying in the right seat, which meant I'd be the one shooting that day. Our squadron commander— the top officer in the unit—had been flying in our team. Prior to the flight, he had told Chris that if I didn't hit the target during test fire I was not allowed to fly as his lead. In that case, we would have to land and Chris and I would have to swap seats so Chris could fly and shoot instead of me.

"You're kidding, right?" I had asked Chris when he told me what the squadron commander had said.

"No, he's serious," Chris said. "Just do a really nice bump and hit the target."

"Chris, I know how to shoot. Thanks." It wasn't Chris's fault, but I was pissed and he was going to hear it. "I've been flying for a few years now, and almost a year of that in combat. I thought I'd be able to put this stupid stereotype shit behind me when I made PC. And real professional of him to set the bar at a new low for how every other pilot should treat the women in this unit."

"I know, it's fucked up," Chris said. "Just use that anger and hit the target, and it'll be a nonissue. Prove him wrong."

Not only did I hit the target that day, I destroyed it. Our squadron commander didn't say a word, and I flew lead for the rest of the mission.

But there was no point lingering on that memory now. I had to get my head into the mission at hand.

The test fire of our .50-cal machine guns went fine, so I turned the helicopter left toward Hawija.

"I'm going to fly on the perimeter of the north side of the city and turn south and fly in a zigzag pattern," I told Chris as we got close.

We would do a quick sweep of the city like we always did, a standard recon. We had divided the city into sectors for airspace control and deconfliction of the different aircraft teams. Our team was covering the west side of Hawija, and our job was to hold the cordon until the ground units were in place. A Kiowa team conducted a recon of Hawija nearly every day, so that's exactly what we wanted the people in the town to think we were doing. We had to make sure we still had the element of surprise for the air assault insert.

"Three minutes," Chris said.

"Roger, moving to the landing zone," I said.

Chris's "three minutes" referred to when we would call the inbound Black Hawks and Chinooks that were transporting all of the soldiers and make the CHERRY/ICE call. CHERRY and ICE were our code words for whether or not it was clear for the helicopters to land in the designated LZ, or helicopter landing zone—ICE for safe and clear,

CHERRY for any sign of the enemy or if it was otherwise not safe for a landing.

I flew near the first LZ, but not over it so we didn't give away its location to the enemy; the same with the second LZ. The LZs were just sandy fields filled with tumbleweeds. I cringed at the thought of how many camel spiders were hiding in that brush. So far it appeared we had been successful at faking out the enemy.

"Looks clear to me," I said to Chris. "I am calling it ICE."

"Roger, I concur," Chris said. "Thirty seconds to call."

It was hot as hell—I had already finished an entire liter of water, but I banked the aircraft right, allowing a refreshing breeze to come through the open cockpit door.

"Lightning Six, this is Annihilator Two-Four, ICE," I said to the commander in the aircraft en route to the LZ.

"Roger, Annihilator Two-Four, ICE."

"All right, let's head their way so we can be in a security overwatch position when they land," Chris said.

I turned the Kiowa to the south. In the distance, I could see a bunch of little black specks on the horizon—the helicopters we were due to link up with. I pulled in the collective to give us some power to increase our airspeed until we found ourselves playing chicken with a bunch of Black Hawks and Chinooks, flying right toward each other.

The sight was unreal—like a scene from *Apocalypse Now*. The sky was filled with helicopters—a glorious sight. *That's what freedom looks like, right there.*

The plan was to fly right under their formation until they passed us, then we would bump the Kiowas up and do a 180-degree turn so we were all flying in the same direction. That way we would be a little above their altitude and in a perfect profile to shoot at any enemy as the Black Hawks and Chinooks approached and landed. We'd do the same for their departure.

Their helicopters were right off my nose. It was still eerie to be flying head-to-head with a row of Black Hawks and Chinooks.

"Here we go," I said to Chris.

I lowered the collective and pointed the nose down to reduce our altitude to ensure that we were adequately separated from the other helicopters. As they roared past us, I could feel the vibrations of their rotors in my body armor and helmet. Passing behind them and turning around, we hit the rough air their massive rotor blades created, and turbulence rocked our little Kiowas. The cyclic moved all over the place, so I tightened my grip to maintain control of the aircraft. It lasted a few seconds, then we were out of it.

The LZs were still quiet. No personnel moving about. Nothing on the LZ that would obscure the landing. It looked like it was going to be the perfect infill. One by one the helicopters touched down, and the soldiers jumped out and took off running toward the birch trees that lined the east side of the LZ. Once the soldiers found cover, they would link up before moving in on the city. Each helicopter was on the ground for less than a minute before it took off and headed south, away from the city.

By this point, everyone in Hawija knew we were there. The people in the city were running from house to house like cockroaches fleeing after a light was turned on. Clearly, word spread quickly throughout the city that a military operation was under way. People gathered at the perimeter of the cordon to flee the city.

Out my door, a group of women in black burkas gathered near a bridge that led out of the city. No one was allowed to cross that bridge. We had no way of knowing whether the group hid some high-value terrorist targets dressed up in burkas. It wouldn't be the first time.

There were no U.S. or Iraqi forces in that part of the city yet, so our mission was to prevent any squirters—people fleeing a cordon—from succeeding in their escape attempts. Iraqi soldiers were using bullhorns and loudspeakers, telling the people of Hawija to stay put. No one was allowed to leave until the operation was over. But this group of women was testing our resolve.

I was flying an inner loop fifty to a hundred feet above the ground. Chris was flying a little higher and wider, so he could cover me if someone started shooting at us. We were easy targets flying that low and slow.

Frank unholstered his M4 rifle from the dash and stuck it out the window. I looked out my side of the helicopter and started to make a 180-degree turn in the opposite direction.

Dat! Dat! Dat! Dat! Dat!

Suddenly, metal was flying through the cockpit and hit the windshield.

I banked the aircraft hard right—the rotor blades making a popping noise from slapping the air so hard in the turn—and started flying erratically to avoid getting shot.

Then I realized what had just happened—those things flying through the cockpit were brass casings from Frank's M4.

"Frank! You jerk! I thought we were getting shot at," I shouted over our internal.

Frank laughed. "Sorry, I thought you knew I was firing, since I took it off the dash."

"I thought you would at least give me a warning before you pulled the trigger! I was looking out my right door when you started firing, which completely screwed me up for a second."

"At least you did some good evasive maneuvers," Frank said, still laughing at me. "I was letting them know that they weren't going to get past us."

After that, the people gathered at the bridge stopped trying to cross.

The operation was successful and surprisingly uneventful. There was little enemy resistance. The ground guys detained a bunch of terrorists, found multiple caches and an IED factory, which they blew up in a controlled detonation. And no one slipped through the cordon. Mission accomplished.

———

A few weeks later, I found myself on my last mission in Iraq. If I made it through this flight, I would have survived the hardest year of my life.

That day's mission out in the AO was route and oil pipeline recon and then picking up convoy security for the infantry platoon that was attached to our unit, call sign Cold Steele. Our job was to escort them back to our base, FOB Warrior in Kirkuk.

This was about as simple and straightforward a mission as it got. But as we finished up the first portion of the mission and flew toward Cold Steele's location, a deep sense of anxiety washed over me as we picked up their convoy.

Last flight. Please don't let them hit an IED.

I could see the dust trail of the Cold Steele convoy up ahead in the distance. We were out in the middle of nowhere, scouting a flat, open asphalt road with plenty of visibility down the route. Previous IED holes littered the road. Those holes were often the hiding places of new IEDs, just waiting for a convoy to drive over them. But those holes also attracted lots of trash and debris, making it hard to tell from the air whether it was harmless trash or camouflage to conceal an IED.

We had to get these guys home safely. They wanted to go home as badly as we did.

We whizzed past the convoy, looking for anything suspicious, including possible triggermen for IEDs—they were usually somewhere in the vicinity of the road with a cell phone or walkie-talkie.

"Cold Steele, we've got a red sedan two hundred meters to the front of your lead vehicle just off the left side of the road in the field. Two military-age males inside. Approach with caution," I said over the radio.

"Roger, Annihilator. Contact," Cold Steele said.

The convoy continued on, slowing as they approached the red sedan.

Boom!

Smoke filled the air as the convoy rolled to a stop.

NO! Let our guys be okay. Let them be okay.

"Cold Steele, are you guys all right?"

"Annihilator, stand by!" Cold Steele said.

I picked up an inner flight pattern and zeroed in on the red sedan.

"Annihilator, we're all accounted for and okay," Cold Steele said.

The soldiers poured out of their Humvees, machine guns cocked, pointed at the sedan. The Iraqi interpreters embedded with Cold Steele sprang from the convoy, ran to the red sedan, and began beating the crap out of the men inside it who had detonated the bomb remotely. Then they threw the two guys on the ground and zip-tied their hands behind their backs and searched the car. They found all sorts of IED paraphernalia in the truck.

Score. These guys had been caught red-handed.

That was close.

While it wasn't the IED-free mission I'd hoped for, since no one got hurt, I was happy. Two more bad guys detained and out of the fight. They wouldn't be placing any more IEDs anytime soon.

On the way back to refuel at Kirkuk, I saw the most incredible sight: a group of about eight Kiowas were flying in formation on short final to the runway. It was 2-6 CAV—our replacement unit out of Hawaii.

The Iraq war was just beginning for 2-6, but we had done our time. The war was over for us. We were going home.

15

SCREAMING EAGLES

Fall 2006

Fort Campbell, Kentucky

Being home in the United States was everything I thought it would be—at first. Everything just seemed a little clearer, a little cleaner, a little brighter. My future. My outlook. My attitude. I enjoyed the small things: going to the grocery store; making fresh salads; going out to dinner; indoor plumbing; a shower whose drain didn't clog. I roamed the aisles of Target enchanted by the options.

But I had fundamentally changed. In a few months, I'd be turning twenty-five. The twenty-three-year old who had set out on her first deployment was gone. I had been young, naïve, eager, and somehow survived the war. My outlook on life had changed completely.

Even things back at the pilots' office at Fort Campbell were different. Before, I was at the very bottom of the totem pole; now I was a PC who had seen combat in Iraq. An influx of new baby warrant officers, pilots fresh out of flight school, all looked at us with big round Bambi eyes filled with wonder and envy.

Our unit, 2-17 CAV, had been a tough place to learn the job, and the troop's acceptance of me hadn't come easily. But it was a rite of passage that I now respected that much more. I'd earned it.

I'd learned to never ever let a mistake go to waste. I learned how to stand up for myself, because if I didn't, no one else would. I learned that no matter what, I could not make everyone happy. I learned to trust my instincts. My confidence grew from having the confidence of others who had trained me—Chris, Brian, Ed, and Mike. I'd made tough, split-second decisions as a PC in Iraq.

More than once I thought I would break. But I kept going. Every time I felt sorry for myself and wished things were easier, I told myself I had two choices: I could quit and prove everyone who'd thought that I couldn't handle it was right; or I could say, "Screw you all." I chose option number two every single time.

———

One day, I was sitting in our pilots' office at Campbell Army Airfield, working on one of our computers. Three of my guys were behind me, shooting the shit. One of them, James, was a CW3—he was new to our unit, but a senior pilot. The conversation turned to women, specifically "banging chicks." Throughout my time at 2-17, I had developed the unique ability to tune out the noise, sometimes even while appearing as if I were listening attentively. But James didn't know me.

"Hey, you guys can't talk like that," James said, a sound of concern in his voice.

Luke, another pilot in the conversation, shrugged him off. "Why?"

"You just can't talk like that in front of Amber," James said. "She's a girl."

No shit, Sherlock. Why are you dragging me into this? I am just sitting here working, minding my own business.

Luke laughed. "You don't need to worry about her. She's cool."

I smiled as I continued working on the computer. I was one of them now. And damn, it felt good to finally be there.

———

After a few weeks, the carefree illusion of life at home was shattered. One day at 6:40 a.m., about ten of us from Alpha Troop had gathered for PT outside the CAV gymnasium.

"Where is everyone?" someone said.

"They are already ten minutes late. Another five and I say we're outta here," someone else said.

Finally we saw one of our Alpha Troop platoon sergeants pull up.

It's about time, I thought.

Sergeant First Class (SFC) Muller walked up to our group in full uniform instead of his PT uniform. He gathered us together; he looked serious.

"Mr. Arrowood was killed last night," Muller said.

We were stunned into silence. I had heard the words, but I'd hadn't *really* heard what he had said.

"He was—"

"WHAT DID YOU SAY? Why did you say Jason Arrowood?" I blurted out.

"Yes, ma'am, he was killed last night in a motorcycle accident," SFC Muller said.

"No, he wasn't. I talked to him yesterday to find out where we were meeting for PT this morning," I said. "I just talked to him."

Jason was married and had two small kids. We had arrived at our unit within weeks of each other, been WOJGs together, and had flown combat missions together. We had constantly flown together in the same flight team with Frank and Chris. We had been back from Iraq for barely a month. How had he survived the entire year in Iraq only to be killed in a motorcycle accident?

Jason's death rocked our tightly knit troop. A week later we attended his funeral in Florida. After that, there was a strange absence back at the office that none of us could really get used to. Jason was the funny, lighthearted guy, the one who made everyone laugh. Now the office seemed so serious, so quiet.

I didn't take Jason's death very well. I'd made it through twenty-four years of my life and a war, and still hadn't known anyone personally who had been killed. One second you're here, the next you're not. It was too hard to believe.

The transition to working at home was tough. Our op-tempo didn't slow down. I had expected a honeymoon phase after coming home from Iraq, some downtime, but rumors were flying that our next deployment would be sooner than later. Things were rapidly changing. We were running from one training exercise to the next aerial gunnery, to JRTC—mock deployments—in Louisiana.

Then it was official: 2-17 CAV was back on the patch chart (the Army's deployment schedule). We heard different stories: One day we were leaving in the fall of 2007, the next early 2008; we were deploying for twelve months, then we were deploying for fifteen months; Alpha Troop was going to Jalalabad, or was it Salerno? Our operations officer told us that Afghanistan was now where the fight was. Terrorist activity was on the rise, and our Kiowas would be extremely effective in that theater of operation.

I was an Afghan novice. All of us in 2-17 CAV were. I didn't even know anyone who'd been there. Our unit was so Iraq-focused that we never really thought about Afghanistan. Suddenly Iraq no longer mattered. We were headed to a new theater of war and we needed to be prepared.

My dream of having a nine-to-five job for a while went out the window, and our pre-deployment training began in full force.

We began by studying the different provinces and cities in the area of operation. The terrain in Afghanistan was different from Iraq's deserts and its extreme temperatures. In Afghanistan, we'd be flying in mountainous terrain at higher altitudes than we were used to. Aircraft performance is reduced at higher altitudes, which puts a higher workload on the pilot. While a year seemed like a significant amount of time to train and prepare, in reality it wasn't long enough.

I began flying with some of the new guys who had just arrived to our unit straight out of flight school. It made me appreciate how much I learned flying with other PCs and copilots in Iraq. But I liked flying with the new guys. I had received fantastic instruction when I was new, so I wanted to pay it forward. Flying with the baby pilots put me in a position to learn a lot, too—having to explain all the different steps and techniques helped me continue to grow as a pilot.

We even got a new female pilot right out of flight school. CW2 Deidra Adams was a former Marine who had switched branches of service to fly. A blonde from Florida with a big personality, she drove a crotch-rocket motorcycle, had an affinity for tattoos, and was the master of the selfie before anyone else. She had multiple deployments under her belt, but our trip to Afghanistan would be her first as a pilot.

Deidra was now one of three female pilots in Alpha Troop. Katie was still in our troop and had just passed her PC ride. Lori had transferred up to 2-17's headquarters unit when she returned from Iraq so her gunshot wound could heal and was in the process of retiring from the Army after twenty years of service.

Our duties at home base often seemed harder than being at war. We were always busy: Army schools, gunneries, mandatory training, casualty assistance officer or casualty notification officer, courtesy patrol, and safety days. We were tasked with being the investigation officer as well as trash detail, guard duty, range control, cleaning detail, kitchen patrol, and staff duty—where we had to work for twenty-four hours at the reception desk at headquarters. And if for some reason you ever found yourself with extra time, you were instantly put on a detail.

One pilot told me, "I just want to hurry up and deploy so things will slow down."

It's a bad sign when people would rather deploy over the chaos of being in training mode. Training is one thing—working so hard that all you want to do is go back to war so the op-tempo will slow down is another. When our unit was on this back-to-back deployment schedule we never got a break. When you get about fifteen months home in the States between wars, but are training nonstop for war, you also never get a break.

On top of everything else, we had to put our Kiowas through reset—maintenance overhauls between deployments. It was like giving them a tune-up. We had to fly the Kiowas to Fort Bragg, North Carolina, for reset, and then once the overhaul was finished, we had to pick them up and fly them back to Fort Campbell.

In April 2007, it was my turn to make the trip. Next stop, Fort Bragg.

16

THE CRASH

Friday, April 13, 2007
Fort Bragg, North Carolina

Beeeeep. Beep. Beeeeep.

It was 4:45 a.m. I rolled over and turned off my cell phone alarm. My eyelids felt like sandpaper. It seemed like I had just closed them. We were staying in a seedy motel on Bragg Boulevard, just outside the base. The area was littered with strip clubs and fast-food joints. I was convinced they rented the rooms in this place by the hour.

We had flown in yesterday from Fort Campbell, ferrying four Kiowas that were scheduled to have maintenance overhauls after our deployment in Iraq. It had been a long eight-hour flight. It shouldn't have taken that long, but the wind had slowed us down and the turbulence was terrible. My arms were exhausted from wrestling the wind by keeping my death grip on the flight controls. I was flying with Charlie Troop, didn't know any of the other six pilots well, and hadn't flown with them before. At least my copilot, Caleb Warns, was from Alpha Troop.

Today we would be picking up four different Kiowas that had just completed their maintenance overhauls and flying them back to Fort Campbell.

I was ready to get back to my base. Cross-country flights with your unit were usually pretty fun, but being the add-on to another troop left me odd man out.

We went to the flight line, cranked up the aircraft, and were on our way to our first fuel stop in Lancaster, South Carolina, a little town just south of the North Carolina border. It was a beautiful day.

"I'm coming in tight off your left rear, about one rotor disk. I want to practice some close formation flight," Matt Murphy said to me over our internal radio. Matt was in Charlie Troop.

I was the third aircraft in our flight formation, and Matt was behind me in the trail aircraft as the flight's AMC.

Ugh. Get off my ass.

I was not a fan of tight formation flight. I'd seen the video in flight school one too many times of two helicopters that got too close to each other in the air. Their blades hit and the helicopters fell out of the sky into a fireball.

Matt wanted to practice formation flight, because he was moving to 160th Special Operations Aviation Regiment, a premier specialized unit that often flies in those tight formations. But as Kiowa pilots, we never flew like that. It would be dangerous for us to do so in mission profile in combat.

"Will you check him and make sure he's not too close?" I said to Caleb, who turned to see the situation behind us.

Fortunately, we were about ten minutes out from Lancaster, so Matt's tight formation flight didn't last more than a minute or two.

As we made our approach to the runway and hovered toward the fuel parking, I noticed that the parking area looked abnormally small. Usually, we would park in designated spots for our helicopter, shut down the aircraft, and a fuel truck would stop at each Kiowa and fill it up. This airport was different. There was no fuel truck, just a hose fixed to an underground tank.

The first two aircraft continued forward toward the fuel hose. I sat my aircraft down and waited for the first two Kiowas to land. I radioed Matt. "Let's just wait for them to gas up and then once they are out of there, we'll go in behind them and get gas?"

"No, there's room, just go in and park behind them," Matt said.

"Roger," I said, and began to hover behind the other two helicopters that were already on the ground.

I turned the helicopter so we were situated directly behind the first aircraft. We would be parked in a perfect square with all four aircraft facing east. To my right was a little shed and a huge hangar that was way too close for comfort.

"Holy shit," I said under my breath as I put the helicopter down on the ground. We were squeezed into this spot, but at least our skids were safely on the ground.

I saw Matt's aircraft hovering next to mine as I pulled my checklist book off the dashboard to begin my shutdown sequence.

"Um, they are REALLY CLOSE!" Caleb said as he glanced nervously out the left door at Matt's aircraft.

We're all too close. This was a bad idea. I shouldn't have listened to Matt. I should have just waited for the first two aircraft to refuel.

The skids of Matt's aircraft touched the tarmac.

Boom!

The explosion of rotor blades colliding, shattering on impact, was deafening. The sound was sickening. The cyclic between my knees starting slamming back and forth, left and right, hitting my thighs. The terrifying sound of shearing metal filled my ears as the transmissions and engines of both Kiowas were ripped apart. The cockpit convulsed, and the whole helicopter began rocking violently back and forth so strongly I thought we were going to tip over.

Boom! Boom!

"I'm hit," I said over the flight frequency so all of the pilots could hear.

"I know," Matt said. "Amber, I'm sorry."

The metal-on-metal screech continued. Matt had sat his helicopter down on the ground with his rotor blades barely overlapping mine. It was snowing white pieces of fiberglass from the shattered rotor blades.

I closed the throttle, cutting off all fuel to the engine, and turned off the battery to stop the flow of electricity, all steps of an emergency shutdown.

I looked over at Caleb and saw him rummaging around the door. Ferrying aircraft for maintenance overhauls was one of the few times that we flew with doors on, and at that very moment, I was very thankful to have them. They were protecting us from the flying projectiles outside of the cockpit.

"DO NOT OPEN THE DOOR!" I yelled to Caleb.

"I'M NOT!" he yelled back.

The doors were the only things protecting us at the moment, and while I was worried about the aircraft possibly catching on fire, right then the pieces of the helicopter blades flying a zillion miles per hour were more of a concern.

Finally, the blades slowed and the metallic grinding sound came to a stop, but my heart was still beating hard and fast.

"You okay?" I said to Caleb.

"Yeah. You?"

I felt strangely optimistic, even though I'd just been hit by another helicopter.

We're all okay. That's what matters. Shit happens. It's going to be okay. Matt hit me while I was on the ground shutting down. I was already parked.

I was thankful to be alive, but I couldn't help thinking what if Matt had hit me in the air as he was practicing that one-rotor disk formation flight?

The next day, all eight of the pilots involved in the crash huddled in one of our hotel rooms.

"Look, we all need to fill out sworn statements describing what happened," Tom, one of the pilots from Charlie Troop, said. "We all have the right to talk to JAG [judge advocate general] and get a lawyer."

A lawyer sounded good to me. I'd been in the Army long enough to know at this point that I needed to look out for myself.

"I think I want a lawyer," I said to the group. Seven pairs of eyes turned in unison and looked at me as if I were crazy.

"Amber, if you get a lawyer, it'll only make you look guilty," Tom said to me.

"How on earth could I look guilty? I was on the ground when my helicopter got hit. I'm not the one who caused this!"

"I know, but just trust me, don't do it. You don't want to be making any waves right now," Tom said.

Everyone else agreed with him.

Two days later I was in a little office at the same Lancaster airport, sitting across the table from four senior officers who were all glaring at me. By then the euphoria of surviving the helicopter accident had worn off. I'd had little sleep since the accident. We were all pulling "guard duty" shifts throughout the night at the airport to make sure no one messed with the aircraft, since it was an active civilian airport. Our Kiowas were still outside on the refuel tarmac where the accident occurred, cordoned off with yellow accident scene tape.

I stared back at the four officers on the other side of the long conference table from me in a backroom office at the airport. The room was silent. And cold. I had my big tan cold-weather flight jacket on over my uniform. The fluorescent light made me squint. I was exhausted.

I was not looking forward to this interview, but all involved had to be interviewed as standard procedure for the safety board. I wasn't nervous. I was just ready to go home. Its findings could not be punitive in any way, so at least I had that going for me.

"Ms. Amber Smith. Thanks for joining us. Can we get you anything? Water?" one of them asked.

"I'm good, thanks," I said.

"We're going to each ask you some questions about the accident. Just answer to the best of your ability. This isn't a test, we're just trying to put the pieces together."

"Okay," I said.

"Will you describe to me how you conducted preflight the morning of the accident?"

"I did it the same way I always do. But we did preflight the night before. I inspected the right side of the aircraft, since I was flying in the right seat, and my copilot did the left side. I went through the logbook with the maintenance guy, since it was just coming out of reset and it needed a thorough review," I said.

"Did you use your checklist?"

"Yes," I said.

"Did you do a crew brief?"

"Yes. Caleb and I flew this mission together the day prior, so we did an abbreviated crew brief," I said.

He raised his eyebrow and wrote something down on his notepad while the rest stared at me silently.

"Who in your flight crew conducted the mission brief?"

"Casey did," I said. "Like I said, we had all flown this mission yesterday, so it was an update brief."

"You were flying a cross-country flight mission and you thought it was okay do an update mission brief?"

"I didn't abbreviate it. I wasn't the AMC doing the brief. I was chalk three. But I got all of the information that I needed," I said.

"But you thought it was okay?"

"I guess," I said.

I felt my heart rate speed up. What was going on here? This wasn't just a couple of questions to figure out what happened. Every single question was accusatory. They took turns berating me. Question after question, accusation after accusation.

"What did you do the night before?"

"I went to bed. I had a four forty-five a.m. or so wake-up after an eight-hour flight," I said.

"You don't know what time you woke up?"

"What? Yes. Four forty-five a.m.," I said.

"When did you land at Fort Bragg?"

"Around six fifty-five p.m. I think," I said.

"What was the temperature when you took off?"

"I think it was . . ."

I drew a blank. I think it was fifty-nine degrees at takeoff. Or maybe it was sixty-three degrees.

"Sixty-three degrees, I think?" I said. "Wait, that might be what it was on our flight the day prior."

They continued to write on their notepads after I spoke.

"What were the winds coming in to land at Lancaster?"

"I think they were about ten to fifteen knots out of the west, so we did a straight-on approach," I said.

"You think?"

My heart was racing. I'd never been in a situation quite like this. And I kept drawing blanks. If only I could go grab my kneeboard with all of my flight notes on it, I could tell them. But they already had my kneeboard—a notepad I kept strapped to my thigh during flights. They knew all of the answers. They were just quizzing me. I was all alone in the room, I had no representation. It was them against me.

"Why did you land so close to the shed?"

"I needed to. All four aircraft landed super close to each other. I was confident in my ability to safely land the aircraft. And I did. Matt was the one who didn't. He hit me," I said.

"So you don't think that you landed too close?"

"I know I did. Would I do it again? Absolutely not. But I didn't hit anything or anyone. I safely landed the helicopter on the ground and was shutting it down when I got hit by another helicopter," I said.

"What if you hit it?"

"I didn't hit it," I said.

I was growing increasingly frustrated. Why were they coming after me? I was shocked at the way they were treating me. It was as if they didn't realize who caused the accident. You can't drive into a parked car and blame the parked car. It's common sense. If you parallel park a car and park a little too close to the car behind you, it doesn't matter unless you hit it. Some people might even call that skill. It was irrelevant to the accident.

"What did you do when your aircraft got hit?"

Well, at least they recognized that it was my aircraft that got hit.

"I completed an emergency shutdown and then stayed in the aircraft until the blades stopped turning and it was safe to get out of the helicopter," I said.

After being berated for more than an hour, I walked out of the interview. I was pissed. These guys weren't being objective. They had it out for me. Even so, I kept telling myself I had nothing to worry about since this was Matt's doing, not mine. Still, I walked away with a bad taste in my mouth.

Suddenly, all that I had worked for was at stake. My reputation and good standing were threatened. This accident made the brigade commander look bad. It was a multimillion-dollar accident. Two Kiowas were destroyed. It was on the local news. Our leadership would be out for blood. But I didn't know why they were coming after me.

When I got back to Fort Campbell after my interview, I was relieved to put the dark moments of Lancaster behind me. But the accident didn't go away. I was not on the flight schedule. When I asked why I wasn't getting my postaccident mishap flight with an IP—which is standard procedure for anyone involved in an accident—I was given the runaround. "We have to wait for the results of the investigation to come out," I was told. Yet Matt was already back up and flying.

The weeks dragged on with little communication about what was going on.

A couple of weeks after the accident I saw Matt in the hallway at work. A guilty look washed over his face when he saw me. I wondered if he'd been avoiding me.

I gave him an annoyed look.

"Amber, I know. I don't know why they are doing this to you. Everyone knows it was my fault and I hit you. You just have to ride this one out. Rocking the boat will seriously only make it worse," he said.

I stood there, shocked at the fact that he had just told me to sit there and take it, while he got to move forward free and clear of the accident as if nothing had happened at all.

I began pressing the senior warrant officer Kiowa pilots in my unit for some intel. I was pleasantly surprised to learn that they, too, were pissed about how and why I was being singled out.

I walked into Greg's office and sat down, hopeful I'd get some answers about what was going on.

"Do you know what 'apathetic' means?" Greg, one of the senior warrant officer pilots who had been defending me, asked.

"Yes."

"Oh. Well, I had to look it up. That's how the investigating officers described you. But I can't believe that they didn't take into consideration the fact that you had just been in an accident. Maybe that's how you act after you get hit by a helicopter. Maybe it's a defense mechanism. Are they psychologists? No. Do they know how a person is supposed to act after an accident? No. But they are using it against you anyway. The only thing that they have succeeded with here is ruining a good warrant officer and pilot. That's all they've accomplished. And it's messed up that you're being targeted."

The insider information Greg had received from Tyler Williams, who was on the investigation board, was that they didn't like my "apathetic" attitude during the interview they conducted with me. They didn't think I showed enough emotion. I didn't attempt to blame someone else for some of my decisions. Williams had made it his personal mission to ruin me as a pilot because of one interview he didn't like, even though he had never flown with me.

It was a sad day for the Army I loved.

For a month, I felt completely destroyed by circumstances that were out of my hands. But some of the senior warrants in my unit had quietly been defending me. These guys knew me as a pilot and PC and had flown with me in combat—not like the guys on the investigation board, who had judged me based on one interaction within forty-eight hours of surviving an accident.

After what seemed like an eternity, I was scheduled for my post-accident mishap evaluation flight. Finally. I was more nervous for that flight than I was for my PC ride back in Iraq.

I flew like I always did, so the eval went smoothly. I made decisions like I always did. And I passed.

The accident Matt caused was bad, but the way the officers on the investigation board handled it was even worse. Other pilots were scared the same thing could happen to them, and that investigators would be more than willing to rush to judgment while ignoring the facts. It made the Army and our unit look bad.

I was thankful to be flying again, but the false accusations and witch hunt had changed me. I no longer trusted that my unit leadership would have my back if something bad happened that was out of my control. And that mind-set could get me into trouble. It's also not safe for the team as a whole. We were headed back to combat in about six months. The last thing unit leadership should want their pilots to think, prior to pulling the trigger in combat—whether it be to help save the ground guys or to lay down suppressive fire to cover another aircraft—is whether they will become an internal target for doing their job.

I had to put it behind me. The next war was on the horizon, and I had to be ready.

17

A NEW WAR

January 2008

Afghanistan

I stepped off the lowered ramp of the C-17 cargo plane onto the flight line in the freezing night air of Afghanistan. The cold air stung my face. I looked up at the billowing cumulus clouds in the sky and did a double take. *Wait, those aren't clouds—they're mountains!* Massive, snow-covered peaks surrounded the basin where the base was located. The Rockies had nothing on these thundering giants.

This was a new theater and a new war. I wasn't anxious, the way I had been when I first flew into Iraq. How different could two theaters of war be? War was war, right?

Just two weeks earlier I had been standing in the parking lot of the Fort Campbell PX, saying good-bye to my parents and my sister Lacey as I got ready to depart on my second year-long deployment, sixteen months after I had gotten home from Iraq.

So since all three of my parents' daughters were in the military with two wars going on, it seemed like one of us was always being deployed. I just wanted to leave and get the deployment started, not stand there and be sad.

Thinking about what might happen to my family while I was gone was the most difficult part. I worried someone might have a heart attack or get in a car accident. It seems morbid, but those what-ifs do happen to soldiers' family members during deployments. As I was about to walk away, it hit me all at once. My mom and dad gave me a big bear hug. Then I gave Lacey a hug. I wouldn't get to see her for about two years—her unit would be replacing mine in Afghanistan, so once my year was complete, hers would just be starting.

"You fly safe over there. We have a deal, don't you forget," my dad said.

We always promised each other that we would stay safe while we were gone. That was our deal.

"I will, Puppy, I'll be fine," I said.

Tears rolled down my checks. I couldn't hold it in anymore, but I was mad that I'd allowed myself to cry in front of them. They looked at me helplessly. I turned around and walked away.

By the time I arrived in Afghanistan, U.S. forces had been there for seven years, having arrived soon after al-Qaeda attacked our country on September 11, 2001. The campaign had successfully weakened al-Qaeda, forcing them to retreat and decreasing enemy activity. For a while, the military had shifted attention and troops to Iraq, which decreased the pressure on Afghanistan, allowing al-Qaeda and the Taliban to recover, recruit, and regain strength. When I arrived in January 2008, the enemy had reclaimed its position as an incubator of terrorism. For the fifth year in a row, we were fighting two wars.

Our unit, 2-17 CAV, had just arrived in Bagram, the largest U.S. base in Afghanistan, on a flight from Manas, the military staging base in Kyrgyzstan for all inbound and outbound troops for Afghanistan.

The experienced pilots in our unit had been to Iraq, but few had been to Afghanistan. The Stan, as we called it, was unknown territory.

"When is the last time you guys got rocketed or mortared?" I asked a young soldier who was driving us in a small bus around the airfield to the transient tents we would be calling home for the next week. At Balad, mortar and rocket attacks had been daily occurrences—and throughout the day—which created a constant, hovering fear. You never knew if your walk to dinner could be the one when you got killed by a rocket that you never even heard coming. That was the thing I hated most about my time in Iraq, and the thing I dreaded most about Afghanistan.

"I think we got rocketed in September," the driver said.

I laughed out loud. I didn't know whether to believe him.

"You mean, like, over four months ago?"

This year might not be so bad after all.

Bagram had been built on top of a minefield. Old Soviet mines were buried all over the countryside from the Soviet-Afghan war in the 1980s. Everywhere we turned, red triangle hazard signs said: DO NOT ENTER, MINES. The airfield was not only built on a minefield, it was also completely run-down. After seven years of war, it looked like no money had been spent there. By contrast, the big Iraq air bases were like small fortified cities with infrastructure. The troops all lived in container housing units. In Bagram, every building was made of flimsy plywood, and most soldiers slept in what we called B-huts, small plywood huts that housed four to eight people. But as new arrivals, we were bound for big transient tents.

After our bus driver dropped us off in the tent city, we had to rummage through the massive piles of green duffel bags and rucksacks that had been dumped in front of the tents. Katie, Deidra, and I headed to the "girl tent" to claim our green Army issue cots. It was always a pain to be separated from the guys, because we never knew our schedule, where we were meeting, or updates for time changes. Communication usually never got to us because for some reason most of the guys were always too nervous to come over to our tent to tell us anything. But being in the transient tent city sucked for everyone. We had to deal with it until we got to Jalalabad—or as we quickly learned to call it, J-bad.

I lifted the big flap on the green canvas tent door and walked into a large space where cots lined the outer walls of the tent with a walkway down the middle. The whole place could probably hold about seventy-five people. We set our bags down on the gravel floor to claim our cots about halfway down.

Other girls were already in the tent, and they gave us a look that said, "We feel sorry for you, but thank God you're here so we can go home." I knew that look. I'd given it to the pilots from 2-6 CAV a year and a half earlier, when their unit replaced us in Iraq.

"Hey!" someone said.

I continued what I was doing without looking up. I'd been in the Army long enough to know that when someone says "Hey" without specifying to whom, you never act as though it was intended for you. It's a good way to get stuck with a random job tasking, have someone yell at you, or something else ridiculous.

"Is that Amber Smith?" the same voice said.

Ugh, great.

I looked up to see who wanted to talk to me. A girl sitting on the opposite row of cots with dark brown hair gave me a big smile. I looked back at her blankly. Then it hit me: Courtney Young. Five years earlier, she and I had been battle buddies at basic training. We'd spent two and a half long months together marching in formation through Fort Jackson, South Carolina, learning how to be soldiers.

"Courtney!" I walked over and gave her a hug. "What are you doing here?" I asked.

"I'm going home!" She was in the National Guard and had been living in eastern Afghanistan in J-bad, where I was headed.

Courtney told me J-bad was tiny compared to Bagram. It was basically an old air base with one runway with a fence around it and some B-huts. The base was on the east side of the city. To the south were the massive Tora Bora Mountains. Out east was Khyber Pass and the Pakistan border. To the north was the entrance to the Konar River Valley.

I was called to dinner and, when I returned a couple of hours later, Courtney's bags were gone and her cot was empty. We never saw each other again.

―――――

We pilots had days of academics ahead of us before we could start flying in Afghanistan. The last thing we wanted to do was sit in a classroom and learn about rules and regulations of the base, especially since we were going to move to J-bad shortly. All of us were eager to get in the air. But as the new unit, we had to get through a check-the-block sequence of events.

Because our unit was replacing the 82nd Airborne, they gave us our introduction-to-Afghanistan classes. We got classes on the Rules of Engagement (ROE), roadside bombs and IED detection, as well as the General Order #1 directive, which was a list of prohibited activities for soldiers. No drinking. No sex. No drugs. No gambling. No adopting pets. Basically we couldn't do anything except eat, sleep, work out, and fly.

The ROE class was important because it outlined what we were authorized to do and what we weren't allowed to do. As the commander of a helicopter that fires weapons, I had to know precisely when I could and could not pull the trigger. Each theater of operation was different, so the rules were different from those we were used to in Iraq. Once we were flying in combat, we couldn't have any ambiguity about the

ROE when we had to make split-second decisions on whether to pull the trigger. American lives depended on it.

After three days of classes, we were given the green light to start conducting our environmental flights and gunnery familiarization. Only a few years before, I was in Kuwait with my old IP and stick buddy Chris Rowley, conducting my environmental flight before heading into Iraq. Now I was one of the experienced PCs in my troops. Once we got to J-bad and started flying missions, I would likely be crewed with one of the new copilots who had never flown in combat. I felt the pressure and responsibility that came with my experience from Iraq, but I was ready to bring the fight to the enemy. We all were. It was what we were here for.

It snowed during my first flight. I flew with CW3 Ed Dalsey, one of our IPs and a truly talented pilot. I'd flown with him for years now, in training and in combat in Iraq, and I always learned something from him. We did a landing approach to a ridgetop, but only to a hover—we weren't allowed to land because of the mines. I hated the thought that, if I got shot down or had maintenance issues that forced us to land, we would have to worry about land mines in addition to every other threat we faced on the ground.

The cold was another challenge. I'd never felt that kind of cold before flying in the Afghan mountains. Bagram was about a fifteen-minute flight from Kabul. J-bad was about a seventy-five-minute flight to the southeast, close to the Pakistan border. Bagram itself was at about five thousand feet MSL—mean sea level. As usual, we flew without doors. The frigid air that came in that cockpit made exposed skin feel as if it were being stabbed with a thousand needles. I was looking forward to getting to J-bad, not only to get settled into my new home, but also because it was supposed to be about ten degrees warmer. J-bad is almost three thousand feet lower than Bagram.

For our flight to J-bad, our troop was split into two flights, five

Kiowas in each. I was flying with CW3 Scott Sherman, an Iraq war vet who had joined our unit the year prior. Before strapping into the cockpit, he knelt on the ground next to our helicopter. On an earlier deployment in Iraq, his Kiowa had been shot down when it took heavy enemy fire, and he and his copilot had had to evade the crash site by running to the safety of the U.S. ground forces. Now, before every flight, he got down on one knee and said a prayer. We all had our own rituals or good-luck charms. Some pilots flew with bobblehead dancing hula girls they'd attach to the dash. Others flew with little mementos their kids had given them. I flew with a tiny stuffed pink pig that I always kept in my flight bag.

The cold air numbed my fingers and toes as we took off from Bagram for the last time, but I shook it off. My adrenaline was pumping. It was go time.

Our flight path took us through an area called the Tagab River Valley, a known hot spot that had received heavy enemy activity reports recently. We had been instructed not to engage with any enemy if we could avoid it on this flight. Our mission was to get the Kiowas to J-bad without sustaining any damage.

As we entered the Tagab, I looked down at the snow-covered fields and mud huts. Cows, sheep, goats, donkeys, chickens, you name it, were on the roofs of some of the primitive huts. We didn't see many people; there didn't seem to be a lot of activity, which we had just learned from our classes was normal for the winter months.

We made it out of the Tagab without incident, even though our route funneled us into a steep canyon with mountains towering above us, blocking any way out. It made my skin crawl, because one of the enemy's tactics for taking down a helicopter is to set up different positions in a canyon or valley, and then as a helicopter flew through, fire at it simultaneously from different altitudes. We had just put ourselves through a dangerous position in a flight of five helicopters all in the exact same flight path through the canyon. But it was the only way to get our Kiowas to J-bad.

The canyon opened onto a vast and beautiful river valley. Out my door was Highway 1, the major road between J-bad and Kabul. Known as one of the most dangerous roads in the world, it had only one narrow lane in each direction, and it was littered with IED holes. This was no freeway.

The lead Kiowa made a radio call to J-bad air control tower declaring we were about to enter their airspace. As we rounded the bend in the river, I glanced ahead. I'd read about Jalalabad in the novel *The Kite Runner*, which made it seem like a majestic, modern place. But after decades of war and Taliban rule, it was just another war-torn shit hole.

Courtney was right. J-bad air base was nothing more than a small runway with a fence around it. With lots of holes in the fence. Cows from neighboring fields constantly made their way inside the wire. On both sides of the runway, smooshed between the fence parts, was our living area. Tents, defac, a couple of gyms, and laundry facilities. Compared to Bagram, which was a city, J-bad was a village.

More tents. I had been secretly hoping we were going to move straight into a B-hut, but construction on them had only begun, on the other side of the airfield. We were stuck in the tents indefinitely.

Over the next few days, we all did our local area orientation flights. This was our one chance to learn our new and vast AO. It was a lot to take in during one flight. We flew up the Konar River Valley toward Asadabad, the area near the Pakistan border where Operation Red Wings had occurred in June 2005, when nineteen Americans, including eight Army Night Stalkers and eleven Navy SEALS, were killed; Navy SEAL Marcus Luttrell was the lone survivor. We flew into the Pech River Valley and the Korengal Valley, or "The Valley of Death," as previous U.S. forces called it. Many helicopters had been shot down here, and dozens of U.S. and Afghan soldiers had been killed.

It would be my home away from home for the next twelve months.

18

CLEARED HOT

January 2008

Jalalabad, Afghanistan

It was nearly dark by the end of our mission. We'd landed at base to refuel, and I was ready to get out of the cockpit after a six-hour time bloc. Before we could shut down and park, though, the aircraft had to be dearmed and refueled by the ground crew. These guys could move at the speed of a NASCAR pit crew, but since we were at the end of our mission, there was no real urgency.

Our reconnaissance and security mission had been uneventful. From J-Bad we had flown southeast to the Tora Bora Mountains, near the Pakistan border, looking for signs of suspicious activity.

I was flying right-seat lead next to my copilot, CW2 Chris Cook. I called him "Astan Chris" (Astan is short for Afghanistan). The other Chris I'd flown with in Iraq, Chris Rowley, was now the standardization pilot—the senior instructor pilot—of a troop based down in Kandahar, so I wouldn't get to fly with him on this deployment.

Astan Chris was originally from Virginia. Though he was new to aviation, he was a war veteran who had survived multiple deployments in special operations units in Iraq—and in other places around the world he couldn't tell me about. As an airborne Ranger, he had para-chuted into Iraq during the invasion, and later he had guarded Saddam Hussein's prison cell in Iraq after his capture.

Chris had a valuable ground-level perspective of the enemy and the war. Chris had a dry sense of humor, sang Shakira in the cockpit, and taught me Spanish. When he was deployed with the Ranger battal-ion, he had loved playing volleyball against Afghan locals, who were, as it turns out, exceptional volleyball players. They regularly kicked Amer-ican ass, and that thoroughly pissed off Chris. Missions with Chris were always entertaining.

We had butted heads at first—he refused to take photos of things I deemed necessary when I asked him to—but after we got to know each other over a few dozen hours of flight time, we became a great team. I could always count on his brutal honesty. I called it "cockpit therapy," the magic of sitting in a four-foot-wide flying confessional for hours. You get to know a side of a person that might not otherwise surface. It's a war thing. A strange trust forms, and people open up.

As the ground crew began refueling and rearming our aircraft, Chris and I relaxed in the cockpit, looking forward to taking off our helmets. This was the point in the flight when your brain starts to shut down and you begin thinking about food, sleep, movies, anything but flying.

Then the radio crackled to life.

"Annihilator Two-One, Annihilator Two-One . . . this is Out Front TOC. What is your location?"

It was our TOC at squadron headquarters in J-bad. It was not nor-mal to hear from the TOC at the end of a mission. Something was up.

"Out Front TOC, this is Annihilator Two-One. We are in the FARP, dearming and refueling. What's up?" reported the voice of CW3 Sammy Puentes, our AMC, who had been flying right-seat trail. He was sitting in his Kiowa on the other side of the T-barrier, the concrete wall that separated our aircraft.

"Roger, Two-One. We've got an ongoing TIC in the mouth of the Korengal and the Pech at COP Michigan. Unit has taken casualties. Sustained enemy contact. They need airpower now. Can your flight be ready to go—NOW?"

The Korengal River Valley was an infamous bastion of enemy operations. Bad shit happened there. A narrow valley flanked by steep, jagged mountains, it was the home turf of the Taliban, who used the terrain to great tactical advantage. Fleet-footed on the rugged trails, they attacked with surprise and vanished like ghosts into the caves and boulder fields. I had flown in the Korengal once, a few weeks earlier, during my orientation flight. But brigade headquarters had since closed the valley to Kiowas because several helicopters had been shot down over the years. Since Kiowas fly low, command didn't want that risk with their helicopters. This TIC was playing out at the mouth of the Korengal, where it forms a T with the Pech River Valley, close to a small combat outpost called COP Michigan.

A second Kiowa team was about to begin their mission block, but they were still in the TOC getting briefed. We were in the cockpit, that much closer to go. Someone up the chain was deciding which team to send. Them or us.

Sammy answered that question: "Roger Out Front. We are rearming, finishing up refuel. We'll be in the air in two minutes."

The jolt of adrenaline woke me right up. All the fatigue of our six-hour mission bloc vanished. We were zero to a hundred in a heartbeat.

"Amber, you ready to go?" Sammy said over our internal frequency.

Hell, yeah, I'm ready to go!

"Roger," I said. "I'll be Red Con One [ready for takeoff] in one minute. I just need them to finish loading my rockets." This was my first TIC call since arriving in Afghanistan.

When you get a call for a TIC, things happen very quickly. Kiowa pilots pride themselves on their ability to respond immediately with little information. It may be just a call sign, a grid, and a frequency. Sometimes it's easier this way. Sitrep information has a short shelf life, and in the time it takes you to reach the TIC, the situation has changed. We normally got updates along the way from the TOC, via Sat-Com radio, but we could not talk to the owning unit until we were within radio range, somewhere at the mouth of the valley.

We were not dressed warmly enough for a night flight. The temperature plunged after sunset, and without our cold-weather gear, the biting wind would cut through our jackets. At least we had our NVGs, which we carried specifically for times like this, when our missions were extended unexpectedly.

Wearing tan gloves, I flashed four fingers at the ammo guys in the FARP who reloaded the four HE rockets they had just removed. I scribbled TIC on my kneeboard and tapped my watch. They immediately amped up to their NASCAR pit crew speed, loading us with extreme precision and efficiency.

Through the open door on my right, the crew held up the grounding cable and weapons pylon pins—visual confirmations that these safety measures were removed and that our weapons were ready to go. When refuel was complete and we were fully rearmed, I gave them the thumbs-up: ready for takeoff.

"Chris, are you ready to go on your side?" I asked.

"Roger, ready," Chris said.

"What's your status?" Sammy barked on the radio.

"Roger," I said. "Annihilator Two-Four—Red Con One."

"J-bad tower: Annihilator Two-Four, flight of two, in the FARP. Request an immediate and direct departure sector Delta for TIC."

"Annihilator Two-Four, Jalalabad tower. Cleared for takeoff. Direct sector Delta."

I pulled up on the collective, increasing the pitch of the blades. A little more collective, and I felt the skids light on the ground. I pushed the cyclic forward, and the aircraft shuddered through effective transitional lift and into forward flight.

We headed north into the Konar River Valley. As we rose into the glow of twilight, the air base shrank behind us, swallowed by the night.

We were still a newly formed crew, having flown together only a handful of times. But we were a good crew, which primarily had to do with the leadership of our AMC, Sammy Puentes. Sammy was an Army Ranger prior to becoming an aviator. He wasn't the most senior guy, but he had a commanding presence and a professionalism that set him apart. No one messed with him.

Sammy was in 2-17 CAV when I joined in 2004, but he had been in Bravo Troop, our sister troop, so our interactions were minimal. I mostly saw him at squadron pilots' briefs or in passing at the hangar. I didn't get to know him until he moved to Alpha Troop in 2007, became one of our IPs, and I started flying with him. Since then he had become a mentor. He trusted my instincts and abilities, not just as a PC but also as the lead of our flight, and was grooming me for the next progression in my career in Army aviation: air mission commander (AMC).

Sammy's copilot was CW2 Deidra Adams.

As I led our team into the mouth of the Konar River Valley, the trail Kiowa slipped into echelon left. The radio crackled to life with Sammy's voice. "Beacon!"

That word signaled we were in flight formation now, and we pulled in max collective to increase our airspeed to get to the TIC as fast as possible. Flying at 95 knots, about 109 miles per hour, I glanced to my right out the open door and noticed the moon's reflection in the river that was gliding by below. Not good. The moonlight made it easier for us to see but also to be seen, and we were deep into enemy territory. When we flew blacked out, we were mostly invisible—except when silhouetted by the moon.

After about fifteen minutes flying up the Konar, we took a left turn into the Pech, where we would link up with the TIC. The mountains rose sharply as we entered the valley. As we climbed in altitude, the air grew thinner, and the Kiowas required more power to stay aloft. In the valley it was darker and harder to see the mountains and the enemy concealed by them.

"Are you ready?" I asked Chris. "Do you know what you are going to say and do?"

"Roger," he said. He sounded confident.

We went over the check-in with the controlling unit of the airspace and AO: "Asadabad Control, Asadabad Control, this is Annihilator Two-Four, flight of two scout weapons team. One hour on station time, eight rockets, six hundred rounds fifty-cal. Transitioning from the south to the north into the Pech to link up with Dagger. Requesting sitrep."

Chris entered the grid to our friendly ground forces into our nav system and punched in their frequency. We were seven minutes out. Asadabad base came over the radio, responding to our check-in. Friendlies in four Humvees were taking enemy fire from the mountain-side. Soldiers had been wounded and they were waiting for a medevac. We were instructed to hold east of the eight-zero grid line until their artillery fire mission was complete.

I saw the lights of FOB Asadabad in the distance. It sat in a river valley surrounded by mountains to the south of Asadabad. As we flew over the base, I saw the long black cylinders of their 155mm howitzers barrels pointed west. I felt their ground-shaking, percussive blasts, even from the air.

To my left, Chris had his head down, reading the grid coordinates that he wrote down on his kneeboard and punching them into our nav system. It was not an easy task in a helicopter during the day, let alone in a blacked-out cockpit. Making things worse, we were flying in Aircraft 014, a Kiowa infamous in our troop for its one-to-one hop. One of the four rotor blades was slightly off balance, causing the helicopter to hop with every rotation. The violent vibration made our NVGs bounce erratically, another distraction we didn't need.

Chris looked up. "Done. Waypoints ninety-eight and ninety-nine are friendly positions, eighty is enemy location. I'm back with you outside."

"Roger. Got it. I'm up with Dagger Six," I said. "Let's see what they've got."

We checked in with Dagger Six, the ground unit involved in the firefight. They acknowledged our arrival on station and told us to hold on the eight-zero easting, our separation boundary, so we kept clear of their friendly artillery fire.

Nothing like a last-minute call-for-fire mission when you're already in their airspace. The last things any pilot wants are artillery rounds flying anywhere near his or her location. Big sky, little bullet is not a comforting thought at the time. I came around to the right, over the eight-zero grid line, staying in the safe zone as artillery zipped through the air.

"We got three ANA KIA."

My stomach dropped as soon as it came over the radio. ANA were Afghani National Army. *Damnit! We were too late.* If we had gotten there sooner, could we have prevented that? Our internal frequency exploded with expletives. Then, radio silence. I had to put out of my mind the potential outcomes of the situation we were about to fly into.

I heard the medevac radio that they were wheels up, which meant they had just taken off from J-bad. They were in a Black Hawk with an Apache escort. They should be here in fifteen minutes.

"I'm going to figure-eight right here until we get the all-clear to move in," I said to Sammy. Loitering around the eight-zero grid line gave us a minute to gain our bearings, since we had flown into the AO with little information.

"Annihilator Two-Four, Annihilator Two-Four! This is Dagger Six. We have contact with three or four enemy personnel maneuvering through the mountainside just above our location. Fire mission is complete. Requesting immediate close combat attack on enemy position. Requesting gun run from north to south over the river at a heading of two hundred degrees. Will lase target with an IR [infrared] laser. Friendlies marked with fireflies. Call eyes on target."

"Roger. Annihilator Two-Four and flight are inbound now. Will call target," I said.

This is what we had been waiting for. I turned the aircraft to the friendly location waypoint on our nav system, looked out my right side, and saw the low-vis IR flashes from the fireflies attached to the friendlies' helmets and the location of the four friendly Humvees. We were on top of them.

"Coming around left. I have eyes on friendlies," I said to Sammy. I saw the Humvees that were pinned down and the soldier swinging a "buzz saw"—an infrared chem light attached to a 550 cord and swung overhead like a lasso—making a circle of light that was only visible through NVGs.

We were flying through the pitch-black darkness a couple of hundred feet above the ground, through a very narrow valley with steep mountains on three sides and filled with active enemy. It was a tight airspace, even with only two aircraft, so we set up a racetrack pattern circling in the sky while monitoring five radios and setting up our gun run.

In addition to the medevac Black Hawk and Apache escort en route from J-bad, we had a second Kiowa team coming in to conduct a battle handover. We would soon have six helicopters maneuvering in the same river valley. Sammy was talking to the inbound Kiowa team while I maintained contact with the ground troops. Headquarters at the TOC was radioing in for an update. It was a lot of radio chatter at once.

"Dagger Six, Annihilator Two-Four. Four enemy on the mountainside. Lasing target. Requesting CCA with fifty-cal machine gun and rockets. Heading two hundred degrees. Cleared hot."

Sammy and I were circling each other, oscillating like two cars on opposite sides of a racetrack. About three hundred feet beneath us, an IR laser beam shone into the mountains, identifying four enemy. To the naked eye, the laser was invisible, so the enemy could not see the beam, but we could through our NVGs.

As I banked left, away from the target, Sammy came around.

"I've got the laser spot," he said. "Inbound hot. Fifty-cal rockets."

"Roger," I said. "I'll be right behind you."

Sammy sprayed the target with the .50-cal, muzzle flash and tracer fire sparking in the night sky. Two rocket explosions flashed on the mountainside.

"Left break, outbound cold," Sammy said.

It was my turn. I came inbound, hot to the target, and bumped the nose of the aircraft slightly up, setting up the perfect angle to shoot. I pressed the trigger.

Nothing.

I pressed it again. And again.

Nothing.

"RECOCK!" I yelled to Chris.

"I already did!"

My gun wasn't firing. Chris looked at the gun and discovered that during the chaos of rearming in the FARP when we got the TIC call our .50-cal machine gun was loaded with bullets, but the ammo belt was never put in the gun chute, so we couldn't fire the ammo.

I quickly switched my weapons page on the multifunctional display (MFD) in the cockpit to the rockets page and fired. Two 2.75-inch high-explosive rockets sailed out of the pod with the familiar *Shoop Shoop*. The mountainside lit up again.

This is the dance of war, two helicopters circling in a ring of fire. I banked left, outbound cold, and Sammy came in hot. Two more rockets. Then he's out, and I'm in. Two more rockets. It happened in seconds.

It was beautiful.

"Winchester!" I said. Out of ammo.

"Target engaged," I radioed to the ground guys. "Rounds complete. Winchester. We'll be breaking station for refuel. Another Condor team will be on station shortly."

"Annihilator Two-Four, Dagger Six. Rounds on target. CCA complete."

We exited our gun run pattern and flew to the west side of the valley to make way for the inbound medevac helicopter. I saw the IR buzz saw spinning again, signaling the landing zone. As the medevac came in on short final for landing, the Apache escort was flying overwatch. The Apache circled the night sky like a shark, menacing and deadly.

We heard the second Kiowa team enter the mouth of the Pech. Our mission was over and our bingo warning was bonging. Before we could leave, we had to conduct the battle handover with the Condor team.

"Dagger Six, this is Annihilator Two-Four. We are CCA complete. Condor has the battle and we are RTB."

"Roger, Annihilator. Just confirmed the battle damage assessment of four enemy KIA. Thanks for your help."

"No problem, Dagger. We'll see you next time."

19

SHOOTING TO KILL

February 2008

Jalalabad, Afghanistan

Our B-huts were finally finished, which meant we got to move out of the tents on the other side of the airfield and into the new plywood structures. Deidra, Katie, I, and a few of our other female crew chiefs moved into one B-hut. Ants and spiders moved in, too. The air-conditioning never worked, because the Afghans who worked on the base would siphon the gas out of our generators. During the winter this was okay, but when the weather warmed up, we had many sleepless nights—or rather, sleepless days after a night shift. There is no successful way to sleep in a plywood box while the sun beats down at 115 degrees. Whenever the gas was replaced and the generators turned back on, those tiny A/C units had to work overtime to cool a B-hut that could be well over 100 degrees, so of course the A/C unit broke from working too hard.

For some reason, Afghans also came around and painted our B-huts with some sort of turpentine paint thinner during the summer months, while yelling in Pashto on the opposite side of our thin plywood walls. Lack of sleep made being on night duty miserable.

Still, we were happy to finally settle into own little space in our B-hut. But we had no downtime. Missions continued.

———

The day after we destroyed the enemy on a mountain at the mouth of the Korengal Valley, we got another TIC call—our ground guys needed Kiowa airpower now. Chris tuned in the radio frequency for the ground unit call sign Rockstar as we flew toward their location.

Below my Kiowa, the moonlight reflected off the river. It looked so peaceful down there, as the river meandered beside the narrow two-lane Highway 1 pocked with IED holes. The river, the road, and the Afghan desert all appeared so quiet, so distant, as though the war were somewhere else, not two hundred feet below me.

"Rockstar, this is Annihilator Two-Four, flight of two Kiowas, loaded with six hundred rounds of fifty-cal, eight rockets, and about one point five hours of station time. We are about five minutes from your location," Chris said over the radio to the ground unit.

Chris had proven to be essential in the cockpit during last night's engagement at the mouth of the Korengal. He communicated well and stayed a step ahead of the aircraft. Not bad for our first engagement of the deployment. I knew I could count on Chris when things got intense, and it sounded as if we were in for another active night.

"Annihilator, we are taking sustained enemy fire! Our vehicles are hit. We are pinned down, we can't move. We need a medevac NOW!" Rockstar said.

Tracer fire lit up the night sky about a mile in front of the aircraft, pinpointing Rockstar's location. It was clear that we were flying into a hot zone.

"Did you see that? And did you get all of that?" I radioed to Sammy Puentes, AMC in the trail aircraft.

"Roger, let's do this," Sammy said.

"Roger, Rockstar, we've got eyes on you, one minute out," Chris said.

As we got closer to their location, we made out our force's stationary Humvees on the road through our NVGs. They were sitting ducks. The enemy had set up the ambush perfectly. The ridge to the south of the road was littered with caves, which made it easy for the enemy to pop in and out of them for cover. It also gave them the strategic advantage of the high ground and ability to shoot down at Rockstar. The vehicles that had been hit were blocking the road for the rest of the convoy, leaving them vulnerable and exposed to the enemy line of fire.

I flew my Kiowa fast and tactically on the north side of the road, the opposite side from where we'd seen the enemy fire, to evade any fire that could be directed at us. I did a quick fly-by of the Humvees to get a visual confirmation of the friendlies' location. Most of our soldiers were taking cover behind their vehicles with their weapons facing the ridge. ANA soldiers gathered on the west side of the road, where a ridge gave them some protection from the attackers.

Chris and I scanned the ridge, looking for signs of the enemy. Nothing. This enemy wasn't stupid; as soon as they heard the sound of the rotors from our helicopter, they knew to take cover or get blown up.

I picked up an inner racetrack pattern with my Kiowa as Sammy picked up an outer. He flew a little higher and wider than my orbit to protect my aircraft as we conducted the close-in reconnaissance. Sammy got on one of the radios to call in the medevac aircraft.

"Rockstar, we've got nothing on the ridge to your south," Chris said. "There are caves all over the place, so I think that's where they are hiding, but we don't have any eyes on the enemy."

Dat! Dat! Dat!

"We're taking fire, we're taking fire!" Rockstar yelled over the radio. "Shoot them! My guys are hit! We need a medevac!"

We couldn't see the tracer fire from where we were. There wasn't much room between the river and the friendlies' location on the road—just a little marsh field with a cluster of trees surrounding a graveyard. I looked left, right, continuing my scan.

Where the hell where these guys hiding?

"Roger, Rockstar," I said. "Where are you guys taking fire from? We've got nothing. Talk me onto the target so we can shoot."

Rockstar was shrieking and hard to make out, so I asked Chris if he had anything.

"Just the friendlies," Chris said. I flew the aircraft in a fast jigsaw pattern over the friendlies. Of course, just because we couldn't see the enemy didn't mean they couldn't see us—the moon was bright tonight.

Rockstar was still almost impossible to comprehend.

"This guy is panicking—I can barely make out what he's saying," I said to Sammy over our internal radio.

"Hey, Rockstar!" Sammy shouted. "SNAP OUT OF IT! Your guys need you right now. Get a hold of yourself and take a breath and tell us where you need us to shoot. We're here to help you guys. The medevac is en route."

Silence.

I was half expecting him to come back and tell us to go to hell.

"Roger, roger!" Rockstar yelled through the radio. "We're taking pop shots from the north side of the road, just to the south of the river! Requesting close combat attack—CCA! NOW!"

"Roger, CCA with fifty-cal and rockets. Can you laze the target so we can get eyes on?" I said.

Immediately I saw an infrared laser beam shining through my NVGs, pointing to a cluster of trees between their location and the river.

"Roger, we have eyes on the target. Do we have a clearance of fire?" I asked Rockstar.

"Roger, you have a clearance of fire and you are cleared to engage!"

"You ready?" I said to Sammy as I set up our gun run flight path.

"Roger, I'm right behind you. Will be in with fifty-cal, then switching to rockets."

"You're armed and ready to go," Chris said to me, ensuring our weapons systems were active.

I banked the Kiowa hard left to turn us toward the target as we flew over the friendlies. The target was far enough away from them that they weren't in the danger close zone. I pulled the cyclic back and bumped the aircraft up about thirty degrees, leveled it out, and pointed the .50-cal machine gun down to the target.

I pulled the trigger.

Dat! Dat! Dat! Our entire aircraft rattled as the gun fired. I clenched my jaws so I wouldn't bite my tongue. A stream of bullets landed perfectly on the target.

That's what I'm talking about. Rounds on target.

"CEASE FIRE! CEASE FIRE!" Rockstar yelled over the radio.

I let go of the trigger. All of the blood drained out of my face. I was suddenly terrified—I had clearly hit the target and possibly killed people, so why the hell was Rockstar yelling at me to stop?

"Why did you just call a cease-fire? What's going on?" I said to Rockstar.

"We don't have all of our friendlies accounted for! We are missing one of our guys!" Rockstar said.

"You've got to be fucking kidding me," I said to our team over our internal radio. "This whole thing is a clusterfuck. What the hell is going on down there?"

"It's okay, we're okay. It's not your fault, they gave us a clearance of fire," Sammy said, clearly reading my mind.

Before we can shoot for the ground guys in combat, they must give us a clearance of fire—which means that they have all their friendly forces accounted for and everyone is a safe distance from the target and kill zone. As pilots we can also get a PID—positive ID of the enemy—ourselves, if we have eyes on the enemy, or if the ground guys can give us their PID, just as they did tonight. Despite all these precautionary regulations, something had gone wrong.

The sick feeling in my stomach grew as we flew circles around the Rockstar convoy waiting for the medevac to arrive. Everything I'd learned—from day one in flight school up to this point; my past five-plus years of Army experience; my entire deployment to Iraq—had all taught me to protect the ground guys. Always.

"Your rounds were right on target, too," Chris said, snapping me back to reality.

"Shit—I know."

This was the first time I wished I had missed a target. I never felt remorse or anguish about killing the bad guys; never questioned whether I could pull that trigger. The guys I shot at were the enemy—they were trying to kill Americans; my fellow soldiers; me. It was my job to stop them.

Please let it be some kind of mistake.

Rockstar was about to be in a world of trouble for calling a scout weapons team of Kiowas in on a target in close proximity to friendlies, and giving us a clearance of fire when he didn't have all of his guys accounted for. Still, it didn't matter if it wasn't my fault or that they had given me the wrong information. The final approval authority lay with me, the pilot in command of the Kiowa. I made the decision to pull the trigger. I'd have to live with it.

"We're missing one of our ANA soldiers that came with us on this mission," Rockstar said. "He may have gotten captured during the attack."

"Roger, Rockstar. So all of your American troops are accounted for? It's an ANA soldier who is missing, but you don't know if he was captured or if he was even on the mission?" I said.

"Roger, Annihilator. We're trying to confirm who saw the missing ANA soldier last so we have a last known location for him."

ANA forces usually worked alongside U.S. troops on ground missions, and we'd been on enough missions to know that they often miscounted their numbers when they left the base, so it wasn't that uncommon for them to realize that their head count was wrong.

We continued our orbit looking for any enemy movement in silence until the crackling of the radio broke it.

"Annihilator Two-Four, we think our head count was just off for our ANA soldiers. Sorry about that. We're good to go," Rockstar said.

I was furious. Rockstar had let me think I could have committed the worst act a pilot could ever do. Nothing seemed to be going right on this mission—except that my rounds were on target when I pulled the trigger. I let it go. Rockstar was having a worse day than I was. I was lucky. I hadn't killed or wounded anyone. But Rockstar's unit had sustained losses and injuries from the enemy before we arrived at their location. And they weren't safe yet.

"Dustoff Three-Three, two minutes out. I have eyes on the Kiowa team," I heard over the common air radio frequency.

A white strobe was flickering in the distant night in the direction of J-bad—it was our medevac helicopter, Dustoff 33, coming in to pick up the wounded.

"I've got eyes on Dustoff," I said to Sammy. "I'm going to widen my flight path over the ground guys' location and set up a pattern over the river to cover the medevac as it comes into the landing zone. That way we'll be able to shoot directly over them if they take enemy fire from the south."

"Sounds good," Sammy said.

"We're getting low on gas," Chris said to me. "We are going to have to leave these guys and head back into refuel in about ten minutes."

The medevac landed on the part of the road between the vehicles of the convoy. Through my NVGs I saw a rush of soldiers moving in unison to take their wounded to the helicopter. The Apache helicopter that had escorted the medevac Black Hawk was hovering above us, ready to lay down suppressive fire in case our aircraft or the medevac took fire while it was on the ground.

The dust began to swirl around the medevac as it pulled in power to take off into the night sky. It had been on the ground for no more than a minute.

"Wheels up," I heard Dustoff say, then it was on its way.

"How are you doing down there, Rockstar?" I said.

"We're good. Waiting on the QRF from Mehtar Lam to get down here to help us get these vehicles out of here so we can head back to the house." QRF was the quick reaction force.

"Roger. We're getting low on gas, so we have to head out of here, but a Kiowa team will be on station to take our place in about five minutes."

I saw the strobe lights of the Kiowa team in the distance as Sammy talked to them over our internal frequency to give them the battle hand-over.

I hoped the worst of the night was over for Rockstar. They'd taken some heavy battle damage during the firefight, including wounded soldiers, and had possibly lost accountability of an ANA soldier.

"Thanks for your help, Annihilator."

"You got it, Rockstar."

I turned the Kiowa toward J-bad and we passed the Kiowa team arriving to replace us.

On the radio, Sammy said, "Saber Three-One, you have the battle," and with that we were gone.

20

CHEATING DEATH

Spring 2008

Konar, Afghanistan

The Chowkay Valley—an offshoot of the main Konar Valley—was a supply route for the enemy moving from Pakistan into the Korengal Valley. Bad stuff always happened in the Chowkay Valley. There was a tiny combat outpost of U.S. troops there—COP Seray, at the bottom of the valley, a place that from the air appeared to be nothing more than a gravel parking lot with a tent and a flimsy fence around it. It ensured that the soldiers there were basically target practice for the enemy, who surrounded them in the mountains. A lot of bases in Afghanistan were like that—it just didn't make any sense. Troops at Seray were regularly attacked and had to live with the constant threat of their little base being overrun.

That particular day, Outlaw—the ground unit in the Chowkay—had just finished coordination for firing artillery at enemy forces on the mountainside. The artillery unit would then set up a mission to fire mortar rounds on the target. We moved to the south side of the valley to make sure we were clear of the enormous projectile rounds flying through the sky toward the target. I was in the left seat of the trail Kiowa today, flying behind Sammy Puentes and Astan Chris in the lead.

The artillery round hit the mountain on the north side of the valley, and white smoke billowed out from the target. The mountains appeared to shake as the rounds exploded.

A voice on the radio said, "Fire mission complete."

The radio operator's voice called in close air support fighter jets above us to drop bombs on the same target.

These guys are going all out!

We set up a racetrack pattern in an area considered the safe zone to ensure we were plenty far away from the bombs that were about to be dropped by the fighter jets. Then everything went wrong: an electrifying white light momentarily blinded us as the bombs hit. The jets were dropping bombs on the wrong grid—right in our safe zone. It looked like a thousand lightning bolts wrapped into a fireball erupted outside my left door.

"GOOOOOOOO! Get out of here!" I screamed.

There was no way we could tell if more bombs were dropping through the sky in which we were flying. If one of them hit us, we'd never even know it.

We broke right, but there was no way a Kiowa could fly fast enough away from the kill zone to avoid a bomb from a jet. It felt like we were moving in slow motion. Where the bombs were falling and where they hit the ground were out of our control.

I don't know where the breakdown in communication was, or why they were attacking the wrong grid, but I just wanted out of there.

"Cease fire! Cease fire!" Sammy yelled over the radio.

Everyone stopped what they were doing immediately—ground forces, artillery, fighter jets, Kiowas. Everyone needed to get reoriented and make sure everyone was safe. Inside the cockpit, we were cursing the pilots who dropped the bombs, while feeling incredibly thankful to be alive. The deployment in Afghanistan was still young, but I'd seen too many close calls already—though usually with the enemy, not the guys on our side. But things rarely went as planned.

We were at the end of this mission bloc and getting low on gas. Sammy turned his helicopter out of the valley and we headed back to J-bad. When we landed at the airfield, we tried to make sense of what had happened. Unfortunately, the reality is that miscommunication happened, and there was nothing we could do about it. Luckily, everyone involved was unharmed.

———

Our team was flying a reconnaissance mission in our AO in the Konar River Valley. The sun had begun to set behind the vast Afghan mountains. The terrain was always intimidating, no matter how comfortable we got with our routine. We knew the enemy were there, watching us. Waiting.

We were closing in on Asadabad, or A-bad, so it was time for Chris and me to halt our banter and concentrate. Flying in the Konar Valley was one thing—the valley was huge, and we constantly changed our flight path to confuse the enemy. But the valley tightened drastically near A-bad, and we had to be vigilant. If we got complacent, the enemy would take advantage. If we flew too slow, too low, too high, or used the same flight path as before, the enemy could get us in their crosshairs more easily.

At a certain point the valley got so tight that we had no choice but to fly in the same flight path each time. All we could do was fly aggressively and erratically to try to prevent the enemy from tracking us. There was nothing but a river beneath us if we got hit and crashed. Flights north of A-bad were pretty stressful.

I turned the aircraft to the left, into the mouth of the Pech River Valley just north of A-bad. Chris contacted Able Main, the call sign of the ground unit in the AO into which we were flying. The ground patrol was working its way up an incredibly steep mountainside, just north of their combat outpost on the opposite side of the river. They had to zigzag to get up. Some mountain terrain had switchback trails, but this one didn't seem to have that much of a trail, making it harder for the guys to make their way up. The ground guys always took fire on it. Our ability to fight back was hindered by car-size boulders that essentially created protective armor for the enemy against our rockets and .50-cal bullets. The enemy also stored caches of weapons and hid personnel in the numerous caves and tunnel systems of the mountains. It was what kept their operations successful in that part of the valley.

Chris began to scan the mountainside with our MMS camera for any hot spots through the thermal imagery. There, on the MMS TV screen in the cockpit, I saw the clearest white silhouette hot spot of an enemy target with weapons clearly defined that I've ever seen. "STOP!" I yelled.

The MMS stopped moving and we had the enemy directly in our sights.

"Where is that?" I said.

The MMS could swivel almost 180 degrees in either direction, so even though it looked straight ahead on the TV screen, it could have been behind us.

"Let me check," Chris replied, lazing the target to get precise coordinates on the enemy hot spot location.

"We've got positive target ID on the enemy," I radioed to Sammy, who was flying behind us as our AMC.

Chris relayed to Able on the mountain what we'd seen so we could get a clearance of fire and set up our close combat attack.

"We've got to set this up quick," I said to Sammy. "I don't want to lose these guys."

By now the enemy knew we were there. We knew they were in

the protection of the cave, and that protection left them feeling cocky enough to come to the mouth of it while we were flying around them. We could actually see them pop their heads out into the opening of the cave. We needed to make sure we shot them as they were standing in the open so they didn't have the protection of the huge boulders, and it would have to be the perfect shot, taken immediately before they got nervous and ran back inside the cave.

I pitched the nose of the helicopter up and climbed to create a perfect diving gun-run approach. The Able element was a safe distance away and significantly below us, so that was one less thing to worry about.

"I'm inbound hot, three hundred fifty degrees, with rockets, right break," I said to Sammy.

If we were going to do any damage, it would have to be with rockets—.50-cal bullets would ricochet off the enormous rocks.

I pulled the trigger. And then again.

Shunt. Shunt.

We watched, eyes on the target, waiting for the explosion. The first rocket exploded in the rocks, but nothing happened with the second rocket. Hmmm. I thought I'd made a perfect shot.

And then, as we began to turn outbound, a huge explosion shattered the mountainside directly above the cave. It was much bigger than the explosion that would have been created by a single rocket. It looked like a huge chimney had just exploded.

"Hell, yeah!" Chris yelled over the radio.

My second rocket had flown directly into the cave and kept going until it was deep inside. Nothing but net. As it detonated so far inside, it created a pressure that amplified the single rocket's power. This indicated that there was likely a tunnel system inside the cave creating the chimney-explosion effect. The rocket may also have hit a weapons cache, creating a secondary explosion. Either way, we significantly damaged their operations on that mountain and likely took out a few of their guys in the process.

Sammy came in right behind me in our racetrack pattern and fired his rockets.

Rounds on target. We unloaded the rest of our rockets into the cave until we were out of ammo.

"Able, this is Annihilator," Chris said. "We just fired eight rockets into the cave where we had positive ID on the enemy. We effectively engaged the target, there was a significant secondary explosion, and I think it's safe to say we got some of them."

We were still riding high from the chance encounter with the enemy, a couple of awesome shots taking out their safe haven and hopefully disrupting their operations for a while. Best of all, it might give Able some peace and quiet for a couple of days. And as much as we wanted Able to go up to the cave and do a battle damage assessment for our engagement, we knew it would take them hours to make it up there. Besides, the caves had been on the side of a cliff, so the access was probably blown up.

"Roger, Annihilator, thanks a bunch," Able said. "We're pretty much done out here for today. I think we're going to head back to the house."

"Sounds good," Chris said. "We're headed back to J-bad. There should be another Kiowa team in the AO shortly, so if you need anything just holler."

———

Chris and I were flying a route recon in the Konar one day when I looked out the cockpit door and saw an Afghan police officer getting out of a green police truck, followed by a brown ball of fur that jumped out after him. "Hey, I think I've got something," I said to Brian Stoner, who was my AMC in the trail Kiowa. Brian had given me my PC check ride in Iraq. "Coming around over this police truck.

"I think I just saw a monkey get out of that police truck," I said.

"What?" Chris said.

I didn't blame him for sounding incredulous. But a couple of days earlier, when I was in our headquarters office, I had overheard a couple of pilots talking about how they had been on a mission and found a bunch of hot spots on the mountainside. Naturally, they thought they'd seen enemy, but after looking more closely, they realized that all they'd found were a bunch of wild monkeys. I didn't believe a word they said—I'd been on the receiving end of stupid jokes and wasn't about to fall for this one. There were no monkeys in Afghanistan. Everyone knew that.

"Look, it's a monkey," I said, swiveling the Kiowa to put the police officer out Chris's door.

"Holy shit, that's a monkey on a leash!" Chris said.

I laughed. What on earth was the monkey doing on a leash? Did this guy take it to work with him? The monkey and his owner paused to look up at the helicopter as we flew slowly by them again and again.

"We have one Afghan policeman and one monkey," I said to Brian over the radio.

After a full-on photo shoot of the monkey, we decided that we had probably terrified the poor police officer and his monkey enough for one day. We flew on.

Unfortunately, the majority of our other animal encounters were not good ones. Sometimes we'd see large groups of men standing in circles while their dogs fought each other. It was a popular, if sickening, sport in Afghanistan, but there was nothing we could do about it. It was notable that when the Afghans came to our base for the bazaar, they were terrified of the stray dogs that we allowed to roam the base. We reckoned it was because dogs recognized the smell of the people who abused them.

One beautiful, sunny day, we were conducting a route reconnaissance for IEDs on the west side of the Konar River. It was just us, no ground troops below us.

I slowed the helicopter and began flying a tight circle around something that had caught my eye. A donkey that appeared to be pregnant because its stomach was so big was tethered to a pole in an open field. The rope was only a couple of feet long, so the donkey couldn't really move. But that wasn't what bothered me.

A boy, maybe nine or ten years old, was standing a few feet away from the donkey and throwing rocks as hard as he could at the donkey's stomach. The donkey tried to run, but the tether kept her in place.

I was infuriated. It was no secret how the Afghans treated animals, nor was it a secret how they treated women. Time and time again our J-bad headquarters would get a call for a medevac helicopter because a little girl had been thrown off a mud hut or doused in boiling water. Women were nothing more than property in Afghanistan, and baby girls were often unwanted, especially if the family already had a daughter. Lots of families decided they couldn't afford extra girls, or that they would be worthless, or for whatever reason decided to literally toss them out. It was a disgusting reality of Afghan "culture."

The boy stopped throwing rocks and looked up at my helicopter to see what we were doing. He knew he'd been caught and he attempted to shoo us away, like we were interrupting some important business he was conducting. We tried hand signals out the door of the helicopter to tell him to leave. I think this kid must have gotten in trouble with helicopters before, because he hurried to the dirt road and ran in the opposite direction. I was certain he'd be back to beat up on the donkey, but at least not while I was flying by.

I wanted to land and cut the donkey free, but sometimes you have to pick your battles. I certainly didn't feel right flying by a helpless pregnant donkey as some horrible kid was beating her up. I'd seen some surreal things since I'd started flying in the eastern mountains of

Afghanistan: there was a goat that climbed a tree, a camel that walked with a car on its back near the Pakistan border, and three grown men riding a single motorcycle. I felt like I had traveled back in time. It was mind-boggling to think that this place was on the same planet as the place I call home more than seven thousand miles away, where people spend money to dress up their beloved pets for Halloween.

21

WAR TESTS YOU

April 2008
Jalalabad, Afghanistan

Days off meant days off from flying, and while I loved flying, I cherished the time on the ground.

We still had plenty to do even when we weren't in the air. I spent most of my time catching up on sleep and answering emails in my six-by-eight-foot room, but there were also official tasks to take care of: cleaning our weapons, Army training, cleaning the NVGs.

Unfortunately, because we had different shifts, I rarely got a day off on the same day as Katie or Deidra. When the stars aligned and we were off at the same time, we would try to come up with ways to pretend that we weren't trapped in eastern Afghanistan. In Iraq, I'd spent the past six months of the deployment doing one of only three things: working in our pilots' office, flying a mission, or sleeping in my CHU. It was miserable. Katie and I had vowed to make this deployment better. It was still early enough that we actually thought we could make our war as normal as possible.

On March 17, we planned a St. Patrick's Day party for everyone not flying that day. People back home had sent decorations, and Deidra had gotten the cooks in the chow hall to make us a green cake. It was like a seventh-grade party, but we didn't care. When we went to pick up the cake, the icing read, "Happy St. Patrik's Day." In the end, the party was fun—a ton of people showed up. We weren't the only ones who wanted momentary relief in Afghanistan.

Katie and I had heard that some of the infantry guys had a fishing spot in one of the ditches on the southeast side of the FOB. Even though it was on the opposite side of the base from where we lived, we decided to give it a try. Turns out it was nothing more than a culvert ditch with some stagnant water in it—swampy, buggy, and disgusting. Nevertheless, a few of us took turns fishing with the two fishing poles we had. But the mosquitoes were so bad that we ended our fishing expedition early.

A few days later, one of our pilots came up to us and gave us some bad news.

"Make sure you guys are taking your malaria medication," he said.

Before we had deployed, our flight doctor had prescribed us doxycycline, an antimalaria medicine. Doxycycline is a strong antibiotic that gives you vivid dreams and makes you wickedly sick if you take it without food. I had learned the hard way once, right before a mission, puking my guts out on the way to my flight brief in the middle of the night. Once I'd stopped heaving, I'd grabbed a Sprite from the chow hall and flew anyway. But I had also stopped taking my doxy after that.

"Why? I hate it, it makes me sick," I said.

"Some soldier here at J-bad just tested positive for malaria, so the mosquitoes here have it," he said.

At the J-bad fishing-hole-mosquito-sanctuary, they had snacked on all of us.

I had no idea if he was just messing with us or not, but I started taking my malaria pills again.

War tests you: your patience, your strength, your will. It pushes you to do things you didn't know you could do. Every time we went out on a mission, a new situation arose, a new decision had to be made, a new test was given. You never knew if you would pass—you just did the best you could with the information you had at the time.

One day we were flying south in the Konar, headed home to J-bad. We decided to check out some NAIs—named areas of interest—places that our intelligence briefer had told us about before our mission. Usually, NAIs were previous rocket or mortar launch sites, places where other Kiowa teams had reported suspicious activity, or where enemy activity is expected.

I turned left into an offshoot valley and headed toward the NAIs. The valley appeared quiet. Nothing going on.

I flew toward a little ridge in the middle of the valley that had built-up fighting positions on it—square walls made of bricks where people could safely kneel during a firefight. Many of them were left over from the Soviet-Afghan war and were all over the place in our AO. I flew low and fast next to one of them. I didn't like what I saw. I yanked the cyclic to the left.

"Hey! I've got a bunch of military-age males in these fighting positions down here. They've all got significant weapons." I yelled to Sammy over the radio, still shocked at what we had stumbled on.

I pulled back on the cyclic to bring the Kiowa up in altitude so we wouldn't be an easy target. I kept expecting to hear the sound of an AK-47 being fired in our direction, so I flew in a large traffic pattern around the ridge to get a better understanding of what we had just discovered.

We'd been in Afghanistan for months now and had picked up on many Afghan customs, but this was really spooky and completely out of the ordinary. These men weren't wearing the customary Afghan outfit for men—*khet partug* or *perahan tunban*—which closely resembled white or blue hospital scrubs and what we called "man dresses." These guys were wearing Western-style clothing—jeans, cargo pants—and one of them was wearing a baseball hat. A couple of them even had light-colored hair.

This felt like a trap.

"Gator Main, Annihilator Two-Four, we've got some suspicious activity to report," Chris said over the radio to the ground unit that owned this AO. "Do you guys have any friendlies outside the wire right now?"

"Negative, Annihilator. All friendlies are at the base right now. What's going on?"

"We ran into multiple military-age males in fighting positions with heavy weaponry at one of our NAIs."

"Roger, Annihilator, stand by," Gator said.

We couldn't wrap our head around this one. Everything pointed to them being bad guys—the weapons, the organized group of men, the fighting positions—but bad guys usually shot at us or started running for cover as soon as they heard or saw us. These guys just sat there.

"Annihilator, this is Gator. Yeah, those guys are bad guys. We're well familiar with that area. Some of our guys have been killed and wounded in that area. You guys are cleared to engage."

What? What the hell is going on?

Gator was a ground unit with close ties to the ground unit in the Chowkay Valley, and their buddies had been getting killed left and right. It was easy to understand that they wanted to take out as many bad guys as they could, and we were right there with them—we hated the bad guys as much as they did. But this situation was different. Something was off.

"Roger," Chris said. "You guys have no friendlies out right now and there are no ongoing U.S. or NATO operations to include any level of special operations missions? Can you double-check that?"

"Roger, just did, no friendlies, no missions," Gator said.

"All right, we're going to hold off for a minute," Sammy said. "Let's get in a bit closer and see what they do."

I did a couple of diving runs on the fighting positions; we even tried to fake them out by pretending to leave the valley and then flying back in from a different direction. The men wouldn't even look at us. It was like they were pretending we weren't there. If the roles had been reversed, and I was the one in the fighting position, I wouldn't have looked at the Kiowa, either, for fear of provoking a firefight and getting my head blown off, but still it was strange.

Sammy flew a little bit higher than us in a protective position to shoot these guys if they made any aggressive move on my aircraft.

Nothing; they didn't move. We concluded that they were scared shitless, and rightfully so.

"Something doesn't seem right," Sammy said. "What do you guys think?"

"Same from us. This is so weird," I said.

"Let's stand down," Sammy said.

"Gator, we've been observing them for a while now. We're not sure if they're bad guys or not, so we're not going to shoot. We're headed back to J-bad, but we'll let the next Kiowa team know what's going on and make sure they come take a look," Chris said.

"Roger, Annihilator."

I turned the aircraft to head out of the valley and head back to J-bad. As we got closer to the airfield, the battle captain from our headquarters came on the radio.

"We have an update for the valley you guys just left," the captain said. "There has been some tribal infighting in that area over mineral and gem rights. They are seriously having to defend their land right now from another tribe, so we think that's what you guys stumbled onto."

Wow. Afghanistan was like the Wild West. We called these Afghans gem farmers—the ones we would find in the hills who dug enormous holes in the side of the mountain to mine for gems. Afghanistan had lots of native lapis and other precious stones, and some tribes made a living from mining.

Chris and I had already come up with a system where we categorized all the Afghans. There were five types of people in this country: rock farmers, dirt farmers, gem farmers, animal farmers, or terrorists posing as one of those four. (We were thinking of adding another category, water farmers, but we hadn't made that one official yet.)

We were tested that day. Fortunately, we let the situation develop and we didn't go in guns blazing, even after we were cleared to shoot. We exercised our best judgment based on what we knew at the time, and we trusted our instincts. Tactical patience and team coordination had paid off.

———

"Chris got hit," Deidra said as she ran into the B-hut.

I was confused. Chris got hit with what? He couldn't have been flying. We were on the same flight schedule and I wasn't flying, so he couldn't have gotten hit by enemy fire. What the hell happened?

Deidra had walked into her mission brief at headquarters and had heard the news. Chris had been walking to our pilots' office to call his wife. Because of the time difference, a lot of us made the trek over to the office late at night to make phone calls back to the States. J-bad is a blacked-out FOB—it has no lights on at night for tactical reasons. Medevac helicopters had just come in to land near the road where Chris was walking, their rotor blades drowning out any other sound. An American soldier on a four-wheeler had come speeding around a corner and hit Chris.

The force of being struck threw Chris flying through the air and broke his right tibia, fractured his pelvis, shifted the bottom portion of his pelvis, dislocated his right hip, fractured his skull and right hand, and broke five vertebrae in his spine.

We had a surgical team at J-bad, so when I heard he'd been flown to Bagram in a medevac, the biggest air base in Afghanistan, I knew his injuries must be life-threatening. No one could tell me if he would survive. All we knew was that he was clinging to life and they were hoping that, if he survived the trip to Bagram, they'd be able to get him to Germany for even better medical care.

The thought of not knowing whether Chris would make it almost killed me. How could this happen to him? The guy who used to sing Shakira to me in the cockpit and teach me Spanish, who had a bright aviation career in front of him. He had to survive. He had to.

If anyone was a fighter, it was Chris.

Chris made it to Germany, and after that to Walter Reed, where he stayed for two weeks. The doctors gave him morphine for the pain and it knocked him out. Eventually Chris was transferred to a VA hospital in Richmond, Virginia, and after that he went back to Walter Reed for the long haul of physical therapy and occupational therapy.

Chris and I never flew together again. But my stick buddy was alive, and that was all that mattered.

22

GOOD-BYE

July 2008

Bagram, Afghanistan

After a long winter and spring of missions, things were changing in Alpha Troop.

Chris was in Walter Reed; Sammy was moving to another troop. Our team would never fly together again. I had assumed we'd spend the whole war together. We had melded into such an effective team, just like my Iraq team. We knew each other's strengths and weaknesses, knew what would piss each other off, and adjusted accordingly. We trusted each other. Then just like that, we were all separated.

It had been hard losing Chris, and it would be hard to lose Sammy, too. Sammy had been putting me through AMC training ever since we arrived in Afghanistan. After about four months of flying in Afghanistan, I was signed off as an AMC. In my almost four years in Alpha Troop, I'd realized that becoming a proficient AMC had about 20 percent to do with training and 80 percent with experience, decision making, and being able to see the mission big picture—from a wide field of view, from the ground perspective, from the Kiowa perspective, and from the headquarters perspective, all at once. At any given time we could be working with the ground guys, a medevac, an inbound Kiowa replacement team, artillery, fighter jets, fuel problems, ammo issues, weather—oh, and the enemy. AMCs have to take all of those different elements of the mission, listening to all of the radio transmissions and replying, and make the best decision for all involved.

Alpha Troop had received orders that a chunk of the unit was moving to FOB Salerno—a base on the southern side of the Tora Bora Mountains near Khost—on the border with Pakistan. The rest of the unit, including Katie and I, would remain in J-bad. The last member of my team, Deidra, was moving to Salerno, too. I was relieved that I didn't have to make the move there, which would involve learning a new AO, as well as new ground guys, but I was going to miss my troop. I didn't like the idea of having to switch saddles and fly with a new gang, but the transition was happening. There was nothing I could do about it.

———

Even with all the bad news, I was happy when my older sister, Kelly, arrived in Afghanistan with her C-130 Channel Islands Air Guard unit out of California. She would be based in Bagram for the next ninety days. J-bad and Bagram were nowhere near each other, but C-130s flew into J-bad all the time. I was determined to see Kelly if she ever flew in.

One day, Kelly emailed me that she'd be coming through J-bad the next day. I was on nights, so it meant I would have to wake up in the middle of the day, but I would have walked to Bagram to see her if they would have let me.

Kelly could give me only a rough estimate of when she would land. Other than that, we'd have no communication to link up. I didn't sleep with earplugs that day so I'd be able to hear the C-130 when it came in. No earplugs meant no sleep, since my bed was less than fifty meters from the runway.

I finally heard the rumble of the C-130 engines as the plane touched down on the runway and taxied over to the transient parking area, right by our B-huts. I jumped up, grabbed my M9 pistol, and put it in my shoulder holster as I ran out. In the aircraft parking area, the C-130 was parked with its engines still running and a long single-file line of soldiers waited their turn to climb on board through the extended back ramp. Kelly and I wouldn't have much time—their turnaround was pretty quick.

It was obvious to the other soldiers that I was not meant to be getting on the plane, since I was wearing my M9 pistol, and most of these soldiers were flying to Bagram for R&R, so they didn't take their weapons with them. (It's the only time you are allowed to travel in Afghanistan without your weapon.) My best chance to make it over to the plane without being noticed (and therefore turned away) was to walk as nonchalantly as possible on the side where no people were, so I headed over to the opposite side of the taxiway.

Then I saw Kelly climbing down the steps from the cockpit wearing her body armor and black sunglasses. She saw me, too, and began walking in my direction. Before we'd even reached each other we both broke out in two huge Smith smiles. Her hug felt like home to me. How crazy it felt to have my sister there, at my "home" in Afghanistan. We could barely hear each other because of the noise from the engines, but we didn't care. Just to be in each other's presence was a much-needed two-minute mental vacation. For those two minutes, we weren't at war; Chris wasn't wounded at Walter Reed; my team hadn't gotten split up; my troop wasn't moving; people weren't dying.

Once we stopped hugging, I got to board the C-130 and climb into the cockpit for a minute to check it out and meet Kelly's other pilots. Eventually, though, the single-file line of soldiers heading for their R&R had almost disappeared, and I gave Kelly one last hug before I climbed down the steps of her C-130 and ran away from the aircraft.

I yelled, "Fly safe!" but I was certain the engine noise was too loud for her to hear me. I walked back to the entrance of our B-huts and watched the C-130 taxi by. I waved and saw Kelly waving back through the cockpit windows. I was so proud of her. She had worked hard to become a C-130 pilot.

Kelly's C-130 roared down the runway and lifted off into the sky. I watched the plane until it was only a little speck in the sky off in the distance. And then it was gone.

More changes were coming.

A C-130 had been reportedly shot at by a missile during takeoff from Bagram air base. There was an increase of attacks at the base and even a perimeter breach. The powers that be decided there needed to be Kiowas at Bagram to conduct recon and security operations to help protect the airfield. A handful of Kiowa pilots would go from J-bad to Bagram to join other Kiowa pilots, who were being moved from Kandahar. In effect, they were creating a new hybrid unit of an attack force—half Apache, half Kiowa.

I immediately volunteered. My troop was already being split up. I wanted to be on the same base as Kelly, but my commander shot down the idea, although the sister factor didn't play into their decision making. I was upset, but it's the Army. I had learned to get over things that were out of my control.

Soon after my commander turned me down, I opened the door to my B-hut and there was Ed Dalsey. As a senior warrant officer and an instructor pilot, he had some pull.

"When does your sister leave Bagram?" Ed asked.

"I think sometime in August, but I'm not sure exactly."

"Mike Slebodnik and I are going to go talk to the commander in the next few days to see if we can straighten this out. They are sending pilots up to Bagram, and there's no reason that it shouldn't be you, especially since your sister is there. You should be first priority," Ed said.

I couldn't believe they were going to do this for me. Mike Slebodnik was now my lead instructor pilot in J-bad, since most of my troop had left. I'd been with him since I first got to Alpha Troop back in 2004.

I walked up to Mike's B-hut and knocked on the door.

"Mike, are you in here?" I yelled as I opened the door a crack.

"Hey!" Mike replied as I saw him appear in the doorway.

"Just wanted to say thanks for your help with trying to get me to move to Bagram," I said.

"Sure, no problem. I think if you have family in-country, and they need people to fill positions, you should be first priority. I don't see why it should be an issue," he said.

I turned to go.

"Oh, hey, can I take you up on your offer to cut hair?" Mike continued. Earlier in the deployment, I'd offered to cut some of the guys' hair. Nothing fancy. Just the standard cut with hair clippers. They needed it.

"Are you sure?" I asked, laughing.

"Yeah, let's do it," he said. "You can't mess it up that bad, just cut it all off."

"You got it."

Mike headed back inside to grab his clippers and a chair.

"Here you go," he said when he came back outside and opened the folding chair outside the entryway of the B-hut.

"Here goes nothing!" I said.

I didn't make him bleed, so the haircut was successful.

———

A few days later I was told I was moving to Bagram and that the Black Hawk to fly me there was leaving early the next morning. I had only a few hours to pack up everything I had brought to Afghanistan and lug it out to Black Hawk parking to load it on the aircraft. My bedding. My clothes. My flight gear and the contents of my desk over in the pilots' office on the other side of the runway.

I was suddenly overwhelmed. *Had I made the right choice? Did I really want to leave all of my people and AO that I knew?* But it was a done deal. I got over it.

The next morning, my stuff and I were on board a Black Hawk headed for Bagram.

23

LUCKY STRIKE

July 2008

Bagram, Afghanistan

"Welcome to Bagram!" Captain Wolfe said, jumping out of his Gator utility vehicle to shake my hand.

I had landed at Bagram airfield to join Lucky Strike, G/6-101, the newly created unit of half Kiowas and half Apaches. It was July 2008, and our unit was halfway through our deployment.

Captain Matt Wolfe was the new commander of Lucky Strike. He had just finished his command of Bravo Troop in Kandahar, and since most commissioned officers would not turn down a second command opportunity, especially in combat, here he was.

Captain Wolfe had a reputation as an awesome commander and a good pilot. He didn't care what anyone thought about him, including his superiors. He was definitely not a kiss-ass, so most warrant officers liked and respected him. Because of his reputation, I was looking forward to joining Lucky Strike.

Once I'd loaded all my gear onto his Gator, Captain Wolfe drove me to my new home: another B-hut. Then I saw the line of Porta Potties. My world was crushed. Down in J-bad, we'd heard that the people at Bagram got to live in real buildings with real bathrooms and showers. Bagram was like this shiny, mythical city to us. The truth, it seemed, was that it was just a really big J-bad.

At least my new B-hut room had a door on it, which I didn't have in my J-bad B-hut. I hoped my laundry would turn out better than at J-bad. I was pretty sure that they had washed our clothes in the little canals that ran next to the base. Anything I turned in that was white came back a grayish-brown color and always smelled bad. That said, pilots still had it better than the ground guys, who had zero options for laundry, but everyone knows that pilots are prissy. Kiowa pilots were just the least prissy of the bunch.

I unpacked my gear to make myself at home. I was in love with my new door, even though it didn't stop a thick layer of dirt, dust, and sand from settling on my laptop and everything else in my room. At least no bugs were visible, which was a welcome change from J-bad's infestations. The wind was incredibly strong at Bagram, blowing sand, dust, and dirt particles constantly. My nose was packed with sand, more like being in Iraq than J-bad.

My first day in Bagram was like a *real* day off. I was free of my duties at J-bad and hadn't yet begun my duties at Bagram. I found Kelly working in the pilots' office and we got some time together after her shift was up.

That first night I awoke to a terrible sound: a grinding, high-pitched whine of afterburner engines. The F-16s always did afterburner takeoffs out of Bagram—essentially they flew straight up into the air to get to a safe altitude as soon as possible. It looked cool, and it even sounded cool—*once*. But it woke me up every two hours, so the novelty wore off fast. Even worse than the F-16s were the EA-6B Prowlers flown by the Navy. The Prowler is a twin-engine plane that resembles a fighter plane but is engaged in electronic warfare—jamming radar and the like.

At six fifteen on my first full morning, I stood awkwardly at the bus stop waiting for a ride to the pilots' office and our helicopters. I felt like the new kid in high school; all the other pilots knew each other. The bus ride took almost thirty minutes to get to the other side of the airfield.

We were driving during restricted hours because the airfield had shut down the main road, allowing soldiers to conduct PT on that route. Our bus had to have a special permit to drive during those hours, even though we had to use that route to get to work. The military police, who wanted to flex their muscles, would always pull us over. It was the most ridiculous thing. Did these people forget that there's a war going on outside the safety of this FOB? I would come to realize that this was one of the most frustrating things about being on a big base such as Bagram. A lot of the people based there never left the safety of the FOB, never saw the war going on outside the wire, so it was easy for them to get wrapped up in driving procedures and pick fights with Kiowa pilots who were trying to get to work to do their jobs (which, in case anyone forgot, was in part to protect this very base).

We made it to the pilots' office without anyone getting arrested. As I walked through the hangar I noticed a pile of fur rugs by the commander's truck, a two-door 1980s Bronco spray-painted flat desert tan. Captain Wolfe and one of his Apache lieutenants were measuring the wheels and the length of the truck for fur hubcaps and side paneling.

Yes. There was a fur-covered Bronco cruising around Bagram. It reminded me of the "Shaggin' Wagon" from the movie *Dumb and Dumber*. It was just one of the many idiosyncrasies that made this mix of Kiowa and Apache pilots very . . . special.

My workdays typically lasted a minimum of thirteen hours. Some days we flew for six or eight of those hours; other days we flew only a couple. I liked flying with the Lucky Strike guys. They were super laid back, both in the way they flew and back at the office. I'm not quite sure how you can be super aggressive and effective on missions and laid back at the same time, but these guys accomplished that.

My new AO included Kabul, the Bagram bowl, and the Tagab River Valley, all the way down to where my old AO at J-bad ended. The Tagab was a known hot spot with a hive of enemy fighters. Back at J-bad we had primarily worked with the 173rd Airborne, which was an incredible infantry unit; it had been an honor to fight alongside them. In Bagram we worked with all sorts of NATO forces: French, Romanian, and German. The only U.S. forces we worked with, aside from patrols directly around Bagram, were a small group of Marines embedded with some ANA soldiers and a Special Forces unit in the Tagab.

Because of all these forces, flying in Bagram airspace was a real shit show. It was actually nice to leave Bagram airspace and get out into the AO where the bad guys would shoot at you, since at least for the most part we were safe from the midairs with friendly helicopters and planes that were a constant risk within the Bagram bowl.

The Russians were a whole other level of problem. "Vodka" was the call sign for the Russian Mi-17 helicopters that often flew into Kabul and Bagram. We always had to be on the lookout for Vodka when we were flying in the Bagram bowl because they never made radio calls to let the other helicopter traffic in the area know their position. These guys constantly busted Bagram airspace without clearance. They spoke with thick Russian accents and didn't seem to understand English at the level that was needed to fly there.

No one was more frustrated with Vodka than the air traffic controllers. But Vodka ignored their scolding. We'd overhear their fights on the radio.

"VODKA! You just broke Bagram airspace without calling me. Say your position and intentions!" the guy in the tower yelled.

A cargo plane on final approach to land had to put in full power to abort because Vodka flew near the approach end of the runway.

"Vodka-come-to-land," Vodka said.

"You have to call me before you come into my airspace!" the controller screamed. "UNDERSTAND? We have other aircraft in this airspace we have to deconflict you with. You just made an aircraft abort its landing!"

"Vodka-come-to-land," Vodka said.

"VODKA, GET OUT OF MY AIRSPACE! NOW! GET OUT! AND DON'T COME BACK!"

"Vodka-arrive-Bagram," I heard over the radio as I saw the Mi-17 come to a hover over one of the helicopter landing areas.

Even though the situation was dangerous, we all laughed. The blood pressure of the guy in the Bagram tower must have been off the charts.

———

When I was on the day shift, I would wake up at 4:00 a.m. and go for a fifty-minute run. It was nice and quiet at that time of the morning. My route took me from my B-hut, on the perimeter road, all the way down to the east end of the runway, past the trash burn pits (which were always disgusting), and over to where the Military Police kept their working dogs. Those German shepherd–type dogs always scared the shit out of me. Every time I ran by them, they barked and snarled at me. I was terrified that one would get free and attack me; their cages didn't look very secure. On the way back I usually got stuck running behind the water truck—it had a little sprinkler on the back that sprayed down the road. But it always stirred up dust, too, which meant I ate a mixture of nonpotable water and Afghan moon dust.

Kelly started waking up early and running with me during the last couple of weeks she was there before heading home. I appreciated being able to be myself and let my guard down around her. I was sad she was leaving, but I was happy for the time we got to spend together and that she was getting out of this place.

A few times I went to dinner with Kelly and her guys. It was such a different dynamic from what I was used to. They still talked to each other, still laughed at the stupid stuff. I missed that life, that easy-going, carefree attitude. My guys and I had gotten to the point in the deployment where there was nothing left to talk about. Even though I was now with a new troop, we were from the same brigade, so we were familiar with one another and we'd all been deployed for the same amount of time. The jokes were no longer funny. We quickly learned as much about one another as we cared to know. Now the bus was silent, the office hushed—boredom had set in. It was like the fun had been sucked out of us. That's what happens when you deploy for a year. We were all sick of one another.

One night, Kelly managed to borrow her unit's truck so she could drive me around the airfield and drop me off at work. It was kind of a big deal. Not having to take the bus to work gave me a sense of freedom and independence I hadn't felt in a while. Kelly had never seen a Kiowa up close in combat before. She'd transported them folded up on her C-130 but had never seen them in action. For transportation, Kiowas can fold their rotor blades to make them more compact and easier to transport.

I had to fly that night, so I still had premission work to do after our mission brief.

"Want to come preflight the aircraft with me?" I asked Kelly once we got to the hangar.

"Sure!" she said.

I got my aircraft assignment, read through the maintenance log-book to make sure the aircraft was good to go, grabbed my helmet and flight bag, and headed out to the Kiowa. I showed Kelly all the parts and pieces of the aircraft. I opened the engine cowling to point out different components of the engine and drive shaft that ran down the tail boom to the tail rotor. We carefully climbed on top of the helicopter to check out the rotor system and inspect the four blades for any sign of damage or wear. After we crawled back down, the ammo soldiers arrived to load the .50-cal machine gun with 350 rounds and four high-explosive rockets.

I spotted my pilots walking toward the aircraft.

"We've got to launch," one of them said.

"I've gotta go," I said to Kelly. "Thanks so much for driving me over and hanging out. It was so much fun to have you here. Love you." I gave her a big hug.

I got in the aircraft and started to put on my seat belt.

"Love you! Be careful!" Kelly yelled as she walked a safe distance away from the helicopter.

I started the Kiowa, picked up to a hover, and began to fly toward the runway. Kelly was still standing there, watching as we took off into the night sky. She waved. I knew she probably couldn't see me, but I waved back. Then I turned off all the lights as we flew across the wire of the base and disappeared into the black Afghan night.

24

KIA

September 2008

Bagram, Afghanistan

On my return trip to Afghanistan after a two-week R&R in the States, we had made a stopover in Kuwait, where I met a Marine who was returning, too. He was cute and smiley and seemed to want to chat. I was wearing my flight suit, which made me stand out a little from everyone else wearing the normal Army combat uniform.

"Are you a pilot?" the Marine said.

"Yep, a Kiowa pilot."

A smile crept onto his face.

"Are you out of Bagram?"

"Yes," I said, wondering where he was going with this.

"Are you Lucky Strike?"

"Yeah! Our troop call sign is Lucky Strike and my call sign is Annihilator Two-Four," I said.

"No shit! You guys fly for us all the time! I'm one of the Marines on the ETT in the Tagab."

"No way! That is so cool that I finally get to put a face to a voice

I always talk to on the radio. Next time we are out there covering you guys, I'll say hello."

"My lieutenant is going to be so jealous I got to meet you," he said, laughing.

"Well, tell him I said hello, too," I said.

Embedded training teams, or ETTs, were small groups of American soldiers who were embedded with the Afghan army to lead, advise, train, and support. They had an extremely dangerous job because they were usually outnumbered and in the middle of nowhere. Additionally, training the Afghan soldiers was a challenge in itself. There was always the threat of green-on-blue attacks—a tactic used by the enemy to join the ranks of the Afghan army with the sole purpose of killing as many American soldiers as possible.

When we arrived at Bagram, we said our good-byes and went our separate ways.

A few days after being back in Afghanistan, I walked up the steps of the little bus stop outside our B-hut living area, kicking up the dirty moon dust with every step. I'd gotten used to eating that moon dust as part of my daily diet. It was 6:30 p.m. but the heat was still in full force and I was on my way to work. I threw my backpack on one of the seats, put in my earphones to listen to my music, and the bus began the thirty-minute drive around the airfield to our hangar for the night shift.

In the office, I saw my friend and fellow pilot CW2 Sam Mansfield, one of the few female pilots in 2-17 CAV when I arrived in 2004. Originally in Bravo Troop, she had come up to Bagram to join Lucky Strike for the rest of the deployment, as I had. We'd gotten to fly together once in combat. I'm pretty sure all the guys thought the aircraft was going to erupt in flames, but what do you know, it didn't. It was pretty rare for two women to fly in the same cockpit, mainly because there were so few of us.

"Just got done with a nine-hour flight," Sam said.

"Yuck. Why?"

"You know the Marine ETT out in the Tagab?"

"Yeah, I actually met one of them coming back from R&R, and apparently their lieutenant has a crush on me," I said.

Sam looked at me without smiling.

"They were out driving through the Afghanya Valley today, hit an IED, and it killed two Marines, a Navy sailor, and their Afghan interpreter," Sam said.

I felt the blood drain from my face. I closed my eyes and saw the Marine I had met in Kuwait. These were our guys, the ones we protected. Based on the information we had about the rank of the Marines killed, I knew the Marine I'd met was okay—but his lieutenant wasn't. He was one of the three killed. I never got the chance to tell him hello.

Every time I heard about a U.S. soldier getting killed, it pained my heart. It was a reality of war I never accepted. When it was someone I'd met, one of their buddies, or someone I'd talked to on the radio, it ripped my heart right open. This was how Afghanistan welcomed me back.

━━━━━━━

It was the seventh anniversary of 9/11, and I was glad to be on the flight schedule. It was an excellent reminder of why we were all here. I was flying lead for Captain Bryan Woody, who had been my Charlie Troop commander for a few months back at J-bad. As I headed toward the crew chief shack to get my aircraft assignment, I saw my friend Sam again. Her eyes locked with mine. From the look on her face, I knew. Someone's dead.

NO! I silently screamed. *Who was it?*

"Amber, I need to talk to you," she said.

I didn't want to know. Knowing made it real, and I didn't want it to be real.

"What?" I finally said. "WHAT?"

"Mike was shot and killed today."

CW4 Mike Slebodnik—my instructor, my friend, the guy who could make anyone smile, and who had helped get me to Bagram.

"I'm so sorry, Amber," Sam said. "They were responding to a TIC and they took small-arms fire. Mike got hit in the leg with an AK-47 round. His copilot was able to land the Kiowa at COP Najil. A medevac took Mike back to Bagram but he didn't make it. Mike bled out."

Najil? I'd flown there many times when I was living at J-bad. It was a tiny U.S. outpost on the east side of the Tagab River Valley Mountains, north of Mehtar Lam. I knew the exact spot.

Mike had won the lottery in reverse. He had been unbelievably unlucky: the bullet that left that AK-47 on the ground and hit Mike's leg had traveled through the air, gone through the gap between the armor plate—meant to protect the pilot—and the seat.

Often during deployments you got immune to the threat of death, which was actually an important defense mechanism because you had to be able to do your job. You had to let go of the fear and tell yourself that things were beyond your control. We all had been lucky when we had responded to TICs, all the times we'd been shot at, the time an AK-47 round stopped twelve inches behind my back in Iraq. Just another close call. But deep down, every time you took off and left the wire, you knew there was a chance that you wouldn't be coming home that day. You just accepted it and charged forward.

We dealt with death on almost every mission. Ground guys, Afghan army, Afghan police, civilians, the enemy. But this time it was Mike.

I closed my eyes and remembered just a few months ago right before I moved to Bagram, Mike had been showing me photos of his wife and kids, and told me how much he was looking forward to October, when he was scheduled to go home for R&R to see them. Now that would never happen.

Captain Wolfe asked me to be a pallbearer for Mike's "ramp cere-mony," also called a fallen comrade ceremony, which is the final transfer of the body from Afghanistan onto the plane that will take the soldier home to the United States. A ramp ceremony is conducted for every soldier who is killed during a deployment. They are always solemn and gut-wrenching. Soldiers line the streets as the Humvee that carries the American flag–draped transfer case—the military's term for casket, a silver-colored metal container—drives by. There is a moment of silence and then in unison every soldier gives a final salute.

I was honored to be a pallbearer, although doing so for one of my friends was going to be one of the hardest things I'd ever had to do. But I knew Mike would have done it for me.

The next morning, the eight pallbearers, including Captain Woody, arrived at the mortuary affairs site to pick up Mike. The transfer case with Mike's body was placed in the back of a trailer pulled by a Hum-vee, and we all crawled in to sit on the bench seats next to Mike. We sat in silence, facing toward one another, the transfer case between us, as we drove along the same road we took to work every day.

Soldiers lined Disney—the road we traveled along to get to the airfield—in their ACUs, coming to attention and raising their right hands to salute as we passed. In that instant, I was so proud to be surrounded by such amazing Americans who understood that freedom was not without a price. They had come out to honor and pay their respects to Mike and others like him, who had paid for our freedoms with their lives.

After a nearly mile-long procession, the Humvee made a right turn onto the airfield, which was lined with soldiers as far as we could see. A small formation of uniformed soldiers stood near the C-17 cargo plane that would carry Mike's body home after the ceremony. As the Humvee neared the plane, it slowed to a stop. We each waited our turn to get out of the trailer. Then, in unison, we slid the flag-draped casket out.

Left left leeeeft right. Left left leeeeft right.

The eight pallbearers silently marched Mike to a stand where his casket would rest for the ceremony, next to the back end of the aircraft where the ramp was lowered. We placed his transfer case on the stand, took a synchronized step back, and saluted. Then we marched to the formation next to the ramp. One by one we took turns walking by the casket to say good-bye.

When it was my turn, I thought, *How could this be happening?* I placed my hand on the field of blue with white stars of the flag. *I'm so sorry, Mike. Thank you for everything. Rest easy.*

I saluted and walked back to formation. I took long, deep breaths, trying to control my tears, but they flowed anyway. As we stood there, our squadron commander from J-bad walked through the ranks. He shook my hand as tears ran down his face, too. We looked at each other in silence. There was nothing anyone could say.

"Taps" began to play. I looked around at all the faces of my fellow Kiowa pilots, people who had known Mike and with whom I had shared both wars. It could have been any one of us. Why were we alive and Mike was in a casket about to be loaded onto the C-17?

Then the ceremony was over.

"Dismissed!" I heard the soldier in front of the formation yell.

I broke away from the group and began to walk back to the entrance of the flight line. I wanted to be alone. Since I'd been told the news about Mike, I pretty much hadn't slept. I needed to process it all somehow, and I didn't want to do it in front of everyone.

As I walked away, I saw a familiar face: Katie. She had been closer to Mike than I was, and she was sobbing. I ran over to give her a hug.

"I just saw him," Katie said. "I just talked with him."

"I know," I said. "Me, too."

A few days later, some of the Kiowa pilots from Bagram boarded a Black Hawk en route to our squadron headquarters in J-bad for Mike's CAV memorial. Kiowa pilots were flying in from all across Afghanistan—Salerno, Kandahar, Bagram—to participate in the ceremony and remember Mike.

On the way, I looked at Afghanistan from the door frame of the Black Hawk. Highway 1 was out my right door and Mehtar Lam my left. I'd spent so much time flying here. The Black Hawk banked right toward J-bad airfield as we flew over the city. Nothing seemed to have changed since I had left.

But it had.

25

THE TAGAB

Fall 2008

Tagab River Valley, Afghanistan

Back in June, before I made the move to Bagram, I had flown lead for Captain Woody, our AMC for the flight. We were headed toward Mehtar Lam, northwest of J-bad, when an ANA unit out on patrol called in a TIC. They had no U.S. forces with them, so we were relaying from the radio operator at the nearby base. As I flew over the ANA location, the Afghan soldiers were pointing to a hill west of them.

"Looks like they are taking fire from the ridgeline," I said to trail over the radio. "I'm going to pick up some airspeed and fly low and fast to the hill and then bump up and see what's going on back there."

I increased the collective flight control to give me more power to gain speed, then I flew the Kiowa low, about fifty feet above the ground. As we approached the ridge, I bumped the aircraft up in altitude and pointed the nose down so my copilot would have a good angle to see the terrain.

Right on the other side of the ridge were three grown men dressed in black man dresses with AK-47s and a bandoleer of brass bullets in an X shape across their chests.

I couldn't believe my eyes. Who did they think they were, Rambo? It was the easiest—and most ridiculous—positive enemy ID ever.

As soon as they realized they'd been caught, the enemy froze. Then as one, they all ran—right into each other, like in a cartoon.

I laughed out loud.

There was nowhere for them to go. We had them in our sights. You can't run from a helicopter once you've been spotted, and they knew it.

Then all of a sudden, they dived off the edge of the ravine and tumbled down the side of the mountain. Luckily for them, the rock face was covered with trees, and we lost them in the terrain. They had chosen to take their chances jumping off a cliff rather than being on the receiving end of a .50-cal machine gun.

I didn't know at the time, but those occasions when we had to do hand and arm signals to communicate with the ANA were actually great practice for what I encountered daily in Bagram working with the French military. A French base in the Tagab River Valley was home to French infantry, and we worked with them nearly every time we flew in the valley. The biggest struggle was communicating with them over the radio.

At J-bad we had worked primarily with U.S. forces, some of whom were embedded with the Afghan National Army. Once in a while we would have to respond to a TIC that solely involved the ANA. To get by, we would talk to a U.S. radio operator who had a translator with him. Sometimes the ANA forces on the ground would call the base to tell the Afghan translator where they were getting shot from and who they wanted the Kiowas to shoot at. The Afghan interpreter would then translate the message, and the U.S. soldier would finally relay the information to us. It was like a child's game of "telephone," only during combat. The reality, of course, was that this form of communication was impractical and extremely dangerous. But the lack of communication I encountered working with the French was at a whole new level.

That autumn in Bagram, after one of our mission time blocks was over, it was time to head home. We had spent most of our mission looking at suspicious areas around the valley in support of the Special Forces team that was based right in the middle of it. That day we were in the middle of the Tagab. It had been an uneventful exercise, which basically meant "not dying," which was, of course, always welcome.

"Are you guys good on gas to get back to Bagram?" I radioed to my trail aircraft. If the answer was "no," we would have to fly up the valley and stop at Morales-Fraiser base, where they had a FARP, and refuel.

"Yep, we're good. Let's head direct to Bagram," CW3 Toby Long said.

"I'm going to climb up to fly over the ridge, then," I said.

"Roger, we're behind you," Toby said.

There was a ridgeline on the west side of the Tagab that separated it from the Bagram bowl. We would have to climb to at least two thousand feet to fly over it.

As we gained altitude, it was nice to see Afghanistan from a different perspective—that is, from a distance. Everything looked quieter, almost peaceful, from above.

When we were almost at the same altitude as the ridge we had to cross, I turned the Kiowa toward Bagram. As I did so, a flash of light north of our location caught my eye. I saw movement at the mouth of the valley but couldn't make out what it was, as it was moving too fast through the air.

"Do you see—" I said, but before I could finish my sentence, an enormous fighter jet roared by the right side of my helicopter and tore between me and my trail aircraft, the sound jarring my brain. White light exploded all around me like fireworks. It was the jet's defensive flares, used as a decoy for heat-seeking missiles. The aircraft's detection system had sensed our Kiowa's heat emission and triggered its flares to shoot off all around us.

Every fighter jet I'd ever worked with flew in pairs, so I knew his wingman was likely right behind him and would be coming through the valley any second.

I pulled in the collective to make us go faster, but it seemed like we were in snail speed mode. Nothing could have gotten us out of that valley fast enough. A few seconds went by before I could make sound come out of my mouth.

"Are you guys okay back there?" I finally managed to ask my trail Kiowa.

"Holy shit, we almost died," Toby said. "I've never been that close to a Mirage before."

A Mirage. The French fly Mirage jets.

"Kutschbach base! This is Annihilator Two-Four. Do you guys have any fixed-wing on station, working in the Tagab?" I radioed to the U.S. base in the Tagab.

"This is Kutschbach, Annihilator. No, you guys are the only air traffic we have right now."

I was furious. What an asshole that pilot was. Fighter jets weren't supposed to be down this low. Rotary wing helicopters and fixed-wing planes are separated by altitude for airspace deconfliction so that once we are outside of a certain radius of an airfield, we never have to worry about planes. Those fighter planes have to request specific clearance and precoordinate with airspace control if they need to fly this low.

For guys who weren't in the fight day in and day out, getting in on some of the action was "fun" for them. I'd seen this kind of showboating before. I knew the pilot didn't have any malicious intent; he was just complacent and stupid.

This was a too-close reminder that it's not only the enemy that can kill you. Mistakes, miscommunication, friendly fire—all of these things can make you just as dead. It's one thing to have the enemy constantly trying to take you out, but when it's someone on the same team, acting idiotically and putting lives at risk, it's infuriating.

Luckily his wingman never came. We continued flying toward Bagram in silence, all four of us shaken at how we had just cheated death.

After that, every time I walked into the hangar and saw that our mission was to work with the French, I was on guard. Most of the Lucky Strike Kiowa pilots needed to get our hearts checked for the stress we faced from working with them every day. We loved the French and we were both out there on the same side fighting the same enemy, but the language barrier was about as frustrating as it got. Plus we used different radio systems, so we had to communicate over the radio with our squelch off, meaning that the function that minimizes background noise wasn't operational, so we had to listen to the equivalent of a screeching fax machine.

One day, after we had broken six hours of flying, and it didn't seem like our mission would be over anytime soon, my upper back and neck were tightening up and the sciatic nerve on the left side of my butt was on fire. It always flared up when we flew this long in the tiny, cramped cockpit of the Kiowa. Working with the French was literally a pain in my ass.

The day had been chaotic. It was a big operation for the French. They had different friendly elements scattered all over the valley— some on the top of the ridgeline, some down in the villages, others on the main dirt roads. There had to be more than a hundred French soldiers out there.

The French were taking fire from the enemy, we were taking fire, they were shooting, we were shooting. Mortars were being launched by the French before airspace had been cleared, and they kept trying to get the U.S. A-10 Warthogs to drop bombs, but those pilots refused in order to avoid collateral damage.

I only wanted us (and them) to get out of there alive. It had taken all four pilots in our Kiowas to make sure nothing bad happened thus far. I was PC in the lead, listening to every radio message, attempting to stay up to date with what was happening on the ground—and not get hit by enemy fire or a rogue mortar. My copilot was trying to translate the broken English of the French radio operator but was having a hard time explaining that all of their friendlies had to be accounted for and clear of the target area before we could shoot.

We didn't always trust the targets the French gave us to shoot at. They had a history of inadvertently giving us the wrong enemy positions—including, once in a while, positions taken by their own infantry. So while we were happy to shoot for the American ground troops, we were often reluctant to pull the trigger for the French.

"We have about eight minutes left here before we have to break station for fuel," I said over the radio to the small element of U.S. ground forces who were out with the French on the main dirt road that ran along the valley. "I think it's time for you guys to get out of there and return to base. The French a couple hundred meters to the east of you are taking heavy fire every time we leave the area for more than thirty seconds and we're leaving in a few for fuel."

"Roger," a U.S. soldier said.

The U.S. guys didn't need to be told twice. They grabbed their stuff and ran to their vehicles to move out. The French who were standing near their position followed their lead.

We flew over what was left of the French ground forces on the front line. They were positioned on a large boulder, their weapons pointed toward the enemy, still taking heavy fire. They began to run back toward to road, taking cover where they could. They needed to make it about two hundred meters north of their location to the main road, where they could rendezvous and head out of the valley and back to safety.

We had no eyes on the enemy's location from the air. They had excellent concealment from the terrain as well as the mud hut villages scattered all over the place.

I turned the Kiowa back to head out of the valley and saw an unbelievable sight: on the road below us a long line of French soldiers was streaming out of the valley, some in vehicles, others running behind them. It was a full-blown retreat.

"Annihilator!" someone in a French accent shouted over the radio. "We left some equipment and need you to blow it up!"

"Roger, we'll check it out, but be advised, as we mentioned earlier, we are almost out of fuel and have to head back to refuel in a few minutes."

"We need you to blow it up before you go," the voice said.

My copilot put the grid in our nav system and I turned the helicopter toward it. Fortunately, it was only thirty seconds away from our position, but when we reached the spot a group of Afghanis had arrived.

And then I saw why.

The French had left three antitank missiles—likely Milans—on the boulder, as well as a scope device on a tripod and a rucksack filled with the equipment required for the Milans to be fired.

Holy shit—this stuff could not fall into the enemy's hands. This was serious weaponry that could be used against U.S. and NATO soldiers, especially their convoys. We circled the weapons, hoping to keep the Afghans from taking them.

"We've got eyes on the weapons," my copilot radioed to the French. "You guys need to come back now and get them. Those weapons CANNOT be left out here. They are going to fall into enemy hands."

"No, you shoot the weapons," a French voice said.

"We can't shoot them! We are out of fuel and there are civilians everywhere!" my copilot said.

"No, no," was all the reply we got.

"Hey, I'm bingo," I radioed to my trail aircraft. We had to get fuel.

"We are, too. Let's go."

We had pushed our fuel limits to stay over the abandoned weapons as long as we could, but now I had to turn the Kiowa in the direction of the Morales-Fraiser base at the north end of the valley, where we would land to get fuel. I was furious. I hated that we had to leave those weapons out there unsecured. It was like handing the enemy a trophy.

We flew as fast as we could to the refuel spot to minimize our turnaround time. Maybe if we were fast enough we could get back out there in time and the Milans would still be there. Even I knew I was being overly optimistic.

As we sat in refuel, I listened to our trail aircraft relay the events to higher headquarters over the radio. I looked over at my copilot, who looked as beat to shit as I felt. This mission had worn out all four of us. By now we had broken the maximum eight-hour flight limit, though we'd been granted an extension.

When we were refuel complete, I waved my hand straight out of the cockpit to the refueler guy, signaling we were full on gas.

"Coming up," I radioed to my trail aircraft.

I picked up the helicopter, turned it around, and took off to the south, back toward the last known location of the Milans. We flew as fast as we could.

We came in low and fast to do a flyby of the boulder. The valley was eerily silent.

No people. No scope. No rucksack. No Milans.

They were gone.

26

HANDING OFF THE WAR

December 2008

Bagram, Afghanistan

December: my favorite month. I'm obsessed with everything to do with Christmas, and it's also my birthday month, but in 2008 it had an extra meaning: I was heading home—for good.

I'd made it this far without starting an official "countdown," as I had in my past few months in Iraq. But now that it was December and the last month of our deployment, I was silently counting. My sister Lacey would be arriving in Bagram in a couple of weeks, and I couldn't wait to see her.

Getting ready to go home had its own set of challenges. We were packing, living out of a rucksack, going through customs, dealing with everyone's bad moods, moving to the transient tents, getting little sleep—we had to deal with all this while still flying missions. The last month of a deployment is often the most dangerous for the outbound unit because pilots are exhausted and excited to be going home. Their minds are elsewhere, and that often leads to complacency. It's a dangerous combination while flying helicopters, especially when training the new, replacement unit pilots. When those pilots are ready, the first flights were manned by one new pilot and one from the old unit, which is not ideal in a combat environment. The risk factor increases.

I was switching from the day shift to the night shift, again, which was never fun. We got a maximum of forty-eight hours to do the 180-degree swap. It was the middle of December and in two weeks we'd be out of here, but for now we had to complete our missions.

After a few night missions, I had a "day" off and was getting some sleep.

Knock, knock, knock.

I pushed open the plywood door of my B-hut. One of our instructor pilots, Brandon, stood there awkwardly, the way most of the guy pilots did when they had to get one of us girls.

"I need you to fly tomorrow night," he said to me with a smile.

What the hell is he smiling about? I don't want to fly, I'm still reversing out. I'm not falling for this little ploy.

"Ha, um, no," I said to Brandon. "Tomorrow night is my day off. Isn't there anyone else who can fly who doesn't have it off?"

"You have to fly, okay?" Brandon said. "Trust me, you will be happy you are flying tomorrow."

Hmmm. Interesting.

"Okay, okay, okay, fine. I'm flying," I said. "See you tomorrow." I shut the door and went back to my bed.

Twenty-four hours later I grabbed my backpack and my cold-weather flight jacket and got on the bus with my new flight crew for the night. My friend CW2 Mel Gresham, one of the pilots who had come up from Bravo Troop in Kandahar to join Lucky Strike in Bagram, was on the team, too. Mel and I had flown together in Bagram.

CW3 Bryan Elwood and I were crewed together for this flight.

I sat down on the bus, and the four of us looked at each other like we were all in on some inside joke, we just didn't know what it was. Brandon had a big smirk on his face that he couldn't seem to wipe off.

The bus slowed to a stop as we approached the hangar.

"I need Amber, Mel, and Bryan to meet me in the IP office," Brandon said as the bus arrived at the hangar.

When we were all assembled, Brandon said, "I bet you guys are wondering what's going on."

"Just tell us already," Mel said.

"We are going to be pulling security for Air Force One when it lands tonight at Bagram," Brandon said. "I wanted to tell you guys yesterday, but the Secret Service guys literally threatened my life if I said that President Bush was coming, or if I told anyone outside of our team tonight."

I was now happy I had been chosen to fly that night.

No one outside of our Kiowa team, the air traffic controllers (because the airspace was shut down), and President Karzai, whom President Bush was meeting, knew he was coming.

Ahead of his arrival in Afghanistan, President Bush had been in Iraq, where an Iraqi journalist had thrown a shoe at him during the middle of his speech. Secret Service had tightened security and didn't want any screwups this time, so we went over a very detailed flight brief. We were going to be the only air traffic in the airspace while Air Force One was on approach and landing at Bagram. Immediately after landing, the president would board a helicopter and fly fifteen minutes south, to President Karzai's palace in Kabul.

———————

We got to work on an elaborate flight and team brief for our mission. Everything was planned down to the smallest detail, no contingency left unchecked. Pulling security for Air Force One and the president of the United States, there was no room for error.

After takeoff, our team began conducting reconnaissance around Bagram, looking for anything suspicious—any holes in the fence, people or vehicles where they weren't supposed to be, as well as searching for any possible rocket or mortar launch sights. Nothing. It was like "Silent Night" out there.

We flew down to Kabul, conducting a wide recon of the path the president would be taking on his Black Hawk ride. When it was time to head back up to Bagram, we prepared for Air Force One's final approach path. We had to be in position to provide security and air cover as it came in to land. We positioned our Kiowas on the southwest side of the runway to stay out of the flight path and to give us an excellent field of view.

"Bagram tower, Air Force One. Inbound for landing," I heard over the tower frequency.

The huge Boeing 747 appeared through my NVGs. It was a beautiful sight.

"Bagram tower, this is Annihilator Two-Four. We've got eyes on Air Force One," I said over the radio.

The enormous 747 flying through the air, completely blacked out, was a surreal sight. At that moment, I was in a unique position: armed with .50-cal and high-explosive rockets with the authority to take out any threat posed to the president or Air Force One. What an incredible honor it was to be handed that responsibility. A swell of pride filled me as I watched the plane touch down.

"Going to transition to the north side perimeter," I radioed to trail.

This position would give us a better vantage point to Air Force One. The airspace was closed, so we had the freedom to move around the airfield as we pleased. I turned the Kiowa to the north.

Air Force One taxied to the parking area. Before it came to a complete stop, a swarm of people dressed in black—who I presumed were Secret Service—came out of nowhere to surround the plane.

"Where the hell did those people come from?" I asked. The Secret Service wasn't messing around.

We had completed our mission successfully. Air Force One and the POTUS were safely on the ground at Bagram.

━━━━━━━━

Flying for the president of the United States was a high moment near the end of my deployment. But I was ready to be done. It'd been a long year.

The war was nearly over for me, but our replacement aviation brigade, 159th Combat Aviation Brigade—the unit my sister Lacey was in—had begun to arrive in Afghanistan. Logistically, getting to see Lacey would be a challenge. We had no way of contacting each other outside of email, and because I had moved into the transient tents, the only access I had to email was at the hangar at work (unless I wanted to wait in line for hours to get a computer at the library center on the opposite side of the base). The last I had heard, Lacey was in Manas, Kyrgyzstan, waiting to get on a flight to Bagram.

Then one December day I was walking back from the showers when someone called my name. I stopped and turned.

"Amber!" someone said. "AMBER!"

"Is that her?" someone asked as I walked by.

"LACEY!" I yelled as I spotted her.

The bitter winter cold seemed suddenly to disappear. I was standing outside the shower tents in Afghanistan with my little sister Lacey.

"How did you know I was here?"

"We've been asking everyone where you were, and we finally found your tent. They said you had left to take a shower," Lacey said.

My time in Afghanistan overlapped with Lacey's for about two weeks. I was still on the flight schedule, and Lacey had to do her Afghanistan introductory classes. Our opportunities to hang out were limited. But I got to give her all of the stuff I had had in my B-hut that I no longer needed—a microwave, sheets, blankets, extension cords, power adapters, storage containers, even a chair. Her room was well equipped after we made the transfer.

We managed to spend Christmas together, although not on the actual twenty-fifth—the date didn't work out with our schedules. When we were kids, my dad was usually flying for the airlines on Christmas Day, so we had celebrated many Smith Family Christmases on the twenty-first, twenty-sixth, or even January 3—whenever we were together. That's what mattered.

My mom, dad, and Kelly had sent Christmas decorations, stockings, and wrapped presents to us both, and we sat on Lacey's bed and opened everything. For a few moments in Lacey's tiny B-hut room, I had no idea I was in Afghanistan—aside from the sound of the F-16s doing their afterburner takeoffs.

I felt guilty knowing that I was going home and Lacey was just starting her year of suck. She seemed so fresh, not yet tarnished by this war, like a younger, earlier version of myself. I was realistic about what she would face. We'd lost helicopters, pilots, friends, Americans. She'd lose people and find herself in situations that would change her forever. There was a possibility that I'd never see her again. But she was a great pilot and would be smart.

Saying good-bye to Lacey was tough. On the day of my troop's departure, she met me at the U.S. Customs building where we would board the plane. I felt like I had so much to tell her, so much advice to give her, but time was short, so I said, "Fly safe, Lace. Never get complacent and always keep your eyes open. Love you."

———

After leaving Bagram, my unit spent five days in Manas, Kyrgyzstan, waiting for our final plane ride home. When our flight finally arrived, I found myself in a middle row of a 757 in the aisle seat. The entire plane smelled like sweaty body armor. We were all exhausted and gross. But we were headed home.

My life had changed during my time at war. I'd made some friends, and lost some. Learned some lifelong lessons, and done things I hoped I'd never have to do again. I'd flown in some of the most rugged and unforgiving terrain in the world. I'd witnessed terrorists, Taliban, and al-Qaeda. I'd been shot at too many times to count, had some close calls, but luckily was not injured by enemy fire. My Kiowa got shot up in Iraq in the same AO where the then leader of al-Qaeda in Iraq, Abu Musab al-Zarqawi, was killed by a U.S. air strike. I spent time in some of the most notoriously dangerous valleys that were witness to some of the most intense and dangerous combat in the world, where many brave soldiers earned the Medal of Honor. Somehow, I'd survived. Most of my fellow pilots had survived—but not everyone. For those of us who had made it, we had a future to look forward to. The war had taken its toll on all of us, but what we made of that was up to us.

The pilot's voice came over the loudspeaker, "I'm happy to announce that we have just entered U.S. airspace. Welcome home."

The plane erupted in cheers.

We had made it.

Epilogue

ALIVE

2013

United States of America

"Amber, it's New York. How do you hear me?" the television producer said through my tiny radio earpiece in my right ear. The lights shone down on me, temporarily blinding me from seeing anything other than the black lens of a camera.

I wanted to say "Roger, lickin' chicken," but I decided against it.

"Looking forward to your thoughts on Afghanistan," the producer said.

It had been four years since I was in Afghanistan and three since I had been in the Army. Where had the time gone? In a weird way it seemed like yesterday, while at the same time it was a lifetime ago.

"Thanks," I said.

"Count down from ten for me," he said.

"Roger," I said. "Ten, nine, eight . . ."

The wheels of the Black Hawk touched down on the tarmac in J-bad, where I was based for the first seven months of my deployment. It had only been two months since I left this AO for Bagram, but I felt as if I were home. Kiowa pilots were flying in from all over Afghanistan today to come to Mike's memorial, which 2-17 CAV was holding in honor of his death three days earlier.

It was like walking into a high school reunion. Most of my Alpha Troop pilots from our Iraq deployment were there. They all had grown disgusting molester-mustaches for their traditional deployment competition. So typical. Chris Rowley, my old stick buddy and IP, had flown in from Kandahar.

It was a somber event that none of us really wanted to talk about. But the realities of war had brought us back together. I had been to war twice with these guys and we shared a common bond that only those who have been there understand. We had been through the unbearable together, the good and the bad, the highs and the lows. These were some of the best men and women I have ever known. They were my Kiowa family. . . .

"Thirty seconds," the producer said.

"Thanks for being with us tonight, Amber," the host said as I smiled into the camera.

"Thanks for having me," I said. "It's great to be here."

"So you've been there. You've fought in Iraq and Afghanistan. What was it like?"

Acknowledgments

Danger Close had been an idea for some time, but would not have come to fruition without the help, guidance, faith, and encouragement of many. I am forever thankful for the amount of support and motivation I've received every step of the way from all involved in this process.

First I want to thank my parents, Lane and Betsy, for not only going on this roller-coaster journey of my book-writing ambitions, but also for living through the real deal throughout my time in the Army and all of my deployments. I can honestly say that I couldn't have done any of it without you. I cannot even imagine what it must be like to have had three daughters in the military at once while we were involved in two wars. Your strength, support, constant encouragement, and unconditional love got me through some of the toughest times in my life. It means the world to me. Thank you for never losing faith in me along the way and for always being my best friends and biggest advocates. You guys deserve the title of editor in chief.

To my sisters, Kelly and Lacey. I am so thankful to not only have you as my sisters but also as my best friends. You are amazing women. Thank you for going on this journey with me from the very beginning. You both have incredible stories of your own and have sacrificed so much through your service to this country. Thank you.

To the men and women of Alpha Troop, 2-17 CAV, 101 CAB, 2004–2010, it was an honor to serve with you. To all the members of

2-17 CAV past and present—pilots, crew chiefs, ammo, refuelers, flight ops, maintenance, and everyone else I am missing—I am so grateful to share the CAV legacy with you. Your professionalism, leadership, and incredible flying skills on and off the battlefield will never cease to amaze me. I can only hope that *Danger Close* gives the world a glimpse into the most prestigious and historic CAV unit out there and does it justice for how essential our mission was in combat and what an asset we were on the battlefield. I am still in awe of the talent of the pilots I got to fly with. For all of you who helped teach me to fly and helped me evolve as a KW pilot—Chris, Sammy, Mike, Brian, Ed—I appreciate it more than you know. I learned so much about flying, the Kiowa, the mission, the Army, and life from all of you. I wish I could go fly with you guys again, just one more time.

To my agent, Jim Hornfischer. Thank you for believing in my story, the need for it to be told, your encouragement every step of the way, and having faith in my writing ability to get it done. I am incredibly grateful for all of your help.

To my editor Elizabeth Stein. It was an absolute pleasure to work with such a talented writer and editor. You taught me so much about everything involved in the book-writing process. Thank you for your always honest opinion, speaking my language, and giving me a push when I needed it—which was often! You are the best. Thank you.

To my editor Leslie Meredith at Atria, thank you for everything. It has been pleasure to get to know you and work with you throughout this process. Thank you for your patience and support.

To my best friend, Gina S. Thank you for being there for me when it mattered most and for every reason I could not have completed this book without you. You are an incredible person and our friendship means the world to me. Thank you.

To Sean and Laurie Parnell. Thank you for your help with this project and steering me in the right direction from day one. Your advice, phone calls, friendship, and guidance throughout this process were lifesavers.

Writing *Danger Close* has been an incredibly challenging but rewarding experience. It was tough going back and reliving some of the most intense times I've been faced with, but it helped in a way I never could have imagined. It gave me an unexpected sense of closure from that time of my life. Reconnecting with my former pilots whom I spent years of my life with and experiences I could only try to recapture with this book was incredible. It was as if no time had gone by at all. To Mike Desmond, Melissa Gresham, Matt Wolfe, Sammy Puentes, Lori Hill, Chris Rowley, Chris Cook, Thomas Hussey, Samantha Weston, Deidra DeJiacomo, Andy Miller, Mike Hambrecht, Frank Villanueva, and Ed Dalsey (and anyone else I am missing), thank you for your time, friendship, patience, and memories.

For all of the ground guys out there we supported in Iraq and Afghanistan, you will always have a special place in my heart. Thank you for everything you did and continue to do. Your hard work, selflessness, and sacrifice do not go unnoticed.

Scouts out.

Glossary

ACU: Army Combat Uniform.

AK-47: A Soviet-made 7.62mm assault rifle.

AMC: Air mission commander. The pilot who is the acting commander of a flight of aircraft.

ANA: Afghan National Army.

ANP: Afghan National Police.

AO: Area of operations. Where missions are conducted in a designated battle space.

BDA: Battle damage assessment. A report generated after a weapons engagement, lethal or nonlethal, that indicated the damage inflicted.

Beacon: Code word pilots use after takeoff to confirm that a flight with two or more aircraft is in mission profile.

Break station: Term used by a Kiowa team when leaving the location of the ground unit they are covering, whether it be for refuel, end of mission, or returning to base.

CHU: Container housing unit. The housing soldiers lived in during the Iraq war.

COP: Combat outpost. Any outpost smaller than a FOB.

CP: Command post. Troop office.

CW2: Chief Warrant Officer 2.

CW3: Chief Warrant Officer 3.

CW4: Chief Warrant Officer 4.

CW5: Chief Warrant Officer 5.

Defac: Dining facility. Also referred to as chow hall.

EOD: Explosive ordnance disposal. Explosives expert responsible for dismantling explosive devices.

EOM: End of mission. The assigned mission is complete.

ETT: Embedded training teams. U.S. military embedded with Afghan National Army to help train and assist.

FADEC: Full authority digital electronics (or engine) control.

FARP: Forward arming and refueling point. The area aircraft land at to refuel and rearm.

FOB: Forward operating base. A fortified military base used to support tactical operations.

Grids: Slang for grid coordinates for MGRS (military grid reference system).

HE: High-explosive; e.g., HE rockets.

IED: Improvised explosive device. An improvised bomb used by the enemy.

IIMC: Inadvertent instrument meteorological conditions. Unintentionally flying into the clouds.

IP: Instructor pilot.

J-bad: Jalalabad, Afghanistan.

JRTC: Joint Readiness Training Center. A military training center in Louisiana at which units often train prior to deployments.

LSA: Logistics support area.

Man dress: Military slang for the clothing we saw men wear in Iraq and Afghanistan.

MFD: Multifunctional display. The computer screens inside the cockpit that control most of the systems: navigation, weapons, communications, MMS, maintenance features, historical engine data, and digital flight instruments.

MMS: Mass mounted sight. Multisensor sight system mounted above the rotor system.

MTP: Maintenance test pilot. A pilot who is responsible for conducting maintenance and test flights on aircraft.

NAI: Named area of interest. Location of interest due to enemy activity.

NCO: Noncommissioned officers. Enlisted leaders.

NVG: Night vision goggles.

On station: Term used by a Kiowa team when covering a ground unit.

PC: Pilot in command. The pilot who is commanding the aircraft and responsible for the final decisions of all actions out of the aircraft.

PT: Physical training.

PX: Post exchange.

QRF: Quick reaction force. Military unit whose mission is to respond to troops who call for help.

R&R: Rest and recuperation. It is a period of scheduled leave soldiers take during deployments.

RFD: Radio frequency display. The RFD is the display for our five radios. Between the two MFDs were the analog standby flight instruments, the remote frequency display (RFD) and RPM percentages, torque, and turbine gas temperature indicators.

RPG: Rocket-propelled grenade.

RPM: Revolutions per minute.

RTB: Returning to base. When a Kiowa team has completed their mission or has completed their scheduled amount of flight time, pilots report that they are returning to base.

Sitrep: Situation report. Information relayed between or among relevant parties of the current situation.

SWT: Scout weapons team. Military term for two Kiowas.

TIC: Troops in contact. Friendly ground troops under attack by the enemy.

TIC call: A report Kiowa teams get with a request to respond to the attack to assist the ground troops with armed aerial power.

TOC: Tactical operations center. Operations center used to manage the battle space.

WO1: Warrant Officer 1.

Index

267

About the Author

Amber Smith is a former U.S. Army OH-58D Kiowa Warrior helicopter pilot in command and air mission commander who flew two combat tours, in Iraq and Afghanistan. She frequently appears on national TV and radio networks, analyzing national security, military operations, and foreign policy. Her articles have been published in *Forbes*, the *Washington Examiner*, *Aviation Week*, and other publications. Smith has traveled across the nation to tell her inspirational story and to speak to military and corporate audiences, veterans organizations, at grassroots events, and on Capitol Hill.

Amber has a master of science degree in safety, security, and emergency management with a specialization and a graduate certificate in Homeland Security from Eastern Kentucky University. She earned a bachelor of science in professional aeronautics from Embry Riddle Aeronautical University. She lives in Washington, D.C.